HENRY FRANCIS LYTE

HEAVEN
WILL BRING ME
SWEETER
REST

SELECTED WORKS OF
HENRY FRANCIS LYTE

Heaven Will Bring Me Sweeter Rest

Selected Works of Henry Francis Lyte

Edited by
Alex J. Webster

SHAZBAAR PRESS |BIRMINGHAM, AL

Alex J. Webster/Shazbaar Press
4936 Mountain View Parkway
Birmingham, Alabama 35244

Heaven Will Bring Me Sweeter Rest/Henry Francis Lyte. --
1st ed. Hardcover
ISBN 978-0-9969880-7-0

For
Jon-Michael
Webster

Still there is comfort left. It still is joy
That they can lift their weeping eyes to Heaven,
And think that one of theirs is settled there;
–HENRY FRANCIS LYTE

Contents

THE SPIRIT OF THE PSALMS

TALES IN VERSE ON THE LORD'S PRAYER

INTRODUCTION

Henry Francis Lyte was born in a small Scottish town near Kelso in 1793. His father has been described as a ""ne-er do-well ... more interested in fishing and shooting than in facing up to his family responsibilities".[1] He had been a military man and there is some question as to whether his parents were actually even married. His mother was basically left to raise their three sons (of whom Henry was the second) alone. It wasn't long before the father deserted his mother completely, right after shipping his two older boys off to boarding school. His mother and younger brother were left destitute and his mother moved to London to find work as a nurse, but died (along with Lyte's younger brother) not long after that. Lyte was only seven when his father abandoned him and his mother passed away, and had quite a difficult childhood. Eventually He was "adopted" by the headmaster of the school, Dr. Burrowes, who encouraged him in his studies and growing literary gifts. Lyte was a frail, but handsome boy, with a real flair for writing poetry and eventually was able to attend Trinity College in Ireland where he won numerous prizes for poetry.

---

[1] H.J. Garland, *Henry Francis Lyte And The Story Of Abide With Me* (Torch Publishing, 1950), 18

Lyte was ordained into the Anglican ministry in 1815, but his true conversion occurred a few years later attending to a fellow clergyman during his last months of life. This clergyman began to read the scriptures in earnest and discovered that neither he nor Lyte understood the new birth. He discovered that what they had both been teaching did not line up with the scriptures, particularly the teachings of Paul and the doctrine of grace. Lyte was converted through this experience and wrote in his diary:

> *"I began to study my Bible and preach in another manner than I had previously done. There were four or five clergyman in my neighborhood whom I had before laughed at and deemed Methodist enthusiasts, weak simpletons, unable to rationally defend their beliefs. These men I now saw (generally speaking) to be in the right and I did my best to follow their example as a preacher and witness of the gospel, and I proclaimed such to my fellow man."*

It was not long however, before Lyte suffered another serious breakdown in his health and had to travel to France in hope of making a recovery. His health struggles would plague him throughout his life. In 1822 he married Anne, and their marriage was said to be a happy one. She was an heiress to a considerable fortune, but also Methodist in her convictions. This was rather unusual for one of her station, and she was persecuted by her family for it, but she remained Methodist her entire life, attending both the Methodist meeting on Sunday mornings and the Anglican church her husband pastored in the evenings. When Lyte's health finally broke down for good, it was a kind providence of God that she was able to support the family with her inheritance.

Lyte was a clergyman of sophisticated literary tastes who amassed one of the greatest libraries in the western part of England. (At his death the library was sold by Sotheby's and the auction lasted 17 days!) But Henry was also a wonderful pastor to the sailors in his parish at Brixham. (In fact his former residence there is now a wonderful inn.) Henry's ministry was regularly interrupted by the need to travel to France for his health but in 1847 he felt that he wanted to try to return to England to preach once more to his people and was able to get home for the summer. However, near the end of the summer he had a relapse of his tuberculosis and felt that he would not recover this time.

It was during this season that he wrote *Abide With Me*, his most famous hymn. It was not actually written on his deathbed, but as he felt the end was drawing near. For all those who are concerned that we should sing the original tunes for hymns it is worth pointing out that Lyte set Abide With Me it to his own tune himself and this tune was used for about 10 years. But the tune Eventide was composed by Monk in 1861 and has been the "traditional" tune used ever since.

He preached his last sermon on September 5th, 1847, and that evening revised Abide With Me. (He would send the final revision to his wife a little later.) He travelled again to France where he died and was buried in Nice in November 1847. His nurse recorded his words as he neared death, "Oh blessed converse, begun on earth, to be perfected so soon in paradise! Blessed faith! Today piercing through the mist of earth! Tomorrow changed to sight! Abiding ever with the Lord!" [2]

I am so excited that Alex has brought forth this new edition of the Poetical Works of Henry Francis Lyte. He is one of England's greatest hymns writers, and one of my favorites. On the second Indelible Grace project, *Pilgrim Days* (named for a phrase in a Lyte hymn), we recorded a version of Lyte's hymn *Jesus I My Cross Have Taken* as well as another classic Lyte hymn *Praise My Soul The King Of Heaven*. It is incredibly powerful to reflect on how God was able to reconstruct for Lyte the Father image. Even though he himself had a wretched father, (or maybe because of it?) the Fatherhood of God is captured in almost every one of his hymns. Lines such as:

> *"Father like He tends and spares us, well our feeble frame He knows, In His hands He gently bares us, rescues us from all our foes"*

Such lines are powerful testimonies to the healing power of the gospel Lyte had experienced.

There are so many wonderful hymns, including many versions of the Psalms, included in this new edition and

---

[2] Garland, pg. 51

I am excited to see what new tunes might be written to accompany them. I wrote a tune for his version of Psalm 103 and included it on our *Look To Jesus: Indelible Grace VII* project and hope that those who acquire this volume will continue to find treasures among his Psalm versions in particular.

May the Lord add His rich blessing to the work Alex Webster has done in bringing this new edition of the Poetical Works of Henry Lyte to us!

Grace and peace,

Rev. Kevin Twit

Founder, *Indelible Grace Music*

GENERAL POEMS
AND
HYMNS

ABIDE WITH ME

Abide with us, for it is toward evening, and the day is far spent. —

Luke 24:29

Abide with me! Fast falls the eventide;
The darkness thickens. Lord, with me abide.
When other helpers fail, and comforts flee,
Help of the helpless, O abide with me!

Swift to its close ebbs out life's little day;
Earth's joys grow dim, its glories pass away:
Change and decay in all around I see.
Thou who changest not, abide with me!

Not a brief glance I beg, a passing word;
But as Thou dwell'st with Thy disciples, Lord;
Familiar, condescending, patient, free, —
Come, not to sojourn, but abide with me.

Come not in terrors, as the King of kings;
But kind and good with healing in Thy wings.
Tears for all woes, a heart for every plea.
Come, Friend of sinners, and then abide with me.

Thou on my head in early youth didst smile;
And though rebellious and perverse meanwhile,
Thou hast not left me, oft as I left Thee.
On to the close, O Lord, abide with me!

I need Thy presence every passing hour.
What but Thy grace can foil the tempter's power?
Who like Thyself my guide and stay can be?
Through cloud and sunshine, O, abide with me!

I fear no foe with Thee at hand to bless:
Ills have no weight, and tears no bitterness.

1

Where is Death's sting? where. Grave, thy victory?
I triumph still, if Thou abide with me.

Hold Thou Thy cross before my closing eyes.
Speak through the gloom, and point me to the skies;
Heaven's morning breaks, and earth's vain shadows
flee!
For life, in death, O Lord, abide with me!

A FALLEN SISTER

She is not dead — she only sleeps:
Life in her soul its vigil keeps:
Though dark the cloud, though strong the chain,
Speak, Lord, and she shall live again!

She is not dead: — it cannot be
That one whose soul so glowed to Thee
Should all that's past renounce, forget:
Oh, speak, and she will hear Thee yet.

I know, I know how once she felt,
Have seen her spirit mount and melt;
Have joined with her in praise and prayer;
And cannot, dare not, yet despair.

She that has fed on heavenly food,
Conversed with all that's great and good,
Can she descend from heights like these,
To the poor worldling's husks and lees?

She, that has bent at heaven's high throne,
And claimed its glories for her own,
An earthworm here again to crawl? —
She cannot long so deeply fall.

I know how many for her feel,
And plead with Thee to come and heal:
I know the power of faith and prayer,

2

And cannot, will not, yet despair.

Sunk as she is in thoughtless sin,
Thou hast a still, small voice within —
A silent hold — a hidden plea —
That needs but quickening. Lord, from Thee.

A look of Thine can life impart;
A tone of Thine can touch the heart:
The very grave Thy voice must hear:
Oh, bid it reach our sister's ear!

Press on her soul each pang and scorn,
Which Thou for her of old hast borne;
And ask how she will dare to meet,
Thy face upon a Judgment-seat.

Talk to her heart, and bid her feel;
Send forth Thy word to wound and heal;
Melt off her spirit's icy chain,
And bid her rise and live again.

She is not dead: Thy voice Divine
Can still revive, and seal her Thine;
And 'neath Thy wing she yet may dwell,
More meek, more safe, than ere she fell.

⚜⚜⚜

TO A BLADE OF GRASS

Poor little twinkler in the sun,
  That liftest here thy modest head,
    For every breeze to blow upon,
  And every passing foot to tread;

The loneliest waste, the humblest bower,
  Content in homely green to dress,

3

And wear away thy little hour
   In meek unheeded usefulness;

No hues of thine attract the eye,
   No sweets allure the roving bee,
Nor deigns the dainty butterfly
   To rest his wing on lowly thee.

All undistinguished and forgot
   Among the myriads of thy kind,
The moral of thy tranquil lot
   Thou wastest on the idle wind.

Be mine, while others pass thee by,
   To win and wear thee in my strain;
And from thy gentle teaching try
   A lesson for my heart to gain.

While brighter children of the sun
   With altering seasons droop and die,
I see thee green and gladsome run
   Through all the changes of the sky.

Where vegetative life begins,
   Thy little flag is first unfurled,
And marks the empire Nature wins,
   From desolation round the world.

Yes; Nature claims thee for her own;
   Her thousand children house with thee:
An insect world, to eye unknown,
   Peoples thy coverts blithe and free.

The partridge, 'midst her speckled brood,
   Leans upon thee her cowering breast;
Thou giv'st the field-mouse home and food;
   Thou curtain'st round the skylark's nest.

Thou feed'st the honest steer by day,
   Thou strew'st at night his open bed;

The young lamb, in his morning play,
  Strikes down the dewdrop from thy head.

Oh, ever pleasing, ever plain,
  Creation's goodly household vest!
By thee is fringed the ruined fane,
  By thee the poor man's grave is drest.

The pilgrim of the sandy waste,
  The roamer of the long, long sea,
The sick-room's or the dungeon's guest —
  'Tis his, 'tis his, to value thee.

Green soother of the burning eye,
  Thou speak'st of sweet and simple things —
Of freedom, health, and purity,
  And all that buxom Nature brings.

Be mine to dwell with her, with thee;
  At eventide the fields to roam;
My God among His works to see,
  And call my wandering spirit home:

And, while I view the Hand that tends
  Ten thousand worlds, so kind to thee,
To feel that He, who so descends,
Will not o'erlook a worm like me.

SHE IS GONE! SHE IS GONE!

She is gone! she is gone! A God of love
Has called her up to His side above;
Has gathered the flower in all its prime,
And bade it bloom in a brighter clime;
Has filled her hand with a heavenly lyre.
And found her a place in His angel choir.

She is gone! she is gone to a land of light,

5

Where the glorious day ne'er sinks in night;
Where a cloud ne'er comes across the sky;
Where the tears are wiped from every eye;
Where all is holiness, love, and bliss,
And none regret such a world as this.

She is gone! she is gone! she passed away
Like the dying close of a summer day:
A dawn of glory round her shone,
A light shot down from the heavenly throne:
The last of her breath in song was spent,
And forth in a smile her spirit went.

She is gone! she is gone to her high reward,
To bask in the looks of her wished-for Lord.
She gained one peep through the golden gate;
She saw the Seraphim for her wait;
And sprang from sorrow and sin away,
To dwell in the light of eternal day.

She is gone! she is gone! And who would chain
Her soul to a world like ours again?
But oh, the blank, the desolate void,
In hearts that her converse here enjoyed!
They long from all upon earth to sever,
And be with their loved and lost for ever.

She is gone! she is gone but a while before,
She waits for them at the heavenly door:
They hear her calling them up on high;
They feel her drawing them on to the sky;
And pray, at their parting hour to be
As ripe, as ready, as blessed as she.

THE PILGRIM'S PROGRESS

Blest is the broken, bleeding heart,
For sin constrained to ache!
Soon Heavenly Hands shall bind it up,
No more to bleed or break.

Blest are the eyes, whose burning tears
O'er past transgressions fall!
The Sun of Righteousness shall rise,
To dry, or light them all.

That broken heart, that tearful eye,
That pensive pilgrim guise,
Are Heaven's own gifts, and more than all
That worldlings seek or prize.

Who has them claims and titles has
Which none beside can own;
Pledges of more than eye hath seen,
Or heart conceived or known.

Through clouds and sunshine, storm and calm,
He on to glory goes,
With hope to light him o'er his way,
And bliss to crown its close.

The wise may slight, the proud may shun!
His God is with him still,
And adds a zest to all his joys,
And lightens every ill.

Through Him he daily triumphs gains,
O'er Satan, self, and sin;
Through Him new blessings smile without,
New joy and peace within.

7

A coal from heaven has touched his lips,
    And filled his mouth with song;
And Faith and Love spring forth to waft
    His fainting steps along.

He goes, he goes, his fadeless crown
    From Christ's own hand to win!
The angels throng round heaven's high gate,
    To hail the stranger in!

The silver cord is loosed at last,
    The fettered soul takes wing;
Assumes its station fast by God,
    His ceaseless praise to sing.

THE WALLFLOWER

Why loves my flower, so high reclined
    Upon these walls of barren gloom,
      To waste her sweetness on the wind,
    And far from every eye to bloom?
Why joy to twine with golden braid
This mined rampart's aged head,
Proud to expose her gentle form,
And swing her bright locks in the storm?

That lonely spot is bleak and hoar,
    Where prints my flower her fragrant kiss;
Yet sorrow hangs not fonder o'er
    The ruins of her faded bliss.
And wherefore will she thus inweave
The owl's lone couch, and feel at eve
The wild bat o'er her blossoms fling,

And strike them down with heedless wing?

Thus, gazing on the loftiest tower
    Of ruined Fore at eventide,
The Muse addressed a lonely flower
    That bloomed above in summer pride.
The Muse's eye, the Muse's ear,
Can more than others see and hear:
The breeze of evening murmured by,
And gave, she deemed, this faint reply:

On this lone tower, so wild and drear,
    'Mid storms and clouds I love to lie,
Because I And a freedom here
    Which prouder haunts could ne'er supply.
Safe on these walls I sit, and stem
The elements that conquered them;
And high o'er reach of plundering foe,
Smile on an anxious world below.

Though envied place I may not claim
    On warrior's crest, or lady's hair;
Though tongue may never speak my name,
    Nor eye behold and own me fair;
To Him, who tends me from the sky,
I spread my beauties here on high,
And bid the winds to waft above,
My incense to His throne of love.
And though in hermit solitude,
    Aloft and wild, my home I choose,
On the rock's bosom pillowed rude,
    And nurtured by the falling dews;
Yet duly with the opening year,
I hang my golden mantle here.
A child of God's I am, and He
Sustains, and clothes, and shelters me.

9

Nor deem my state without its bliss:
   Mine is the first young smile of day;
Mine the light zephyr's earliest kiss;
   And mine the skylark's matin lay.
These are my joys: with these on high,
In peace I hope to live and die,
And drink the dew, and scent the breeze,
As blithe a flower as Flora sees.

Bloom on, sweet moralist! Be thine
   The softest shower, the brightest sun!
Long o'er a world of error shine,
   And teach them what to seek and shun!
Bloom on, and show the simple glee
That dwells with those who dwell like thee;
From noise, and glare, and folly driven,
To thought, retirement, peace, and heaven.
Show them, in thine, the Christian's lot
   So dark and drear in worldly eyes;
And yet he would exchange it not
   For all they most pursue and prize.
From meaner cares and trammels free,
He soars above the world, like thee;
And, fed and nurtured from above,
Returns the debt in grateful love.
Frail, like thyself, fair flower, is he,
   And beat by every storm and shower;
Yet on a Rock he stands, like thee,
   And braves the tempest's wildest power.
And there he blooms, and gathers still
A good from every seeming ill;
And, pleased with what his lot has given,
He lives to God, and looks to heaven.

'MY BELOVED IS MINE, AND, I AM HIS'

Imitated from Quarles

Long did I toil, and knew no earthly rest;
Far did I rove, and found no certain home:
  At last I sought them in His sheltering breast
Who opens His arms, and bids the weary come.
With Him I found a home, a rest Divine;
And I since then am His, and He is mine.

Yes, He is mine! and nought of earthly things,
  Not all the charms of pleasure, wealth, or power,
The fame of heroes, or the pomp of kings,
  Could tempt me to forgo His love an hour.
Go, worthless world, I cry, with all that's thine!
Go! I my Saviour's am, and He is mine.

The good I have is from His stores supplied:
  The ill is only what He deems the best.
He for my Friend, I'm rich with nought beside;
  And poor without Him, though of all possessed.
Changes may come — I take, or I resign,
Content, while I am His, while He is mine.

Whate'er may change, in Him no change is seen,
  A glorious Sun, that wanes not, nor declines:
Above the clouds and storms He walks serene,
  And on His people's inward darkness shines.
All may depart — I fret not nor repine,
While I my Saviour's am, while He is mine.

He stays me falling; lifts me up when down;
  Reclaims me wandering; guards from every foe;

11

Plants on my worthless brow the victor's crown.
　　Which in return before His feet I throw,
Grieved that I cannot better grace His shrine,
Who deigns to own me His, as He is mine.

While here, alas! I knew but half His love,
　　But half discern Him, and but half adore;
But when I meet Him in the realms above,
　　I hope to love Him better, praise Him more,
And feel, and tell, amid the choir Divine,
How fully I am His, and He is mine.

WINTER

The billowy shore is booming loud,
The sky is black with storm and cloud,
The fields are bare, the air is chill,
And winter reigns from vale to hill.

The shortening day, the muffled sky,
The wild wind whistling bleakly by,
The naked fields, the leafless tree,
Speak, mortal man, speak all to thee.

They talk of sin, they talk of woe,
Of ruin wrought to all below:
They taunt the author of their doom,
And point him onward to the tomb.

The waves lift up their voice; the woods
Make solemn answer to the floods:
They bid us stand abased and awed,
And own an Omnipresent God.

Calm on the tempest's hurrying wings,

He walks His trembling earth, and flings,
Unmoved by elemental din,
His scourges o'er a world of sin.

Almighty! be it mine to lie
Adoring as Thou passest by,
And hear Thee at the close proclaim
The gentler glories of Thy name!

The fire, the earthquake, and the wind —
In these my God I would not find —
But in the Voice still, small, and dim,
That speaks of Christ, and peace through Him.

ASPIRATIONS

I would not always sail
Upon a sunny sea:
  The mountain wave, the sounding gale,
  Have deeper joys for me.

Let others love to creep
  Along the flowery dell:
Be mine upon the craggy steep,
  Among the storms, to dwell.

The rock, the mist, the foam,
  The wonderful, the wild —
I feel they form my proper home,
  And claim me for their child.

The whirlwind's rushing wing,
  The stem volcano's voice,

To me an awful rapture bring:
    I tremble and rejoice.

I love thy solemn roar,
    Thou deep, eternal sea,
Sounding along from shore to shore,
    The boundless and the free.

I love the flood's hoarse song,
    The thunder's lordly mirth,
The midnight wind, that walks along
    The hushed and trembling earth;

The mountain, lone and high,
    The dark and silent wood,
The desert stretched from sky to sky
    In awful solitude.

A presence and a power
    In scenes like these I see:
The stillness of a midnight hour
    Has eloquence for me.

Then, bursting earth's control,
    My thoughts are all at flood:
I feel the stirrings in my soul
    Of an immortal mood.

My energies expand;
    My spirit looks abroad;
And, midst the terrible and grand,
    Feels nearer to her God.

Let others tamely weigh
    The danger and the pain:

I do not shrink the price to pay,
  To share the joy and gain.

SPARE MY FLOWER

O spare my flower, my gentle flower,
  The slender creature of a day!
    Let it bloom out its little hour,
  And pass away.
Too soon its fleeting charms must lie
  Decayed, unnoticed, overthrown.
O hasten not its destiny, —
  Too like thy own.

The breeze will roam this way to-morrow,
  And sigh to find his playmate gone:
The bee will come its sweets to borrow,
  And meet with none.
O spare! and let it still outspread
  Its beauties to the passing eye,
And look up from its lowly bed
  Upon the sky.

O spare my flower! Thou know'st not what
  Thy undiscerning hand would tear:
A thousand charms thou notest not
  Lie treasured there.
Not Solomon, in all his state,
  Was clad like Nature's simplest child;
Nor could the world combined create
  One floweret wild.

Spare, then, this humble monument
  Of an Almighty's power and skill;

And let it at His shrine present
   Its homage still.
He made it who makes nought in vain:
   He watches it who watches thee;
And He can best its date ordain
   Who bade it be.

O spare my flower — for it is frail;
   A timid, weak, imploring thing —
And let it still upon the gale
   Its moral fling.
That moral thy reward shall be:
   Catch the suggestion, and apply: —
'Go, live like me,' it cries; 'like me
   Soon, soon, to die.'

ELLEN

She rests beneath her native earth,
Close to the spot that gave her birth.
   Her young feet trod the flowers that bloom-
   Meet emblems — on her early tomb:
   Her living voice was wont to cheer
   The echoes which our sorrows hear.

She rests beneath her native earth;
And few remain to speak her worth.
   Her little sojourn here was spent
   In unobtrusive banishment:
   A flower upon the desert thrown,
   That lived and breathed to God alone.

Yet long her gentle ways shall dwell
In hearts that knew and loved her well;
   And oft they lift their tearful eyes,

16

To hear her calling from the skies;
And ill could they her absence bear,
But that they hope to join her there.

PARTED CHRISTIANS

When reft of the converse of those that they love,
    The godless may fret and repine:
        'Tis ours to look up to a Father above,
    And try to His will to resign.
The friends in a Saviour need not be deplored,
    Wherever their lot may be cast:
Tho' severed on earth, we are one in the Lord,
    And shall meet in His presence at last.
Our Guardian all-wise and all-merciful is;
    He knows, and will give us, the best:
Assured we shall still be each other's and His,
    To Him we relinquish the rest.
We each commend each to Omnipotent hands,
    And calm on His promise repose;
And know that, though scattered o'er seas and o'er
    lands,
        We are sure to reach home at the close.

Meanwhile, we kneel down at the same throne of
    grace;
        We breathe up the same daily prayer;
We march the same road to the same happy place,
    The same Spirit guiding us there.
Sweet hope realizes the things that shall be,
    And memory those that have been;
And, reaching by these to what sense cannot see,
    We lose the dark present between.

We strive to be all that the absent would love;
    To flee from what they would condemn;
Intent, when we meet, upon earth or above,
    To be found the more worthy of them.

17

With aims so exalted, and trust so secure,
    All else is in lovely accord,
All holy, all happy, all peaceful and pure —
    Oh, who would not love in the Lord?

FLY, YE HOURS

Fly, ye hours, the best, the brightest:
Best are they that fleet the lightest!
        Man, be wise:
        Thy earthly joys
Are poor, compared with those thou slightest.

        The world we roam
        Is not our home:
We seek a rest that aye remaineth.
        Through weal or woe,
        From all below
We haste to scenes where nothing paineth.
                        Fly, ye hours, etc.

        It is not life,
        This toil and strife:
These only serve from God to sever.
        We hope to rise
        Above the skies;
And there shall live, and live for ever.
                        Fly, ye hours, etc.

        Can that be gain,
        Whose charms detain
The soul from glory's richer treasures?
        Can that be woe,
        That serves to throw
A brighter hue o'er coming pleasures?
Fly, ye hours, the best, the brightest!
Thou that in the world delightest,
        Rise, O rise,
        To nobler joys.

And taste the bliss which now thou slightest.

THE SAILOR'S MEDITATION ON WATCH AT NIGHT

Above me hangs the silent sky;
  Around me rolls the sea;
   The crew is all at rest; and I
  Am, Lord, alone with Thee!

Go where I may, from all remote,
  Thou, Lord, art ever near:
No secret thought, but Thou canst note;
  No word, but Thou canst hear.

When all around are sunk to sleep,
  Thy presence here I find:
To me Thou walkest o'er the deep,
  Or speakest in the wind.

I look up to the starry sky;
  And read Thy glories there:
I look down to myself, and sigh,
  'Can I be still Thy care?'

I think of days and dangers past,
  When I have found Thee nigh;
And wonder how Thy love can last
  To such a worm as I.

I think of terrors yet at hand,
  Of judgment, and the tomb;
And ask my soul how it shall stand
  To hear its final doom!

Ah, then, how all I've been and done
  Would fill me with despair,
If to the Cross I could not run,
  And find a Saviour there!

19

I know He has the power to aid;
   I know He has the will:
And He, who once for sinners bled,
   Will rescue sinners still.

Lord, arm my soul with faith in Thee,
   And fill my heart with love;
My path from sin and danger free,
   And guide me safe above.

And while at night the waves I beat,
   Lord, often thus descend,
And grant me here communion sweet
   With Thee, the sailor's Friend.

AUTUMNAL HYMN

The leaves around me falling
   Are preaching of decay;
   The hollow winds are calling,
'Come, pilgrim, come away!'
The day, in night declining,
   Says, I must too decline:
The year its life resigning —
   Its lot foreshadows mine.

The light my path surrounding.
   The loves to which I cling,
The hopes within me bounding.
   The joys that round me wing —
All melt like stars of even,
   Before the morning's ray,
Pass upward into heaven,
   And chide at my delay.

The friends gone there before me
   Are calling me from high,

And joyous angels o'er me
    Tempt sweetiy to the sky.
'Why wait,' they say, ' and wither,
    'Mid scenes of death and sin?
O rise to glory hither.
    And find true life begin!'

I hear the invitation,
    And fain would rise and come —
A sinner, to salvation;
    An exile, to his home:
But while I here must Unger,
    Thus, thus, let all I see
Point on, with faithful finger.
    To heaven, O Lord, and Thee.

INVOCATION

Altered from Quarles

Spirits of light and love, who pace around
  The city's sapphire walls; whose stainless feet
    Measure the gem-paved paths of sacred ground,
    And trace the New Jerusalem's jasper street!
Ah you, whose overflowing hearts are crowned
    With your best wishes; who enjoy the sweet
Of all your hopes; when next ye come before
My absent Lord, O say how I implore
From His reviving eye one look of kindness more.

Tell Him, O tell Him, how my widowed breast
    Beneath the burden of His frown has pined:
Tell Him, O tell Him, how I lie oppressed
    In all the tempest of a troubled mind.
O tell Him, tell Him, I can know no rest
    Till He shall smile, as once, appeased and kind.

Tell Him, I think upon the vows He sware —
His love. His truth. His grace — and thus I dare
To come before Him now with penitence and prayer.

Say, the parched soil desires not so the shower
    To quicken and refresh her embryo grain;
Say, the fallen crestlet of the drooping flower
    Woos not the bounty of the genial rain,
As my lorn spirit looks out for the hour
    When her lost Lord shall visit her again.
Then, gentle spirits, should ye hear your lays,
And seem to melt, your best hosannahs raise;
And with your heavenly notes sustain my feeble
    praise.

THE PILGRIM'S SONG

My rest is in heaven; my rest is not here;
Then why should I murmur when trials are near?
Be hushed, my dark spirit! the worst that can come
But shortens thy journey, and hastens thee home.

It is not for me to be seeking my bliss,
And building my hopes in a region like this:
I look for a city which hands have not piled;
I pant for a country by sin undefiled.

The thorn and the thistle around me may grow:
I would not lie down upon roses below:
I ask not my portion, I seek not a rest,
Till I find them, O Lord, in Thy sheltering breast.

Afflictions may damp me, they cannot destroy;
One glimpse of Thy love turns them all into joy:
And the bitterest tears, if Thou smile but on them,

Like dew in the sunshine grow diamond and gem.

Let doubt, then, and danger, my progress oppose;
They only make heaven more sweet at the close.
Come joy, or come sorrow, whate'er may befall.
An hour with my God will make up for it all.

A scrip on my back, and a staff in my hand,
I march on in haste through an enemy's land:
The road may be rough, but it cannot be long;
And I'll smooth it with hope, and I'll cheer it with
song.

EVENING

Sweet evening hour! sweet evening hour!
That calms the air, and shuts the flower;
That brings the wild bird to her nest.
The infant to its mother's breast.

Sweet hour! that bids the labourer cease;
That gives the weary team release,
And leads them home, and crowns them there,
With rest and shelter, food and care.

O season of soft sounds and hues,
Of twilight walks among the dews.
Of feelings calm, and converse sweet.
And thoughts too shadowy to repeat!

The weeping eye, that loathes the day.
Finds peace beneath thy soothing sway;
And faith and prayer o'ermastering grief.
Burst forth, and bring the heart relief.

Yes, lovely hour! thou art the time
When feelings flow, and wishes climb;
When timid souls begin to dare.
And God receives and answers prayer.

Then trembling through the dewy skies
Look out the stars, like thoughtful eyes
Of angels, calm reclining there.
And gazing on this world of care.

Then, as the earth recedes from sight,
Heaven seems to open her fields of light.
And call the fettered soul above,
From sin and grief, to peace and love.

Sweet hour! for heavenly musing made —
When Isaac walked, and Daniel prayed;
When Abram's offering God did own;
And Jesus loved to be alone.

Who has not felt that evening's hour,
Draws forth devotion's tenderest power;
That guardian spirits round us stand.
And God Himself seems most at hand?

The very birds cry shame on men.
And chide their selfish silence, then:
The flowers on high their incense send;

And earth and heaven unite and blend.
Let others hail the rising day:
I praise it when it fades away;
When life assumes a higher tone.
And God and heaven are all my own.

MORNING THOUGHTS

Again, O Lord, I open my eyes.
  Thy glorious light to see,
    And share the gifts so largely lent
  To thankless man by Thee.

And why has God o'er me this night
  The watch so kindly kept?
And why have I so safely waked?
  And why so sweetly slept?

And wherefore do I live and breathe?
  And wherefore have I still
The mind to know, the sense to choose,
  The strength to do Thy will?

Is it, to waste another day,
  In folly, sin, and shame?
To give to these my heart and hand,
  And spurn my Maker's claim?

Is it, to grow unto the world,
  As glides the world from me;
Be one day nearer to the grave,
  And further, Lord, from Thee?

No! thus too many days I've spent!
  To Thee, then, this be given:
Teach what I owe to man below,
  And to Thyself in heaven.

Oh, bring me to my Saviour's cross,
  For mercy for the past;
And make me live the coming day
  As if it were my last!

25

NOVEMBER

The autumn wind is moaning low the requiem of the
year;
The days are growing short again, the fields forlorn
and sere;
The sunny sky is waxing dim, and chill the hazy air;
And tossing trees before the breeze are turning brown
and bare.

All Nature and her children now prepare for rougher
days:
The squirrel makes his winter bed, and hazel hoard
purveys;
The sunny swallow spreads his wings to seek a
brighter sky;
And boding owl, with nightly howl, says cloud and
storm are nigh.

No more 'tis sweet to walk abroad among the evening
dews:
The flowers are fled from every path, with all their
scents and hues:
The joyous bird no more is heard, save where his
slender song
The robin drops, as meek he hops the withered leaves
among.

Those withered leaves, that slender song, a solemn
truth convey, —
In wisdom's ear they speak aloud of frailty and decay:
They say that man's apportioned year shall have its
winter too;
Shall rise and shine, and then decline, as all around
him do.

They tell him, all he has on earth, his brightest,
dearest things,
His loves and friendships, joys and hopes, have all
their falls and springs:

A wave upon a moon-lit sea, a leaf before the blast,
A summer flower, an April hour, that gleams and
hurries past.

And be it so: I know it well: myself, and all that's
mine,
Must roll on with the rolling year, and ripen to
decline.
I do not shun the solemn truth; to him it is not drear,
Whose hopes can rise above the skies, and see a
Saviour near.

It only makes him feel with joy, this earth is not his
home;
It sends him on from present ills to brighter hours to
come:
It bids him take with thankful heart whate'er his God
may send,
Content to go through weal or woe to glory in the
end.

Then murmur on, ye wintry winds; remind me of my
doom:
Ye lengthened nights, still image forth the darkness of
the tomb.
Eternal summer lights the heart where Jesus deigns to
shine.
I mourn no loss, I shun no cross, so Thou, O Lord, art
mine!

AGNES

I saw her in childhood —
  A bright gentle thing,
    Like the dawn of the morn,
  Or the dews of the spring:
The daisies and harebells
  Her playmates all day;
Herself as light-hearted
  And artless as they.

I saw her again —
  A fair girl of eighteen.
Fresh glittering with graces
  Of mind and of mien.
Her speech was all music;
  Like moonlight she shone;
The envy of many.
  The glory of one.

Years, years fleeted over —
  I stood at her foot:
The bud had grown blossom,
  The blossom was fruit.
A dignified mother,
  Her infant she bore;
And looked, I thought, fairer.
  Than ever before.

I saw her once more —
  'Twas the day that she died;
Heaven's light was around her.
  And God at her side;
No want to distress her.
  No fears to appal —
O then, I felt, then
  She was fairest of all!

ON A NAVAL OFFICER BURIED IN THE ATLANTIC

There is, in the wide lone sea,
    A spot unmarked, but holy;
    For there the gallant and the free,
    In his ocean bed lies lowly.

Down, down, within the deep,
    That oft to triumph bore him,
He sleeps a sound and pleasant sleep,
    With the salt waves washing o'er him.

He sleeps serene, and safe
    From tempest or from billow,
Where the storms that high above him chafe,
    Scarce rock his peaceful pillow.

The sea and him in death,
    They did not dare to sever:
It was his home while he had breath;
    Tis now his rest for ever.

Sleep on, thou mighty dead!
    A glorious tomb they've found thee.
The broad blue sky above thee spread,
    The boundless waters round thee.

No vulgar foot treads here;
    No hand profane shall move thee;
But gallant fleets shall proudly steer,
    And warriors shout, above thee.

And when the last trump shall sound,
    And tombs are asunder riven,
Like the morning sun from the wave thou'lt bound,
    To rise and shine in heaven.

STABILITY

There is a change in all below;
　　Nought sure beneath the sky:
　　　Suns rise and set, tides ebb and flow,
　　And man but lives to die.

Our joys and sorrows, hopes and fears,
　　Still course each other on:
A blessing in our path appears —
　　We grasp, and it is gone!

No drop of honey, but a sting
　　Within it lies concealed;
No hour that passes, but its wing
　　Away some good has wheeled.

The joyous sun that lights to-day
　　But clouds to-morrow's sky:
The stars but shine to fall away;
　　The world but lives to die.

And let them pass — each earthly thing —
　　While, Lord, 'tis mine to stand
On Thy eternal word, and cling
　　To Thy almighty hand.

Though sun and moon should sink in gloom,
　　Thy promise ne'er declines:
Dissolving worlds but leave Thee room
　　To work Thy vast designs.

Linked to Thy truth I hold me up,
　　Though earth from 'neath me slide;
And take content whatever cup
　　Thy wisdom may provide.

Bitter or sweet, I little heed:
　　All, all is sweet to me.
While I my title clearly read
　　To joys at last with Thee.

'THE UNKNOWN GOD'

Based upon Acts 17:24

The Lord hath builded for Himself;
   He needs no earthly dome:
      The universe His dwelling is,
      Eternity His home.

Yon glorious sky His temple stands,
   So lofty, bright, and blue,
All lamped with stars, and curtained round
   With clouds of every hue.

Earth is His altar: Nature there
   Her daily tribute pays:
The elements upon Him wait,
   The seasons roll His praise.
Where shall I see Him? How describe
   The dread Eternal One?
His footprints are in every place,
   Himself is found in none.

He called the world, and it arose;
   The heavens, and they appeared:
His hand poured forth the mighty deep;
   His arm the mountains reared.

He sets His foot upon the hills,
   And earth beneath Him quakes;
He walks upon the hurricane,
   And in the thunder speaks.

I search the rounds of space and time,
   Nor find His semblance there:

31

Grandeur has nothing so sublime,
   Nor beauty half so fair.

Yet all I am, or meet, proclaim
   His wisdom, love, and power:
They shine from all yon rolling worlds:
   They bloom in every flower.

He is; He was; He aye shall be.
   But how, my soul? and what?
Where is He? — say, ye works of His —
   Vain thought! where is He not?

Thou Omnipresent, dread Unknown,
   Engage for evermore:
Enlarge my views, exalt my soul,
   And help me to adore!

THE APPROACH OF SPRING

O! Springtime now will soon be here —
The sweetest time of all the year;
When fields are green, and skies are blue,
And the world grows beautiful anew.

The storms and clouds shall pass from high;
And the sun walk lordly up the sky,
And look down love and joy again,
On herb, and beast, and living men.

Then the laughing flowers on plant and tree.
Shall bud and blossom pleasantly;
And spirits through the buxom air,
Drop health and gladness everywhere:

The birds shall build their nests, and wake
Their roundelays in bush and brake;

And the young west- wind on joyous feet,
Go wooing along from sweet to sweet.

Then lives lithe Hope, live Love and Mirth;
Then God in beauty walks the earth:
The heart is in tune, and the life-blood plays,
And the soul breaks out in songs of praise.

O! Springtime now will soon be here,
The sweetest time of all the year;
When green leaves burst, and flow'rets spring,
And young hearts too are blossoming.

'Twas then I ventured first to twine
My Annie's trembling arm in mine;
And trod — with her I cared not where —
Through vocal fields and scented air.

O days of sunshine, song, and flowers!
O young Love's early haunts and hours!
tones and looks! O smiles and tears!
How shine ye still through lapse of years!

There was one bank we loved to climb,
All matted o'er with fragrant thyme,
And screened from every vagrant breeze,
But the sweet south, up with the bees

Came musical; and there we stood,
And gazed down on the ocean flood,
That slept beneath us, heaving mild
Between his shores, like a cradled child;

Or turned where on the orchard trees
Young Spring sat swinging in the breeze,
Unfolding buds, and tending flowers,
For summer's future fruits and bowers.

All, all was bright! — at times like this,
No sight or sound comes in amiss;
But things around appear to win
A colour from the mood within.

The earth laughed into flower: the sky
Cleared off the cloud from its brow on high;
And God — ^the God of grace — unfurled
His flag of peace o'er a fallen world.

These youthful days are past and gone;
The autumn of my years comes on;
I much am changed in mind and frame;
Yet Spring, sweet Spring, comes still the same.

I grow young with the young year then;
I live my past lot o'er again;
And in these hours of song and bloom,
See types of those beyond the tomb.

O! Springtime now will soon be here,
The Spring of Heaven's millennial year;
When God again o'er Nature's night,
Shall say, 'Be light,' and there is light.

O Thou that into glorious birth,
Shalt wake at last this fallen earth,
While humbler things Thy influence share,
Be not the soul forgotten there!

Rise, Sun of glory I rise, and shine
Within this wintry breast of mine;
And make my inward wastes and snows
Rejoice and blossom as the rose.

Oh, while I seem to catch the sound
Of vegetation swelling round,
Grant me within a growth to prove,
Of faith, and hope, and joy, and love!

Springtide of grace, thy course begin;
Chase the dark reign of sense and sin;
From light to light advance and shine,
Till Heaven's eternal Spring is mine!

MARY'S GRAVE

Mary, thou art gone to rest;
    Why should we deplore thee?
    Light the turf lies on thy breast,
  Soft the winds breathe o'er thee.
Here within thy native clay,
    Calmly thou art sleeping,
Safer, happier, far than they,
    Who are o'er thee weeping.

Pleasant is thy lowly bed,
    Close to those that bore thee;
Trees, 'neath which thy childhood played,
    Gently waving o'er thee.
Hark the thrush! how sweet his lay!
    See the flowers, how blooming!
'Weep not for the dead,' they say,
    'Though in earth consuming.

'Weep not for her — she is gone
    Where no cares can move her;
All her earthly labours done,
    All her trials over.
Weep not — she has found a home
    Where no sorrow paineth:
Sin, nor tears, nor terrors come.
    Where a Saviour reigneth.'

❦❦ ❦❦ ❦❦

PARAPHRASE OF THE FORTY-SIXTH PSALM

God is our hope and strength! a present help
In time of trouble! therefore though the earth
Be moved, and her mountains 'midst the deep
Be headlong tumbled, though the waters there
Shall rage till every hill shall shake around,

35

We will not fear! The roaring winds and waves
Shall only glad the dwelling of the Lord,
The seat in which the Mightiest deigns to bide.
God in the midst forbids her to be moved!
God shall assist her timely as before!
The kingdoms threatened, and the proud of heart
Combined in arms. But God gave forth His voice,
Earth melted at the sound! The Lord of Hosts
Is with us, Israel's Monarch is our shield!
Come hither and behold His glorious works;
What desolation in His wrath He brings
O'er all the earth; what gladness when appeased!
See how He quells the storm of war, how breaks
The sword, and snaps the spear, exalts the weak,
And pulls the mighty down. Be still then. Earth,
Tremble, ye kings, and know that I am God.
I will defend My people, I will bend
The stubborn knee of pride I The Lord of Hosts
Is with us, Israel's Monarch is our shield!

ADDRESSED TO MY FRIEND J. K.

And then those nights, those attic nights we've passed
    With the fond few who felt and thought as we,
Chiding the hours that stole away so fast,
    On wings of reason, wit, and minstrelsy:
When my young Muse would list and learn from thee,
    Strains she had envied any tongue but thine,
Or from discussions fanciful and free,
    On books, men, things gay, moral, and Divine,
    Glean'd much to please and mend, enlighten and
    refine.

THE ALPS

The Alps — the Alps — the joyous Alps,
 Are all around me heaving high.
  I bow me to their snowy scalps,
   That rush into the sky.

Hail, lordly land of storm and strife,
 To poetry and wonder dear!
'Tis worth an age of common life
 To feel as I do here:

To look down on that deep blue lake;
 To look up in that glorious sky;
To feel my soul within me wake,
 And ask for wings to fly:

To bound the airy heights along;
 Above the floating clouds to stand;
And meet creation's God among
 The wonders of His hand.

Hail, scenes of holy grandeur! hail!
 Where mortal sense stands hushed and awed.
Oh, who could gaze on such, and fail
 To think of Thee, my God?

Alone and dread Thou dwellest here,
 The source and soul of all I see.
I look around in joy and fear,
 And feel I am with Thee!

I see Thee on the mountain sit,
 At summer's noon, sublime and still,
Or, in the giant shadows flit
 Along from hill to hill.

I read Thy presence and Thy power,
 In each eternal rock I meet;
I trace Thy love in every flower,
 That blossoms at my feet.

37

Thou speakest from each rolling cloud,
    That pours its stormy mirth on high,
When cliff to cliff is shouting loud,
Responsive to the sky.

Thy voice at night is in the sound
    Of sinking glaciers, rushing rills,
And avalanches thundering round,
    Among the startled hills.

The mountain mists, in all their moods,
    The snows by earthly feet untrod,
The fells, the forests, and the floods,
    Are all instinct with God.

O regions, wonderful and wild,
    Sublimity's inspiring home,
Scenes I have dreamt of since a child,
    And longed as now to roam!

And I am here! and I may range
    Your length and breadth without control:
And feel a world all new and strange
    Break in upon my soul!

Hail! mountain monarchs, hail! Again
    Before your reverend feet I bow:
How poor is language to explain
    The thoughts that fill me now!

ELIJAH'S INTERVIEW WITH GOD

Based on I Kings 19: 11, 12

On Horeb's rock the prophet stood:
The Lord before him passed:
   A hurricane in angry mood,
   Swept by him strong and fast.
The forests fell before its force;
The rocks were shivered in its course:
   God rode not in the blast!
'Twas but the whirlwind of His breath,
Announcing danger, wreck, and death.

It ceased: the air was mute. A cloud
   Came muffling up the sun:
Went through the mountain deep and loud,
   An earthquake thundered on.
The frighted eagle sprang in air;
The wolf ran howling from his lair.
   God was not in the stun!
'Twas but the rolling of His car.
The trampling of His steeds from far.

It ceased again: and Nature stood
   And smoothed her ruffled frame:
When swift from heaven a fiery flood,
   To earth devouring came.
Down to his depths the ocean fled;
The sickening sun looked wan and dead.
   Yet God filled not the flame!
'Twas but the fierceness of His eye,
That lightened through the troubled sky.

At last a voice all still and small,
   Rose sweetly on the ear;
Yet rose so calm and clear that all
   In heaven and earth might hear.
It spoke of hope; it spoke of love;
It spoke as spirits speak above;
   And God himself was here!
For, oh, it was a Father's voice,
That bade His trembling world rejoice.

Speak, gracious Lord, speak ever thus;
   And let Thy terrors prove
The harbingers of peace to us,
   The heralds of Thy love!
Shine through the earthquake, fire, and storm,
Shine in Thy milder, better form,
   And all our fears remove!
One word of Thine is all we claim;
'Tis. 'mercy' through a Saviour's name.

FLOWERS

Children of dew and sunshine, balmy flowers!
   Ye seem like creatures of a heavenly mould,
      That linger in this fallen earth of ours,
      Fair relics of her paradise of old.

Amidst her tombs and ruins, gentle things,
   Ye smile and glitter in celestial bloom;
Like radiant feathers dropped from angel wings,
   Or tiny rainbows of a world of gloom.

Yes; there is heaven about you: in your breath
    And hues it dwells. The stars of heaven ye shine;
Bright strangers in a land of sin and death,
    That talk of God, and point to realms Divine.

O mutely eloquent! the heart may read
    In books like you, in tinted leaf or wing,
Fragrance, and music, lessons that exceed
    The formal lore that graver pages bring.

Ye speak of frail humanity: ye tell
    How man, like you, shall flourish and shall fall.
But, ah! ye speak of Heavenly Love as well,
    And say, the God of flowers is God of all.

While Faith in you her Maker's goodness views,
    Beyond her utmost need, her boldest claim.
She catches something of your smiles and hues,
    Forgets her fears, and glows and smiles the same.

Childhood and you are playmates; matching well
    Your sunny cheeks, and mingling fragrant breath.
Ye help young Love his faltering tale to tell;
    Ye scatter sweetness o'er the bed of Death.

Sweet flowers, sweet flowers, be mine to dwell with
    you!
    Ye talk of song and sunshine, hope and love:
Ye breathe of all bright things, and lead us through
    The best of earth to better still above.

Sweet flowers, sweet flowers! the rich exuberance
    Of Nature's heart in her propitious hours:
When glad emotions in her bosom dance,
    She vents her happiness in laughing flowers.

I love you, when along the fields in spring,
　　Your dewy eyes look countless from the turf;
I love you, when from summer boughs you swing,
　　As light and silvery as the ocean surf.

I love your earliest beauties, and your last:
　　Come when you may, you still are welcome here;
Flinging your sweets on Autumn's dying blast,
　　Or weaving chaplets for the infant year.

I love your gentle eyes and smiling faces,
　　Bright with the sun, or wet with balmy showers;
Your looks and language in all times and places,
In lordly gardens, or in woodland bowers.

But most, sweet flowers, I love you when ye talk
　　As Jesus taught you when He o'er you trod;
And, mingling smiles and morals, bid us walk
　　Content o'er earth to glory and to God.

LO, WE HAVE LEFT ALL, AND FOLLOWED THEE

Jesus, I my cross have taken,
All to leave and follow Thee:
Destitute, despised, forsaken.
Thou from hence my all shalt be.
Perish, every fond ambition.
All I've sought, and hoped, and known
Yet how rich is my condition, —
God and heaven are still my own.

Let all the world despise and leave me —
They have left my Saviour too —
Human hearts and looks deceive me;
Thou art not, like man, untrue:
And while Thou shalt smile upon me,
God of wisdom, love, and might.
Foes may hate, and friends may shun me:
Show Thy face, and all is bright!

Go, then, earthly fame and treasure!
Come, disaster, scorn, and pain!
In Thy service, pain is pleasure;
With Thy favour, loss is gain.
I have called Thee Abba, Father;
I have stayed my heart on Thee:
Storms may howl, and clouds may gather;
All must work for good to me.

Man may trouble and distress me;
'Twill but drive me to Thy breast.
Life with trials hard may press me;
Heaven will bring me sweeter rest.
Oh, 'tis not in grief to harm me!
While Thy love is left to me!

43

Oh, 'twere not in joy to charm me,
  Were that joy unmixed with Thee.

Take, my soul, thy full salvation;
  Rise o'er sin, and fear, and care;
Joy to find in every station.
  Something still to do or bear!
Think what spirit dwells within thee;
  What a Father's smile is thine;
What thy Saviour died to win thee, —
  Child of Heaven, shouldst thou repine?

Haste, then, on from grace to glory,
  Armed by faith, and winged by prayer;
Heaven's eternal day's before thee;
  God's own hand shall guide thee there.
Soon shall close thy earthly mission;
  Swift shall pass thy pilgrim days;
Hope soon change to glad fruition,
  Faith to sight, and prayer to praise.

HARK! ROUND THE GOD OF LOVE

Composed for the Sunday-School Anniversary of All Saints', Brixham, and a great favorite among the children.

Hark, round the God of Love
  Angels are singing!
    Saints at His feet above
  Their crowns are flinging.
And may poor children dare
  Hope for acceptance there,
Their simple praise and prayer,
  To His throne bringing?

Yes! through adoring throngs
  His pity sees us,
    'Midst their seraphic songs.
Our offering pleases.
  And Thou who here didst prove.
To babes so full of love,
  Thou art the same above,
Merciful Jesus!

Not a poor sparrow falls.
  But Thou art near it.
When the young raven calls.
  Thou, Lord, dost hear it.
Flowers, worms, and insects share.
  Hourly Thy guardian care —
Wilt Thou bid us despair?
  Lord, can we fear it?

Lord, then Thy mercy send.
  On all before Thee!
Children and children's Friend,
  Bless, we implore Thee!

Lead us from grace to grace,
 On through our earthly race,
Till all before Thy face
 Meet to adore Thee.

'IT IS I: BE NOT AFRAID'

L oud was the wind, and wild the tide;
 The ship her course delayed:
 The Lord came to their help, and cried,
 'Tis I: be not afraid.'

Who walks the waves in wondrous guise,
 By Nature's laws unstayed?
'Tis I,' a well-known voice replies;
 'Tis I: be not afraid.'

He mounts the deck: down lulls the sea;
 The tempest is allayed;
The prostrate crew adore; and He
 Exclaims, 'Be not afraid.'

Thus, when the storm of life is high,
 Come, Saviour, to my aid!
Come, when no other help is nigh,
 And say, 'Be not afraid.'

Speak, and my griefs no more are heard;
 Speak, and my fears are laid;
Speak, and my soul shall bless the word,
 'Tis I: be not afraid.'

When on the bed of death I lie,
 And stretch my hands for aid,

Stand Thou before my glazing eye,
　And say, ' Be not afraid.'

Before Thy judgment seat above.
　When nature sinks dismayed,
Oh, cheer me with a word of love —
　'Tis I: be not afraid.'

Worlds may around to wreck be driven,
　If then I hear it said,
By Him who rules through earth and heaven,
　'Tis I: be not afraid.'

NEW YEAR'S HYMN

Hail to another year,
The year that now begins!
　All hail to Him who led us here,
　Through dangers and through sins.

Hail to another year!
　Peace to the year that's past!
May this one at its close appear,
　Less worthless than the last!

Hail to another year!
　Ere round its wheels are driven,
Each to the grave will stand more near-
　Will each be nearer heaven?

Hail to another year!
　Ere half its race is sped,
Ourselves, with all we treasure here,
　May rest among the dead.

47

Hail to another year!
　　Though yet unknown, untrod,
Whate'er may come, we need not fear,
　　If friends, through Christ, with God.

Hail to another year,
　　A year of peace and love!
Oh, may it prove a foretaste here,
　　Of endless years above!

SAD THOUGHTS

Yes, I am calm, am humbled now;
　　The storm is rocked to rest;
　　　And I have learnt my head to bow,
And count my lot the best.

I would not struggle with my God,
　　Or chide what He has given:
Why should I murmur at the rod.
　　That drives me on to heaven?

Yet withering thoughts at times will break,
　　Across my calmer frame:
And then I feel how hearts may ache,
　　Though still they bow the same.

Dark moods, too long and fondly nursed,
　　Will o'er me come unsought:
And thou, ah thou, beloved the first,
　　To be the last forgot!

I meet thy pensive, moonlight face;
　　Thy thrilling voice I hear;
And former hours and scenes retrace,
　　Too fleeting, and too dear!

Then sighs and tears flow fast and free,
    Though none is nigh to share;
And life has nought beside for me,
    So sweet as this despair.

There are crushed hearts that will not break;
    And mine, methinks, is one;
Or thus I should not weep and wake,
    And thou to slumber gone.

I little thought it thus could be,
    In days more sad and fair —
That earth could have a place for me,
    And thou no longer there.

We met in childhood's morning road;
    Our love with life began;
And on through years the current flowed.
    And deepened as it ran.

Yes: on we loved, and loved the same,
    Though little either said:
It burned, that sad and secret flame,
    Like lamps among the dead.

I knew her heart was all my own;
    She knew the same of mine;
Though caution guarded every tone,
    And checked each outward sign.

To selves or others unexpressed,
    The truth within us waked —
A conscious wound in either breast,
    That inly bled and ached.

At last it came, the day to part!
    And feelings, long repressed,
In bitter shrift from heart to heart,
    Were all at length expressed.

That trying hour all barriers broke;
    A frenzy o'er me fell:

Spirit to spirit briefly spoke,
    And then — Farewell! Farewell!

From that dark day I walked alone,
    In this wide world of care.
My widowed heart regardless grown,
    Of aught that wooed it there.

Its joys and griefs I learned to view,
    Without a smile or sigh;
And naught seemed left me now to do,
    But lay me down and die.

Bereavement was not long her dower;
    She feels no more its sway:
She pined, she drooped, my severed flower!
    And passed from earth away.

No plaint she breathed, no pain confessed,
    But calmly fell asleep;
She stole into her grave for rest,
    And left me here to weep.

While thou wert here, there was a hope,
    All dimly as it shone:
'Tis gone! and I am left to cope
    With this cold world alone.

Yet death cannot our hearts divide,
    Or make thee less my own.
'Twere sweeter sleeping at thy side,
    Than watching here alone.

Yet never, never can we part,
    While Memory holds her reign:
Thine, thine is still this withered heart,
    Till we shall meet again.

That meet we shall, I do not fear:
    The thought was joy to thee:
And I have now but little here,
    To part my God and me.

I feel, too, in my darkest mood,
    How much my soul has won:
I know 'twas needful all, and good;
    And say, 'Thy will be done!'

Still, thoughts like these at times will come,
    My firmness to surprise.
When shall I be with thee at home,
    Beyond the reach of sighs?

❦❦❦ ❦❦❦ ❦❦❦

DOMESTIC LOVE

How lovely is domestic harmony,
Where mind on mind and heart on heart repose
Undoubting; and the friends, whom Providence
Has cast together, sharing each with each
Their hopes, their joys, their cares, appear to live
One common life, and breathe one common will!
This fallen world brings forth no other flower
So beautiful as this; and where the love
Of God is added to this love of man,
Somewhat of heaven itself to earth descends.
For what is heaven, but one immortal home,
Where all are brother, parent, child, or friend,
And all are happy, loving, and beloved?
And what is hell, but the abode of hate
And envy, where discordant elements
Mingle, and hiss, and jar eternally?
Bright comes the morn and soft descends the night
On the fair dwelling-place of love and peace;
And from the buffetings of this rude world
Its happy inmates, like the wandering dove
Home to her ark, for refuge there can fly.

51

Prayer meets no hindrance there; and praise from thence,
Of hearts and lips in unison, ascends
More acceptable to the God of Love.
The idol self is from his throne cast down,
And God set up instead; and where He reigns
There must be happiness, there must be heaven.

＊＊＊

THE HEART IN TUNE

Be the heart in tune within,
All without runs smooth and even,
And earth's objects seem to win
Something of the hues of heaven:
Clouds from off our sky are flown;
All grows bright around and o'er us;
Life acquires a loftier tone,
And hope dances light before us:
Music comes in every gale;
Flowers in all our paths are blowing;
Prosperous winds fill every sail;
Tides are ever fair and flowing;
Time adds feathers to his wing;
Grief of half his load is lightened;
Life's distresses lose their sting,
And its every joy is heightened.

Then the waste, where'er we roam,
Gushes with refreshing fountains;
Then between us and our home,
Open the seas, and sink the mountains:
Faith is strong, and views are clear;
Foes or fears no more confound us;
Ministering angels near,
And an Eden opening round us:

Nature through her wide domain,
Quits her air of ruined sadness,
Kindles into smiles again.
Wakes anew to song and gladness:
God amid His works appears,
Calls His creatures to adore Him;
And this world of sin and tears,
Blossoms as the rose before Him.

If His gospel then be heard,
Soon the inmost soul it reaches;
God speaks home in every word,
Christ again in person teaches;
Every promise is applied,
Power to every precept given.
And the Spirit and the Bride,
Point to woo us on to heaven.

Prayer and praise are easy then,
From the soul spontaneous flowing;
And with love to God and men,
Tenderly the heart is glowing.
All our duties lighter grow;
Pleasant seems the meanest station;
And from light to light we go,
To the fullness of salvation.

Be our spirits ever such,
Turned into harmonious meetness,
Till their chords to every touch,
Answer in some tone of sweetness;
Quickened by celestial grace,
Purified of earthly leaven,
Shining, like the prophet's face,
With a glory caught from heaven.

THE PRAYER-ANSWERING GOD

I stand in a world where there's nothing my own,
Where the lightest event is beyond my control;
But to Him that is Ruler supreme and alone,
I gladly resign, for I know Him, the whole.
How pleasant, 'mid changes and chances unthought,
On His wisdom and love to disburthen our care;
And to know, that the God who disposes our lot.
Is a God that will hear and will answer our prayer!

There are those that I love, far away from me now,
And roaming through danger by shore and by sea;
And what were my feelings, my Father, if Thou
Wert less than Almighty for them and for me?
I cannot command the wild winds to be still;
I cannot compel the dark waves to forbear;
But One is above them who can, and who will:
In Him I am strong, for He answereth prayer.

Ah me! I gaze round me, — and what are the smiles
And the looks that give life all its zest and its soul?
Mortality claims them, and sternly reviles
Affection's vain struggle against her control.
I own it, I feel it; yet, humbled and awed,
I still dare to love them, all frail as they are;
For I know we are both in the hands of our God,
The Father of Jesus, the Hearer of prayer.

Then here be my resting-place! here will I sit
Secure 'mid the shiftings of time and event;
For Fate has no power but what He may permit,
And the Hand that must take is the same that hath
lent
On His wisdom and goodness I calmly rely;
Whate'er He assigns He can aid me to bear:
He knows what is good for me better than I,
And will give it, I hope, in despite of my prayer.

THOUGHTS IN WEAKNESS

PART I

Encouragement

Three mighty companies compose
　The armies of the Lord;
　　Upon His love they all repose,
　　And wait upon His word.
Unlike the offices they fill,
　　The homage that they bring,
But one their ceaseless object still —
　　To glorify their King.

The first in rank and station — they
　　The bright angelic train,
Who never bowed 'neath sorrow's sway,
　　Nor felt corruption's stain.
And yet they feel for man's distress,
　　His every trial share,
Nor spurn the meanest services
　　To help salvation's heir.

The next — a band of humbler birth,
　　But scarce of humbler place.
Who fought and bled for Christ on earth,
　　And triumphed through His grace.
Their secret wrestlings, hidden life,
　　To Him were not unknown:
His arm sustained them through the strife,
　　And now they share His throne.

The last are they who still maintain
　　The conflict here below,
Whose portion still is sin and pain,
　　The danger and the foe.

55

They oft are foiled, they oft despair,
    But help from high is given;
They struggle on through faith and prayer,
    And fight their way to heaven.

And these — though poor and weak they be,
    The Saviour owns them still;
They serve Him, though imperfectly,
    And yearn to work His will.
Temptation's tide they strive to stem.
    Though faith at times burns dim,
Nor find the Lord deserting them,
    While they depend on Him.

The world, the flesh, the Evil One,
    Assault them hour by hour;
And soon must all their hopes be gone,
    If left to Nature's power.
But armed by Christ's own plighted word,
    When fiercest foes assail,
They meet them with the Spirit's sword,
    Nor find the weapon fail.

Oh, mighty is the power of prayer,
    The promise large and true;
The feeblest heart need not despair
    With these to bear it through.
Though darkest clouds o'ercast the sky,
    Though wave call out to wave,
Enough to know the Saviour nigh,
    To bless, to guide, to save.

Shall flesh and blood presume to shrink
    While He vouchsafes to aid?
Shall Nature hear that voice and sink —
    'Tis I, be not afraid'?

Behold — 'tis Jesus walks the deck;
    What fears our hearts o'erwhelm?
Can wildest waves the vessel wreck
    While He is at the helm?

Oh, strange our courage e'er should reel
    With Him so near and kind;
So often rescued — yet to feel
    So trustless and so blind!
Oh, strange to know all heaven to be
    Upon our side arrayed,
All cheering, strengthening us, and we
    By every breath dismayed!

Go, ask those victors now on high
    What helped them on to heaven —
'The very arms,' they all reply, —
    'To you as freely given.
Our hearts, like yours, were faint and frail,
    Our foes as hard to tame;
But grace we found o'er all prevail.
    Oh, try and find the same!'

PART II

Submission

Yet think not, O my soul, to keep
    Thy progress on to God,
    By any road less rough and steep
    Than that thy fathers trod.
In tears and trials thou must sow,
    To reap in joy and love.
We cannot find our home below,
    And hope for one above.

No — here we labour, watch, and pray,
    Our rest and peace are there —

God will not take the thorn away,
    But gives us strength to bear.
The holiest, greatest, best have thus
    In wisdom learnt to grow:
Yea, He that gave Himself for us
    Was perfected by woe.

Thou, Man of Sorrows, Thou didst not
    The bitter cup decline.
Why should I claim a better lot —
    A smoother path than Thine?
Thou sought'st no treasure here on earth,
    No glory 'neath the skies;
And what Thou deem'dst so little worth,
    Shall I so highly prize?

Did not reproach and wrong rain down
    Upon Thy hallowed head?
Didst Thou not strip off glory's crown,
    To wear the thorns instead?
When foes reviled, didst Thou reply,
    Or render ill for ill?
Didst Thou for man bleed, faint, and die?
    And shall I falter still?

In early life to Thee I was
    Consigned by solemn vow:
Enlisted 'neath Thy Holy Cross —
    Shall I desert it now?
I then, 'gainst every hostile power,
    Engaged to follow Thee;
And shall I, at the trying hour.
    Be found the first to flee?

Thou didst not flee, O King of Love,
    When Thou wert sorely tried;

When all men fled, and God above
　　Appeared His face to hide.
Intent that guiltless Blood to shed,
　　That should for guilt atone,
The mighty winepress Thou didst tread,
　　Unshrinking, though alone.

And shall I murmur or repine
　　At aught Thy hand may send?
To whom should I my cause resign,
　　If not to such a Friend?
Where Love and Wisdom deign to choose,
　　Shall I the choice condemn;
Or dare the medicine to refuse
　　That is prescribed by them?

Oh, small the gain when men aspire
　　Their Maker to control!
He gives, perhaps, their heart's desire,
　　And leanness to their soul.
Not His to quench the smoking flax,
　　Or break the bruised reed;
Or with one pang our patience tax,
　　But what He knows we need.

Yet must our steadfastness be tried —
　　Yet must our graces grow
By holy warfare. What beside
　　Did we expect below?
Is not the way to heavenly gain
　　Through earthly grief and loss?
Rest must be won by toil and pain —
　　The Crown repays the Cross.

As woods, when shaken by the breeze,
　　Take deeper, firmer root,

As winter's frosts but make the trees
    Abound in summer fruit;
So every Heaven-sent pang and throe
    That Christian firmness tries,
But nerves us for our work below,
    And forms us for the skies.

PART III

Action

A way, then, causeless doubts and fears
    That weaken and enthral;
    Wipe off, my soul, thy faithless tears,
    And rise to duty's call.
How much is there to win and do,
    How much to help and cheer!
The fields are white, the labourers few;
    Wilt thou sit 'plaining here?

Awake, my soul, to duty wake;
    Go, pay the debt thou ow'st.
Go forward — and the night shall break
    Around thee as thou go'st.
A Red Sea may before thee flow,
    Egyptian hosts pursue;
But He that bids thee onward go
    Will open a pathway, too.

Swift fly the hours, and brief the time
    For action or repose; —
Fast flits this scene of woe and crime,
    And soon the whole shall close;
The evening shadows deeper fall,
    The daylight dies away.
Wake, slumberer, at the Master's call,
    And work while it is day!

THE WORLD RENOUNCED

Go, worthless world! I've tried and found
    Thy hollowness at last:
    I know thee now an empty sound,
    And spurn at all thou hast.

Thy smiles, thy flatteries, thy deceit,
    I've scanned them o'er and o'er.
Go, other hearts to snare and cheat;
    Thou holdest mine no more.

I've been thy dupe, I've been thy scoff,
    For years I've worn thy chain:
My Saviour came and called me off,
    And I am free again:

Free with the freedom Christ bestows;
    Divinely, greatly free;
Redeemed from follies, sins, and woes;
    Redeemed, false world, from thee!

Still must I linger 'mid thy slaves,
    A stranger yet a while;
Must toss on thy uncertain waves,
    And meet thy specious smile:

The scoffs of pride, the snares of sense,
    Must still my firmness try;
Till Christ returns to call me hence.
    To peace with Him on high.

I know me weak, and prone to fall;
    Yet know, with Him my Friend,
I still may pass unhurt through all,
    To glory in the end.
And while my sojourn here I make,
    This, this my maxim be, —
To love mankind for Jesu's sake,
    And spurn, false world, at thee.

A SUMMER DAY IN WINTER

The winter wears a summer hue —
   The sun is on the wave;
     The sky is one unclouded blue;
    The winds begin to rave;

The feathery frost melts fast away
    From every glittering stem;
And cottage eaves in morning's ray
    Are dropping gold and gem.

That ray the silver feet unlocks,
    Of all the tiny floods;
They leap again down o'er their rocks,
    And prattle through the woods.

The cattle in the field rejoice,
    The birds upon the wing,
And from the brake a doubtful voice
    Half warbles, 'Welcome, Spring!'

The wave that flew o'er yester cliff,
    Is sleeping 'neath it now;
And from its creek the summer skiff
    Steals out with timid prow.

The anchored ships, their voyage o'er,
    Shake out their sails to dry;
The fisher spreads his net on shore,
    Beneath the glowing sky.

The old man from his chimney nook
    Creeps out into the sun:
All Nature wears her own sweet look
    Of springtide just begun.

O earth, all fallen as thou art,
   How soon thy darkest day
Can into life and beauty start
   Beneath thy monarch's ray!

Nor less the contrast that awakes
   The wintry soul within,
When, Lord, Thy gladdening Gospel breaks
   On Nature's night of sin.
The Sun of Righteousness ascends;
   The clouds and storms depart;
And Heaven-born grace implants and lends
   Her Eden in the heart.

Yet earth's best joys are brief and base
   To those which Heaven supplies;
A summer smile on winter's face,
   A gleam through clouded skies.

I would not spurn these wayside flowers,
   That strew my pathway home;
But look through all to heavenly hours,
   And bid their fullness come.

INSCRIPTION ON A MONUMENT AT BRIXHAM

HERE LIES VAR
(Lapdog of the Right Honourable Lady Farnham)

Breathe, gentle spring, breathe on this grassy mound,
And sing, ye birds, and bloom, ye flowers, around.
Ye suns and dews, make green the resting-place
Of honest Var, the noblest of his race.
Gentle, yet fearless, active, fond, and true,
He reads, proud man, a lesson here to you;
And bids you (happy might you hear) to be
Guiltless in life, and calm in death as he.
Go, and as faithful to your Master prove,
As firm in duty, and as strong in love.
You will not find this moment here misspent
In musing o'er a spaniel's monument.

RECOLLECTIONS

'Twas a sweet April morning: I traversed the glade
Where my light foot in infancy often had played:
Each object recalled to my lingering view,
The hours that there once so delightfully flew.

Dear scenes of enchantment, for ever gone by!
How brightly they danced before memory's eye!
I numbered their fugitive blisses all o'er:
They were flown, and I sighed I had prized them no
more.

Oh, why is it thus, that we never discover
The worth of our joys till possession is over?
That we only can gaze on the sun of delight,
When its fast-fading glories are setting in night?

All aimless and wild as the zephyr, we fleet
O'er a thousand fair flow'rets that smile at our feet:
Though they lure us to pluck them, and woo us to
stay,
We trample, we slight them, and flutter away.

Then, when life brings its crosses, its cares, and its
fears,
When disaster beside and before us appears,
Then we pause, and look back, and our folly discern;
Then we prize, bless, and mourn what can never
return.

When all that hope hung on for comfort is flown,
When delights from the past must be gathered alone,
How dimly they shine through the distance of years!
How ill can they chase present shadows and tears!

Woe, woe to the heart that is destined to ache
In a world whose gay bustle it loathes to partake!
Where nothing is left that is moving or dear.
That can light up a smile, or elicit a tear!

When conscience is sickened on looking within,
When without there is little to wish or to win,
When Memory shrinks back from the things that have
been,
And Hope looking onward grows pale at the scene.

Oh, where to find comfort? Oh, whither to fly,
Scarce wishing to live, and yet dreading to die?
Thus helpless, thus reckless, pierced, lost, unforgiven;
Heart-broken on earth, and desponding of heaven!

Lord, Thou canst give light in this hour of despair;
Canst ease us of anguish, or teach us to bear:
And good is the pressure of pain and distress,
If they lead to a Saviour to heal and to bless.

'Tis good that our props should from 'neath us be fled.
If we drop into Arms Everlasting instead;
That thistles and thorns in our pathway should rise,

If they send us but on for repose to the skies.

When all else is changing within and around,
In God and His goodness no change can be found.
In giving or taking His end is the same,
His creatures to quicken, exalt, and reclaim.

Such terrors to drive, and such love to allure,
Lord, add but Thy grace, and the issue is sure.
My trials may thicken, my comforts may flee;
I'm rich amid ruins with heaven and Thee.

THE MOTHER AND HER DYING BOY

Boy

My mother, my mother, O let me depart!
Your tears and your pleadings are swords to my heart.
I hear gentle voices, that chide my delay;
I see lovely visions, that woo me away.
My prison is broken, my trials are o'er!
O mother, my mother, detain me no more!

Mother

And will you, then, leave us, my brightest, my best?
And will you run nestling no more to my breast?
The summer is coming to sky and to bower;
The tree that you planted will soon be in flower;
You loved the soft season of song and of bloom;
Oh, shall it return, and find you in the tomb?

Boy

Yes, mother, I loved in the sunshine to play,
And talk with the birds and the blossoms all day,
But sweeter the songs of the spirits on high.
And brighter the glories round God in the sky:
I see them! I hear them! they pull at my heart!
My mother, my mother, O let me depart!

Mother

O do not desert us! our hearts will be drear,
Our home will be lonely, when you are not here.
Your brother will sigh 'mid his playthings, and say,
I wonder dear Willie so long can delay.
That foot like the wild wind, that glance like a star —
O what will this world be, when they are afar?

Boy

This world, dearest mother! O live not for this;
No, press on with me to the fullness of bliss!
And, trust me, whatever bright fields I may roam,
My heart will not wander from you and from home.
Believe me still near you on pinions of love;
Expect me to hail you when soaring above.

Mother

Well, — go, my beloved! The conflict is o'er: —
My pleas are all selfish; I urge them no more.
'Why chain your bright spirit down here to the clod,
So thirsting for freedom, so ripe for its God?
Farewell, then! farewell, till we meet at the Throne,
Where love fears no partings, and tears are unknown!

Boy

O glory! O glory! what music! what light!
What wonders break in on my heart, on my sight!
I come, blessed spirits! I hear you from high.
O frail, faithless nature, can this be to die?
So near! what, so near to my Saviour and King?
O help me, ye angels. His glories to sing!

INSCRIPTION ON A MONUMENT TO S. P. S.

What shall we write on this memorial stone?
Thy merits? Thou didst rest on Christ's alone.
Our sorrows? Thou wouldst chide the selfish tear.
Our love? Alas, it needs no record here.

67

Praise to thy God and ours? His truth and love
Are sung in nobler strains by thee above.
What wouldst thou have us write? A voice is heard, —
'Write, for each reader write, a warning word.
Bid him look well before him, and within;
Talk to his heedless heart of death and sin;
And if at these he tremble, bid him flee
To Christ, and find Him all in all, like me.'

PLEADING FOR MERCY

When at Thy footstool, Lord, I bend.
   And plead with Thee for mercy there,
     O think Thou of the sinner's Friend,
  And for His sake receive my prayer!
O think not of my shame and guilt.
  My thousand stains of deepest dye:
Think of the blood which Jesus spilt.
  And let that blood my pardon buy.

Think, Lord, how I am still Thy own,
  The trembling creature of Thy hand;
Think how my heart to sin is prone.
  And what temptations round me stand.
O think how blind and weak am I,
  How strong and wily are my foes:
They wrestled with Thy hosts on high;
  How should a worm their might oppose?

O think upon Thy Holy Word,
  And every plighted promise there —
How prayer should evermore be heard,
  And how Thy glory is to spare.
O think not of my doubts and fears.
  My strivings with Thy grace Divine:
Think upon Jesu's woes and tears.
  And let His merits stand for mine.

Thine eye, Thine ear, they are not dull;
    Thine arm can never shortened be:
Behold me here — my heart is full —
    Behold, and spare and succour me.
No claim, no merits. Lord, I plead;
    I come a humbled, helpless slave:
But, ah! the more my guilty need.
    The more Thy glory. Lord, to save.

AN INFANT'S ADDRESS TO DEPARTING DAYLIGHT

Beautiful daylight, stay, oh, stay,
Nor fly from the world and me away,
To darken the skies, so blue and bright,
And take the green fields from my lonely sight.
No birds then will talk to me from the tall tree,
Nor flowers appear looking and laughing on me.
Kind voices I hear, and kind faces I view;
But I can't talk with them, little birds, as with you:
I know not their language, their ways, and their looks,
Nor care for their candles, pens, pencils, and books.
Then, beautiful daylight, fly not yet!
Few suns have I ever seen rise or set;
And when each day with its pleasures is o'er,
I fear they will never come back any more.
A stranger I am in this world below,
And have much of its wonders to mark and know:
I want to see more of each new fairy scene,
To trace sounds and objects, and learn what they
mean;
To gaze on the features of her in whose breast
I am fed, and folded, and sung into rest,
Who kisses me softly, and calls me her dear,
And all the new friends that are kind to me here.

Then stay, sweet daylight, mine eyes to bless!
I know night little, and love it still less.
The place that I came from had nothing of shade,
In beauty and glory for ever arrayed:
There angel forms were smiling and singing,
And waving their wings in the daylight springing
From God's own face, like a fountain flowing
With rays sun and moon must fail in bestowing.
I scarcely remember that land of bliss;
But I love what is brightest and purest in this:
And if upon one of those clouds I could lie,
That have run to the verge of the western sky,
And there, in rosy companionship seated,
Look down on the sun from earth retreated;
If aloft in its bright fleecy folds I could lay me,
And call on the winds through the skies to convey me,
I'd ride round the world the perennial attendant
On daylight, wherever it shone most resplendent;
Over hills, over fogs, I would take my glad flight,
And bathe and revel in rivers of light.
The moon and the stars I would leave behind;
Nor stoop any object on earth to mind;
Unless for her baby dear mother should cry:
Then I'd glide down to tell her how happy was I;
I'd kiss off her tears, and wish her good-day,
And again on my travels away, away!
Sweet bird, thy suit it is vain to press,
The daylight heeds not thy fond address;
On glittermg pinion away he hies,
To meet other wishes, and light other skies:
The will of his God he goes to obey,
Nor at earthly bidding will haste or stay.
A child of light, sweet bird, thou art now,
Nor needest a veil for thy conscious brow:
No deeds thy tiny hands have done,
Need fear the broad eye of the flaring sun;

And the pleasant and pure of this world of woe,
Is all thy delicate spirit can know.
But ah, my baby! the day may appear,
When the light shall be loathed as it now is dear;
When thy red-rolling eye, that can weep no more,
The relief of night shall in vain implore!
The billows and storms of a heart-breaking world,
O'er each young illusion too soon may be hurled;
May wring thee, may wreck thee, till all is riven,
But the friendship of God and the refuge of heaven.
Yet, baby, my baby, if these shall be thine,
Thou'lt not want a spot where thy head may recline;
Thou 'lt not want a light in this world of dismay,
To guide thee from danger, or solace thy way:
The bright Sun of Righteousness never declines,
The light of the Gospel eternally shines;
Adds zest to our joys, plucks the sting from our woes,
Sends peace to our life, and joy to its close.
This light, my boy, be it thine to prize:
It ne'er will withdraw from thy favoured eyes:
Come joy, or come sorrow, the same it will stay,
And shine more and more to the perfect day;
Till grace is glory, and faith is sight,
And God, as at first, 'mid His sons of light,
Receives His homage of song and love,
And thou art with Him for ever above.

IS THIS THY KINDNESS TO THY FRIEND?

Altered from Quarles

O think how He, whom thou hast wounded,
  Hast scourged, and scorned, and spit upon.
    Hath paid thy ransom, and compounded.
  For thy distresses with His own!
How He, whose blood thy sins have split,
  Whose limbs they to the cross have nailed.
Hath freely borne thy load of guilt,
  And made supply where thou hast failed.

He died, to save thy soul from dying;
  Was bound Himself, to set thee free;
And where there was no power of flying,
  He came, and met the blow for thee:
And all this dying Friend requires,
  For all His pity, all His pain,
Are simple aims, and pure desires,
  And for His love like love again.

O loose then, Lord, my tardy tears,
  And break this fleshly rock asunder,
And on my night of doubts and fears,
  Pour a new day of joy and wonder.
This deadness from my soul remove;
  Melt down my icy unbelief;
Let grief add feeling to my love,
  And love pluck out the sting from grief.

Then rise, poor earthworm, from the dust;
  Enjoy thy new and large condition;
Walk with thy God in humble trust,
  And ripen for His full fruition.
No more rebellious, dark, exiled,
  Adore, and love, and praise Him rather;
Return a lost, but contrite, child,
  And find a kind, forgiving Father.

'JESUS WEPT'

Enlarged from Beddome

Did Christ o'er sinners weep?
   And shall our cheeks be dry?
Let floods of penitential grief,
   Burst forth from every eye.

The Son of God in tears,
   The angels wondering see:
Hast thou no wonder, O my soul?
   He shed those tears for thee!

He wept that we might weep,
   Might weep our sin and shame;
He wept to show His love for us,
   And bid us love the same.

Then tender be our hearts,
   Our eyes in sorrow dim,
Till every tear from every eye,
   Is wiped away by Him!

'WHITHER SHALL I FLY FROM THY PRESENCE?'

Where shall I fly? What dark untrodden path
Will lead a sinner from his Maker's wrath?
Alas! where'er I bend my outcast way,
His eye can search. His mighty hand hath sway.

Is there no island in the depths of space,
No distant world, where I may shun His chase?

73

Ah no! Of all He is the spring and soul:
All feel His care, all own His high control.

But there is night: — perhaps her murky womb
May wrap and hide me in its depths of gloom?
No: He that says, 'Be light, and there is light,'
Can look Omniscience thro' the dunnest night.

Give me, then, morning's wings; I'll fling me where
The desert waste ne'er claims His eye or care.
Vain hope! If He were absent, conscience then
Would act the God, and scare me back to men.

Well, then, the ocean: she my head shall hide,
And quench His bolts in her o'ersheltering tide.
Fool! The dark waves cleave wide at His command;
And, lo. He walks them as He walks the land.

What say the rocks? Stern marble, open thy breast,
And lock me in to monumental rest.
Vain, vain! His voice the rocks have often heard;
Nay, worlds dissolve before His lightest word.

Be death, then, mine! At least the grave, or hell,
Will yield some sullen nook where I may dwell.
No: the last trump shall burst the bars of death;
And God's stern presence felt makes hell beneath.

Where, then, to flee? How shun His arm, His eye?
Where find what earth, and heaven, and hell deny?
How pass beyond His infinite patrol,
Who fills, pervades, informs the mighty whole?

O where to flee? There is but one retreat —
'Tis that which brings me contrite to His feet:
A change of heart, and not a change of place,

That flees from Justice to the arms of Grace.

The Saviour calls: 'Come, trembler, to My breast;
Beneath My cross thou may'st securely rest:
Washed in My blood, thy guilt will all remove;
And wrath eternal grow Eternal Love.'

'RETURN UNTO ME, AND I WILL RETURN UNTO THEE'

Wilt Thou return to me, O Lord,
   If I return to Thee?
     O heavenly truth! O gracious word!
   My Hope and Refuge be!

Since from Thy foot I dared to roam,
   My soul has found no rest,
Chastised and contrite, back I come,
   To seek it in Thy breast.

And dost Thou say Thou wilt receive,
   And call me still Thy own?
My spirit, hear, accept, believe!
   And melt my heart of stone!

Again that gracious word to me!
   O speak that word again!
My guilt is pardoned? — can it be? —
   And loosed my every chain?

No, blessed Lord; not every chain,
   Not every bond, remove:
Let one, at least, unloosed remain —
   The bond of grateful love.

'HOW SHALL WE SING THE LORD'S SONG IN A STRANGE LAND?'

The song of God, so nobly sung,
   By angels in a higher sphere.
    Shall my unworthy heart and tongue,
    Attempt its numbers here?

With spirit cleaving to the dust,
   How should I hope to glow and soar?
How speak of heavenly joy and trust,
   Till I have felt them more?

An heir of guilt, a child of sin,
   An exile in a world like this,
What should I find without, within.
   To match with Him and His?

In vain I spread my flickering wings;
   In vain I strive aloft to flee:
Great Lord of lords, and King of kings,
   I cannot sing of Thee!

I want a seraph's lofty voice,
   I want a seraph's soaring wing,
Before I make such themes my choice,
   And God's dread glories sing.

Thou needest not a note of mine,
   To swell the triumphs of Thy throne,
Where myriads round Thee bend and shine,
And Heaven is all Thy own.

No, rather let me sit and sigh,
   And drop contrition's silent tear:
Praise is the task of saints on high;
   But prayer for sinners here.

The song of God, that glorious song,
   From me in such a world as this!
O no! a worthier heart and tongue
   Must speak of Him and His.

HYMN OF PRAISE

Praise the Lord! ye heavens, adore Him;
   Praise Him, angels, in the height;
   Sun and moon, rejoice before Him,
   Praise Him, all ye stars and light.
Praise the Lord! for He hath spoken;
   Worlds His mighty voice obeyed;
Laws which never shall be broken,
   For their guidance hath He made.

Praise the Lord! for He is glorious;
   Never shall His promise fail:
God hath made His saints victorious,
   Sin and death shall not prevail.
Praise the God of our salvation;
   Hosts on high, His power proclaim;
Heaven and earth and all creation,
   Laud and magnify His name!

SABBATH HYMN

A wake, ye saints, awake!
And hail this sacred day:
    In loftiest songs of praise,
    Your joyful homage pay:
Come, bless the day that God hath blest,
The type of Heaven's eternal rest.

On this auspicious morn,
    The Lord of life arose;
He burst the bars of death,
    And vanquished all our foes:
And now He pleads our cause above,
And reaps the fruit of all His love.

All hail, triumphant Lord!
    Heaven with hosannas rings,
And earth, in humbler strains,
    Thy praise responsive sings, —
Worthy the Lamb that once was slain,
Through endless years to live and reign.

Great King! gird on Thy sword,
    Ascend Thy conquering car;
While justice, power, and love,
    Maintain the glorious war:
This day let sinners own Thy sway,
And rebels cast their arms away.

MY PRAYER

W hen at Thy footstool. Lord, I bend,
    And plead with Thee for mercy there,
        Think of the sinner's dying Friend,
    And for His sake receive my prayer.

O think not of my shame and guilt,
  My thousand stains of deepest dye;
Think of the blood which Jesus spilt,
  And let that blood my pardon buy.

Think, Lord, how I am still Thy own,
  The trembling creature of Thy hand;
Think how my heart to sin is prone,
  And what temptations round me stand.

O think upon Thy holy Word,
  And every plighted promise there;
How prayer should evermore be heard,
  And how Thy glory is to spare.

O think not of my doubts and fears,
  My strivings with Thy grace Divine:
Think upon Jesus' woes and tears,
  And let His merits stand for mine.

Thine eye, Thine ear, they are not dull;
  Thine arm can never shortened be;
Behold me here; my heart is full;
  Behold, and spare, and succour me!

FRIENDS LOST IN 1833

Gone? — Have ye all, then, gone, —
  The good, the beautiful, the kind, the dear?
    Passed to your glorious rest so swiftly on,
  And left me weeping here?

I gaze on your bright track;
  I hear your lessening voices as ye go.
Have ye no sign, no solace, to fling back
  To us who toil below?

They hear not my faint cry;
    Beyond the range of sense for ever flown,
I see them melt into eternity,
    And feel I am alone.

Into the haven pass'd,
    They anchor far beyond the scathe of ill;
While the stern billow, and the reckless blast.
    Are mine to cope with still.

Oh! from that land of love,
    Look ye not sometimes on this world of woe?
Think you not, dear ones, in bright bowers above,
    Of those you've left below?

Surely ye note us here,
    Though not as we appear to mortal view;
And can we still, with all our stains, be dear
    To spirits pure as you?

Do ye not loathe, — not spurn, —
    The worms of clay, the slaves of sense and will?
When ye from God and glory earthward turn,
    Oh I can ye love us still?

Or, have ye rather now
    Drunk of His spirit whom ye worship there,
Who stripped the crown of glory from His brow,
    The plaited thorns to wear?

Is it a fair fond thought,
    That you may still our friends and guardians be.
And Heaven's high ministry by you be wrought,
    With abjects low as we?

May we not sweetly hope,
    That you around our path and bed may dwell?
And shall not all our blessings brighter drop,
    From hands we loved so well?

Shall we not feel you near,
    In hours of danger, solitude, and pain,
Cheering the darkness, drying off the tear,
    And turning loss to gain?

Shall not your gentle voice,
    Break on temptation's dark and sullen mood,
Subdue our erring will, overrule our choice,
    And win from ill to good?

O yes! to us, to us,
    A portion of your converse still be given:
Struggling affection still would hold you thus,
    Nor yield you all to Heaven!

Lead our faint steps to God;
    Be with us while the desert here we roam;
Teach us to tread the path which you have trod,
    To find with you our home!

IT DOTH NOT YET APPEAR WHAT WE SHALL BE

Ye lingering hours, wheel swift away,
And usher in the joyful day.
When, rising from a world like this.
My soul shall dwell where Jesus is!

Too long I've waited here below,
And spread my wings, and sighed to go!
Too long I've cried, 'Blest Saviour, come.
And bear me to Thyself and home!'

How favoured they, who once on earth,
Enjoyed Thy converse, felt Thy worth;

Who had Thee for their Friend and Guest,
And leaned their heads upon Thy breast!

How blest, to look up in Thy face,
And there Thy Father's image trace!
To hear the music of Thy tongue.
And learn from thence how angels sung!

A lot like this is not for me.
On earth to thus converse with Thee;
And tell what I have seen, and heard,
And handled, of the Incarnate Word.

Yet do I hope at last to rise,
And join my Lord above the skies;
Close by His feet to take my place.
And see and praise Him face to face;

To view Him 'mid His flock, and share.
With them the mighty Shepherd's care;
To hear His saints their tributes pay.
And be myself as loud as they.
Till time shall bring this glad event,
I linger here in banishment;
And but for what I taste of Him,
My lot were yet more blank and dim.

But through the gloom at times He looks,
My hopes revives, my fears rebukes.
And bids me here a foretaste prove,
Of all I seek with Him above.

Then haste, ye lingering hours, away,
And bring the full unclouded day.
That bears me from a world like this.
And lands me safe where Jesus is!

ON DREAMING OF MY MOTHER

Stay, gentle shadow of my mother, stay:
Thy form but seldom comes to bless my sleep.
Ye faithless slumbers, flit not thus away,
And leave my wistful eyes to wake and weep.
Oh! I was dreaming of those golden days
When, will my guide, and pleasure all my aim,
I rambled wild through childhood's flowery maze.
And knew of Sorrow scarcely by her name.
Those scenes are fled! And thou, alas! art fled,
Light of my heart, and guardian of my youth!
Then come no more to slumbering fancy's bed,
To aggravate the pangs of waking truth:
Or, if land sleep these visions will restore.
Oh, let me sleep again, and never waken more!

TO ELLEN

Weeping in Church on the Anniversary of her Father's
Death, when Fifteen Years Old

Ah! wherefore should the silent tear,
Down Ellen's youthful visage stray,
When such a Hand unseen is near.
To wipe each falling drop away;
A Hand that bears a balm from high,
For every earthly tear and sigh?

And wherefore mourn a parent's doom,
When such a Parent from above.

83

Extends His arms and bids her come,
    And dwell with Him whose name is Love;
Who ne'er that orphan will disown,
Whom Jesus' blood has made His own?

That gentle Hand, ah! would she see
    And prove its power to soothe and heal!
Ah! would she to that Father flee,
    And know how well He loves her weal!
Ah! would she learn how sweet it is
    Through Christ to be for ever His! —

Come, then, and give that heart to Him,
    Which long has dwelt on meaner things:
Come, find thy song a worthier theme,
    And learn to soar on loftier wings.
He who has died that thou mightst live,
Deserves the best 'tis thine to give.

The Spirit seeks to live thy Friend,
    And Christ thy Brother deigns to be;
The joys, that know nor bounds nor end.
    To thy possession all are free.
Whate'er is lovely, pure, or great,
On Ellen now vouchsafes to wait.

Expectant angels cry, 'O come!'
    And saints prepare their gladdest song,
Those wandering feet to welcome home,
    Which fifteen years have strayed too long:
Come, then, and all shall triumph o'er
One dear, lost, rescued sinner more.

LONGINGS FOR HOME

Stern Britain, why a home deny
To one who loves thee well as I?
Who woos thee with as warm a zeal
As sons for tenderest mothers feel,

Would hold to thee through good and ill,
Yet find thee but a step-dame still?
Earth has for me no place of rest
So dear as thy parental breast,
No spot to which so close I cling
As to the shelter of thy wing;
And yet thou spurn'st me from thee, yea,
Spurn'st like a prodigal away;
Thou fling'st me suppliant from thy side,
To float a wreck upon the tide;
A boundless world at will to roam,
And sigh and think of thee and home!

Here, amidst fabled woods and streams,
The classic haunts of youthful dreams,
'Mid crumbling fanes and ruins hoary,
Rich with the hues of ancient glory;
Where every hill and every dell
Has its own stirring tale to tell,
And thoughtful pilgrims oft compare
The things that are with things that were.
Yes, here, where seems so much combined
To soothe the sense and fill the mind,
All rich, all bright, around, above,
As soft as is the voice of love, —
While at my feet in silver flakes
The evening billow gently breaks, —
I stand and muse, and o'er the sea,
My thoughts roam off to home and thee.

O what is all that earth bestows,
All that mere sense enjoys and knows.
The fairest fields, the sunniest skies,
To life's diviner charities?
Perchance this eve, so lovely here,
In my own land is bleak and drear;

And clouded skies and blustry weather,
Drive my own dear ones close together;
And round the hearth their beaming faces
Perhaps take now their wonted places,
Each with his little social mite
To aid the general stock to-night;—
His floweret on Time's path to fling,
Or add a feather to his wing.
O, loved ones, at this happy season
Of tender thought and social reason,
When hearts are full, and fancy free,
O, do you sometimes think of me? —
Think of your absent wanderer, who
So fondly hangs on home and you,
And would this moment rather share
Your homely fireside converse there,
And smile with you 'neath wintry skies,
Than reign in this fair paradise!

Alas! 'tis by their loss alone
Our truest blessings oft are known.
If earth wears here a sunnier hue,
Man is the plant that thrives with you;
A plant matured by want and toil,
And noblest oft on poorest soil.
If bleak your hills and rough your clime,
They are not rank with weeds of crime;
The social virtues there take root,
And freedom bears her richest fruit,
While industry and skill supplies
What niggard nature else denies.
The poor man's rights have honour due,
The wronged and weak redress with you.
And boundless as yon rolling sea,
Large as the world, your charity.
Within your happy homes meanwhile

Order, and peace, and comfort smile;
And fertile are your rugged lands
In manly minds, and hearts, and hands,
In generous aims and thoughts elate,
And all that makes men good and great.
And more than all to you is given
High intercourse with God and Heaven.
Religion walking through your land
Showers down her gifts with liberal hand,

And bids the desert, as she goes,
Rejoice, and blossom like the rose.
This is thy glory, Britain; this
Makes thy fair island what it is —
With all its faults, in moral worth,
The Eden of this fallen earth.

Oh, gifts too lightly valued — how
My thirsty soul would prize them now!
Those hallowed Sabbaths, calm and fair,
That still well-ordered house of prayer,
The call that bids the weary come,
The ray that lights the wanderer home;
The Spirit's whisper from above,
The still small voice of truth and love.
O when, my own loved lost ones, when
Shall we such blessings share again?
Drink of the sacred springs that flow
With balm for every want and woe,
Lift up our hearts in prayer and praise
Bequeathed from wiser, better days,
And round the holy altar fare
On food that angels may not share? —
When shall such joys be ours? From high
Heard I a solemn voice reply:
'Live to your Saviour: watch and pray,

Grow in His image day by day;
And know, the souls which thus improve
In meekness, duty, faith, and love,
Though severed in this world of pain,
In earth or Heaven shall meet again!'

GRACE DARLING'S DEATH-BED

O wipe the death-dews from her brow! — prop up her sinking
    head! —
And let the sea-breeze on her face its welcome
    freshness
    shed!
She loves to see the western sun pour glory o'er the
    deep;
And the music of the rippling waves may sing her into
    sleep.
Her heart has long, 'mid other scenes, for these
    poured out the
    sigh;
And now back to her Highland home she comes —
    but comes
    to die.
Yes, fearful in its loveliness, that cheek's prophetic
    bloom;
That lustrous eye is lighted from a world beyond the
    tomb;
Those thin transparent fingers, that hold the book of
    prayer,
That form, which melts like summer snow, too plainly
    speak
    despair.
And they that tend around her bed, oft turn to wipe
    the tear

That starts forth, as they view her thus, so fleeting,
    and so
    dear.

Not such was she that awful night when o'er
    Northumbria's
    foam,
The shipwrecked seaman's cry was heard within that
    rocky
    home.
Amid the pauses of the storm it loud and louder came,
And thrilled into her inmost soul, and nerved her
    fragile
    frame:
'O, father, let us launch the boat, and try their lives to
    save.'
'Be still, my child, we should but go to share their
    watery
    grave.'

Again they shriek: ' O father, come! the Lord our
    Guide will
    be:
A word from Him can stay the blast, and tame the
    raging sea.'
And lo! at length her plea prevails; their skiff is on the
    wave.
Protect them, gracious Heaven! protect the gentle,
    kind, and
    brave!
They reach the rock, and, wond'rous sight to those
    they succour
    there,
A feeble girl achieving more than boldest men would
    dare!

Again, again her venturous bark bounds o'er the
    foaming tide;
Again in safety goes and comes beneath its Heavenly
    Guide.
Nor shrinks that maid's heroic heart, nor fails her
    willing hand,

Till all the remnant of the wreck are ferried safe to
    land.
The cord o'erstrung relaxes then, and tears begin to
    fall; —
But tears of love and praise to Him whose mercy
    saved them
        all.

A deed like this could not be hid. Upon the wings of
    fame,
To every corner of our isle, flew forth Grace Darling's
    name;
And tongues were loud in just applause, and bosoms
    highly
        beat.
And tributes from the great and good were lavished at
    her feet;
While she, who braved the midnight blast, and rode
    the stormy
        swell,
Shrank timid, trembling, from the praise that she had
    earned
        so well.

Why did they tempt her forth to scenes she ill was
    formed to
        share?
Why bid her face the curious crowd, the question,
    and the
        stare?
She did not risk her life that night to earn the world's
    applause:
Her own heart's impulse sent her forth in pity's holy
    cause.
And richly were her toils repaid, and well her soul
    content
With the sweet thought of duty done, of succour
    timely lent.

Her tender spirit sank apace. O, bear the drooping
    flower

Back to its native soil again — its own secluded
    bower!
Amidst admiring multitudes, she sighs for home and
    rest:
Let the meek turtle fold her wings within her own
    wild nest;
And drink the sights and sounds she loves, and
    breathe her
    wonted air.
And find with them a quiet hour for thoughtfulness
    and
    prayer!

And she has reached her sea-girt home — and she can
    smile
    once more;
But ah, a faint and moonlight smile, without the glow
    of yore!
The breeze breathes not as once it did upon her
    fevered brow;
The waves talk on, but in her breast awake no echoes
    now:
For vague and flickering are her thoughts, her soul is
    on the
    wing
For Heaven, and has but little heed for earth or
    earthly thing.

'My father, dost thou hear their shriek? dost hear their
    drowning cry?'
'No, dearest, no; 'twas but the scream of the curlew
    flitting by.'
Poor panting, fluttering, hectic thing, thy tossings
    soon will
    cease.
Thou art passing through a troubled sea, but to a land
    of
    peace!
And He who to a shipwrecked world brought rescue,
    O may He
Be near thy dying pillow now, sweet Grace, to
    succour thee!

NAPOLEON'S GRAVE

Addressed to the French nation on their proposing to remove
Napoleon's remains from St. Helena to France.

Disturb him not! he slumbers well
   On his rock 'mid'the western deep,
      Where the broad blue waters round him swell,
   And the. tempests o'er him sweep.
Oh, leave him where his mountain bed
   Looks o'er the Atlantic wave,
And the mariner high in the far grey sky,
   Points out Napoleon's grave.

There, 'midst three mighty continents
   That trembled at his word,
Wrapt in his shroud of airy cloud,
   Sleeps Europe's warrior lord:
And there, on the heights, still seems to stand,
   At eve, his shadowy form;
His grey capote on the mist to float.
   And his voice in the midnight storm.

Disturb him not: though bleak and bare,
   That spot is all his own;
And truer homage was paid him there,
   Than on his hard-won throne.
Earth's trembling monarchs there at bay,
   The caged lion kept;
For they knew with dread that his iron tread,
   Woke earthquakes where he stept.

Disturb him not! vain France, thy clime
   No resting-place supplies,
So meet, so glorious, so sublime,
   As that where thy Hero lies.

Mock not that grim and mouldering wreck!
    Revere that bleaching brow!
Nor call the dead from his grave to deck,
    A puppet pageant now!

Born in a time when blood and crime,
    Raged through thy realm at will,
He waved his hand o'er the troubled land,
    And the storm at once was still.
He reared from the dust thy prostrate State;
    Thy war-flag wide unfurled;
And bade thee thunder at every gate,
    Of the capitals of the world.

And will ye from his rest dare call,
    The thunderbolt of war!
To grin and chatter round his pall,
    And scream your 'Vive la gloire'?
Shall melodramatic obsequies
    His honoured dust deride?
Forbid it, human sympathies!
    Forbid it, Gallic pride!

What! will no withering thought occur,
    No thrill of cold mistrust,
How empty all this pomp and stir,
    Above a little dust?
And will it not your pageant dim,
    Your arrogance rebuke.
To see what now remains of him.
    Who once the empires shook?

Then let him rest in his stately couch,
    Beneath the open sky,
Where the wild waves dash, and the lightnings flash,
    And the storms go wailing by;
Yes, let him rest! Such men as he
    Are of no time or place;
They live for ages yet to be,
    They die for all their race.

DECLINING DAYS

Why do I sigh to find
　　Life's evening shadows gathering round my
　　　　way?
The keen eye dimming, and the buoyant mind
　　Unhinging day by day?

Is it the natural dread
　　Of that stern lot, which all who live must see?
The worm, the clay, the dark and narrow bed, —
　　Have these such awe for me?

Can I not summon pride
　　To fold my decent mantle round my breast;
And lay me down at Nature's eventide,
　　Calm to my dreamless rest?

As nears my soul the verge
　　Of this dim continent of woe and crime,
Shrinks she to hear Eternity's long surge
　　Break o'er the shores of time?

Asks she, how shall she fare
　　When conscience stands before the Judge's throne,
And gives her record in, and all shall there
　　Know, as they all are known?

A solemn scene and time —
　　And well may Nature quail to feel them near —
But grace in feeble breasts can work sublime,
　　And faith o'ermaster fear!

Hark! from that throne comes down
　　A voice which strength to sinking souls can give,
That voice all Judgment's thunders cannot drown;
　　'Believe,' it cries, 'and live.'

Weak — sinful, as I am,
　　That still small voice forbids me to despond;

Faith clings for refuge to the bleeding Lamb,
    Nor dreads the gloom beyond. —

'Tis not, then, earth's delights
    From which my spirit feels so loath to part;
Nor the dim future's solemn sounds or sights,
    That press so on my heart.

No! 'tis the thought that I— -
    My lamp so low, my sun so nearly set,
Have lived so useless, so unmissed should lie: —
    'Tis this, I now regret. —

I would not be the wave
    That swells and ripples up to yonder shore;
That drives impulsive on, the wild wind's slave,
    And breaks, and is no more! —

I would not be the breeze,
    That murmurs by me in its viewless play.
Bends the light grass, and flutters in the trees,
    And sighs and flits away!

No! not like wave or wind
    Be my career across the earthly scene;
To come and go, and leave no trace behind,
    To say that I have been.

I want not vulgar fame —
    I seek not to survive in brass or stone;
Hearts may not kindle when they hear my name,
    Nor tears my value own. —

But might I leave behind
    Some blessing for my fellows, some fair trust
To guide, to cheer, to elevate my kind
    When I am in the dust.

Within my narrow bed,
    Might I not wholly mute or useless be;
But hope that they, who trampled o'er my head,
    Drew still some good from me!

Might my poor lyre but give
   Some simple strain, some spirit-moving lay;
Some sparklet of the soul, that still might live
   When I have passed to clay! —

Might verse of mine inspire
   One virtuous aim, one high resolve impart;
Light in one drooping soul a hallowed fire,
   Or bind one broken heart. —

Death would be sweeter then,
   More calm my slumber 'neath the silent sod;
Might I thus live to bless my fellow-men,
   Or glorify my God.

Why do we ever lose,
   As judgment ripens, our diviner powers?
Why do we only learn our gifts to use,
   When they no more are ours?

O Thou whose touch can lend
   Life to the dead, Thy quick'ning grace supply,
And grant me, swanlike, my last breath to spend
   In song that may not die!

A RECALL TO MY CHILD, A. M.

Come back, come back, my blessed child!
   Come home, my own light-hearted!
    Papa, they say, has rarely smiled,
   Since from his side you parted. —
That face which beams like opening day,
   That laugh which never wearies;
Why do they linger still away?
   Come home, dear girl, and cheer us!

I saunter sadly through my hours, —
   They want one voice to mend them;

A spell is o'er my drooping flowers, —
    They pine for you to tend them.
The fairest now look all amiss,
    Too dingy, or too flaunting. —
And are they changed? ah, no, 'tis this —
    The sweetest flower is wanting!

Young spring at last, despite the shocks
    Of winter's lingering bluster,
Has flung her mantle o'er our rocks,
    And clothed our lulls with lustre.
Music and balm, and beauty play,
    In all around and o'er us.
'Come, truant, come,' all seem to say:
    'Come, join our happy chorus.'

'Come,' cries the cowslip's fading bell;
    'Come,' cries the ripening cherry;
'Come, ere the bloom in every dell,
    Is turned to pod and berry;
Come, ere the cuckoo change his tone;
    Ere from her nest the linnet,
With all her little ones is flown,
    And you've ne'er peeped within it.'

The sun sets not so brightly now,
    Across the golden water,
As when it gleamed upon the brow,
    Of my loved absent daughter.
Home has no more its cheerful tone,
    Its healthful hue about it: —
When from the lyre one chord is gone,
    The rest sound ill without it.

Come back; the city's flaunting crowd,
    The concert's formal measures,
The din of fashion, false and loud,
    Are not like Nature's pleasures. —
These, these alone, the heart can touch,
    Are simplest and sincerest.
You have an eye, a soul for such:
    Come home, and share them, dearest.

Come, at my side again to walk,
   Beside the fresh'ning billow.
Come, where the waves all night will talk,
   To you upon your pillow.
Come, where the skiff on sunny seas,'
   For you is lightly riding;
Where health and song in every breeze,
   My absent girl come chiding.

Come back! we all from your glad eyes
   New light and life will borrow.
'Tis not papa alone that sighs,
   'Why leave me to my sorrow?'
Each, all, in your loved converse miss
   Some wonted source of pleasure,
From look, or tone, or smile, or kiss:
   Come home, come home, my treasure!

DAVID'S THREE MIGHTY ONES

2 Samuel 23:15

Faint on Rephaim's sultry side,
   Sat Israel's warrior King;
   'O for one draught,' the hero cried,
   'From Bethlehem's cooling spring! —
From Bethlehem's spring, upon whose brink
My youthful knee bent down to drink!

'I know the spot, by yonder gate,
   Beside my father's home.
Where pilgrims love at eve to wait,
   And girls for water come.
O for that healing water now.
To quench my lip, to cool my brow!

'But round that gate, and in that home,
   And by that sacred well,

Now hostile feet insulting roam,
 And impious voices swell.
The Philistine holds Bethlehem's halls.
While we pine here beneath its walls.'

Three gallant men stood nigh, and heard
 The wish their King expressed;
Exchanged a glance, but not a word,
 And dashed from 'midst the rest.
And strong in zeal, with ardour flushed,
They up the hill to Bethlehem rushed.

The foe fast mustering to attack,
 Their fierceness could not rein;
No friendly voice could call them back. —
 'Shall David long in vain?
Long for a cup from Bethlehem's spring.
And none attempt the boon to bring?'

And now the city gate they gain,
 And now in conflict close;
Unequal odds! three dauntless men,
 Against unnumbered foes.
Yet through their ranks they plough their way,
Like galleys through the ocean spray.

The gate is forced, the crowd is passed;
 They scour the open street;
While hosts are gathering fierce and fast,
 To block up their retreat.
Haste back! haste back, ye desperate three!
Or Bethlehem soon your grave must be!

They come again; — and with them bring —
 Nor gems nor golden prey;
A single cup from Bethlehem's spring,
 Is all they bear away;
And through the densest of the train,
Fight back their glorious way again.
O'er broken shields and prostrate foes,
 They urge their conquering course.

Go, try the tempest to oppose,
    Arrest the lightning's force;
But hope not, pagans, to withstand
The shock of Israel's chosen band!

Hurrah! hurrah! again they're free;
    And 'neath the open sky,
On the green turf they bend the knee,
    And lift the prize on high;
Then onward through the shouting throng,
To David bear their spoil along.

All in their blood and dust they sink,
    Full low before their King.
'Again,' they cry,' let David drink,
    Of his own silver spring;
And if the draught our lord delight,
His servants' toil 'twill well requite.'

With deep emotion David took,
    From their red hands the cup;
Cast on its stains a shuddering look,
    And held it heavenward up.
'I prize your boon,' exclaimed the King,
    'But dare not taste the draught you bring.

'I prize the zeal that periled life,
    A wish of mine to crown;
I prize the might that in the strife,
    Bore foes by thousands down: —
But dare not please myself with aught,
By Israel's blood and peril bought.

'To Heaven the glorious spoil is due;
    And His the offering be,
Whose arm has borne you safely through,
    My brave, but reckless, three!' —
Then on the earth the cup he poured,
A free libation to the Lord.

There is a well in Bethlehem still,
    A fountain, at whose brink,

The weary soul may rest at will,
    The thirsty stoop and drink:
And unrepelled by foe or fence,
Draw living waters freely thence.

O, did we thirst, as David then,
    For this Diviner spring!
Had we the zeal of David's men
    To please a Higher King!
What precious draughts we thence might drain,
What holy triumphs daily gain!

SEA CHANGES

From shore to shore the waters sleep,
    Without a breath to move them;
        And mirror many a fathom deep,
        Rocks round and skies above them.
I catch the sea-bird's lightest wail,
    That dots the distant billow,
And hear the flappings of the sail,
    That lull the sea-boy's pillow.

Anon — across the glassy bay,
    The catspaw gusts come creeping;
A thousand waves are soon at play,
    In sunny freshness leaping.
The surge once more talks round the shore,
    The good ship walks the ocean;
Seas, skies, and men all wake again,
    To music, health, and motion.

But now the clouds, in angry crowds,
    On Heaven's grim forehead muster,
And wild and wide sweeps o'er the tide,
    The white squall's fitful bluster.

The stout ship heels, the brave heart reels,
    Before the 'whelming breaker;
And all in Nature quakes, and feels
    The presence of its Maker.

O, glorious still in every form.
    Untamed, untrodden ocean;
Beneath the sunshine, or the storm,
    In stillness, or commotion;
Be mine to dwell beside the swell,
    A witness of thy wonders;
Feel thy light spray around me play.
    And thrill before thy thunders!

While yet a boy I felt it joy
    To gaze upon thy glories;
I loved to ride thy stormy tide,
    And shout in joyous chorus.
With calmer brow I haunt thee now,
    To nurse sublime emotion;
My soul is awed, and filled with God
    By thee, majestic ocean!

STANZAS TO J. K.

What strains are these, what sweet familiar
    numbers,
        From old Ierne o'er the waters wend?
How welcome, wakening from its lengthened
    slumbers,
        Sounds the heart-music of my earliest friend!
Well might that hand amid the chords have faltered,
    That voice have lost the power to melt and move:
How pleasant, then, to find them still unaltered,
    That lyre in sweetness, and that heart in love!

Shall not my tuneful powers, too long neglected,
    Revive to answer that persuasive call? —
Like the old harp that, mould'ring and rejected,
    Hangs up in silence in some lonely hall,
When youth and beauty's train there reassembles,
    And mirth and song once more begin to flow,
Light o'er the chords a mimic music trembles,
    Responsive to the notes that swell below!
Ah me! — what thoughts those few bold notes
    awaken,—
    Bright recollections of life's morning hours;
Haunts long remembered, and too soon forsaken;
    Days that fled by in sunshine, song, and flowers;
Old Clogher's rocks, our own sequestered valley;
    Wild walks by moonlight on the sounding shore,
Hearts warm and free, light laugh, and playful sally,
    All that has been, — and shall return no more —

No more, — no more, — moods ever new and
    changing,
    Feelings that forth in song so freely gushed,
Winged hopes, high fancies, thoughts unfettered
    ranging —
    Flowers which the world's cold ploughshare since
    has crushed.
Dear early visions of departed gladness,
    Ye rise, ye live a moment in that strain,
A gleam of sunshine on life's wintry sadness,
    Ah! why so bright, to flit so soon again?

Friend of my heart! — since those young visions
    perished
    We've trod a chequered path of good and ill;

We've seen the wreck of much that once we
   cherished,
   But not the wreck of love and friendship still.
No, hand in hand we've met life's stormy weather,
   Sustained the buffetings of foe and friend.
And hand in hand and heart in heart together,
   We'll help and cheer each other to the end.

Strike then the chords! — alas, too rarely stricken,
   And I will answer in my humbler style:
No voice like thine can soothe, can urge, can quicken,
   —
   Why has it been so little heard ere while?
Yes, strike the chords! high thoughts and aims
   inspiring;
   And up the narrow way we'll homeward move,
Mingling our pilgrim songs, and here acquiring,
   New hearts and voices for the songs above.

THE CZAR IN ROME

Explanatory note:

In December 1845, Emperor Nicholas of Russia, after being at Palermo and Naples, came to Rome, but met with no welcome or greeting there. His reputation had come before him, and all were indignant at his tyrannical conduct towards his Polish subjects, and his persecution of the unfortunate Roman Catholics in his dominions, whom he wished to compel to conform to the Greek Church.

One of the unfortunate nuns from the convent of Minsk, of whom more than thirty had perished under the frightful persecutions to which they were subjected, escaped from Russia, and found her way to Rome, and was thus in a great measure the means of informing the world of the cruelties that were going on in Russia.

On the morning after his arrival the Emperor had an audience with the Pope, who appears to have spoken with great firmness and dignity upon the occasion; and when the Emperor left his presence his face was flushed, the sweat stood on his brow, and he was evidently ill at ease. After leaving the Pope, the Emperor went into St. Peter's, where he seemed awed with the majesty of the place, and fell prostrate before St. Peter's shrine, and kissed the ground. (The Greeks are worshippers of the saints even more than the Roman Catholics.) It is even said that there he told his attendants that if the Roman Catholics had been persecuted in Russia they should be so no more.

The mighty Caesar of the North
   Has entered Rome to-day.
     Why peal her bells no greetings forth,
  Her crowds no tributes pay?
'Stranger, we love the great and good;
  But honour not the man of blood!

'The man of blood! can one so high
  Upon the lists of fame,
Who looks and moves thus loyally,
  Deserve so dark a name?'
'Yes! let the pining exile tell.
  The bleeding martyr say, how well!'

While through these streets he sweeps to-day,
  The gaze of thousand eyes,
A victim of his iron sway
  In yonder convent lies,
And pleads for her oppressor there. —
  O King of kings, fulfil her prayer!

The soul that looks through such an eye,
  That sits on such a brow;

105

Must have its instincts rare and high,
  Though undeveloped now;
And moral music, strong and deep,
  Among its chords must surely sleep.

And who shall say, within that breast,
  What throes e'en now may work?
Seems there no signs of strange unrest,
  Beneath that brow to lurk?
No troubled wave to heave and roll,
  O'er the proud stillness of his soul?

This morn St. Peter's courts he trod,
  With stately step and stern,
Encountered there the man of God; —
  And how did he return?
With faltering foot, and darkened look,
  That spoke confusion and rebuke.

Did some strong truth, all new and strange,
  Blest by the great 'I am,'
Drop from those reverend lips, and change
  The lion to the lamb?
Did pride feel there abashed and awed,
  And conscience own the voice of God?

This morn before St. Peter's shrine,
  In lowly guise he knelt.
Fell on him there some grace Divine,
  With power to move and melt?
And flew to him some wing of Love,
  Charged with an unction from above?

While prostrate 'neath that ample dome,
  Amidst the holy dead,
Touched with the claims of injured Rome,
  His soul may well have said,
'Surely the Lord is in this spot,
  And I, insensate, knew it not!'

Might one such feeling reach his heart,
  One thought like this prevail,

'Remember, mortal, what thou art.
    Accountable and frail!'
The crowns and sceptres of this earth,
    Weighed with that thought, had little worth.

And where so well might moods like these,
    Upon the spirit come,
As here, where sighs the autumn breeze,
    O'er desolated Rome;
Where every stone its moral brings;
    Where tread we on the dust of Kings?

Saw ye a shadowy hand sublime,
    Write on that ruined wall?
Heard ye a voice, the voice of Time,
    From yon grey turret call?
'All fleets, all fades beneath the skies;
    O man, be humble and be wise!'

Go forth then, King of nations; march
    Along the sacred way;
Stand 'neath the yet unbroken arch [3]
    Of him who lost a day,
When he had done no generous deed;
    And wilt thou there no lesson read?

Go where the Coliseum rears
    Its sad, majestic pile, —
The pride and shame of former years: —
    Go, when the moonbeams smile.
And talk with the historic dead,
    Who there have revelled, — or have bled!

The tyrant's trophies sink to dust;
    The hero's still arise,
True to their monumental trust, —
    Lo, in the evening skies,
How freshly bright file columns shine,
    Of Trajan and of Antonine!

---

[3] Arch of Titus

Go, then, to these mute teachers, go!
    And if, like genial rain,
Their lore upon thy heart shall flow,
    Thou cam'st not here in vain;
Nor shalt thou fail to carry home,
    A blessing from Eternal Rome!

✿✿✿ ✿✿✿ ✿✿✿

FRAGMENTS OF AN UNFINISHED POEM ENTITLED *LILLA*

A Fairy Tale

'Tis pleasant to walk the broad seashore
When the soul is dark, or the heart is sore.
The waves give forth a soothing sound,
As they boom along the shelving ground;
The crispness of the salt sea air,
Breathes fresh on the fevered brow of care:
And the waters, melting into the sky,
Send the spirit on to Eternity!
So felt Sir Rupert, as o'er the sands
That skirted his own brave house and lands
He paced, but in dark regardless mood
Of aught that there his attention wooed.
The sky was clear, and the sun was bright.
The blue waves danced in the shifting light,
And the foam-bells on the sand uprolled,
Tike silvery fret on a floor of gold.
The fair white ships sailed stately by,
The seamew[4] flitted and laughed on high.
But all appeared in vain to woo
Sir Rupert's thoughts to a livelier hue.

---

[4] Sea gull

From that mysterious race I'm sprung
That lived with man, when the world was young:
But ever since envy and lust possessed,
And ruled and sullied his own pure breast,
They have fled from earthly folly and art,
And dwell in a world of their own apart:
Hiding in Nature's secluded bowers,
Watching and tending her fruits and flowers,
Giving the blossom its scent and hue,
And the fainting leaf its drink of dew;
Spanning the shower with its bright brief arch,
Leading the seasons their stately march,
Staying the storm in his fierce career. —
These are the tasks which engage us here.
Not that we less count man our friend,
Or fail on his homely wants to tend.
We note the housewife's honest cares,
And speed her labours all unawares.
We succour the mower down in the mead,
And help the ploughman to sow his seed.
We smooth the pillow where sickness lies,
And shake sweet sleep o'er the infant's eyes.
But we mingle not in man's vain affairs,
Nor darken our path with his fears and cares;
And the Court, the city, the festive hall,
We feel as strangers amidst them all

'Tis merry, 'tis merry in Colmar towers,
On Rostan's hills, and in Binda's bowers,
In humble cot, and in stately hall;
There are happy looks and hearts in all.
The cloud that hung o'er the whole is fled,
And the broad clear sun laughs out instead.
One influence sweet, one presence bright,

Has quickened the darkness into light.
Woman's soft smile is in Colmar found,
And it blesses and gladdens all around.
This Rupert felt, as from day to day,
Lilla spread round her gentle sway;
All, all beneath her influence grew
To a better tone, to a brighter hue.
Old Colmar's Courts no longer wore,
Their lorn and desolate air of yore;
A cheerful bustle ran through the place,
Content sat beaming on every face;
And active feet and diligent hands,
Eager to work her light commands;
And all on their various tasks intent,
At their lady's bidding came and went.
All into life by her eye seemed warmed;
All to her own sweet will conformed;
Till throughout that grim old Gothic pile,
Order and neatness began to smile;
And comfort lighted up there a home,
That stole from the heart all wish to roam.
Nor less did improvement win its way,
O'er all that around the castle lay.
The lawn, of late so rugged and wild,
Like emerald velvet now glowed and smiled.
The walk with mosses and weeds overspread,
Wooed the light step o'er its gravelly bed.
Trees and shrubs that had wont to swing
Their long lank arms on the wild wind's wing,
Were taught to conform their savage will
To the eye of taste and the hand of skill.
The fount, that long had forgot to play,
Sparkled once more in the morning ray.
The vine clung again to the elm-tree tall,
And the plum hung blue on the garden wall. —
And then the flowers, the laughing flowers,

The playmates of Lilla's earliest hours,
How did she revel among them! how
Watch, and nurse, and enjoy them now!
Whether they grew on the wild bank, known
To the wandering bee and the lark alone;
Or bloomed in the garden's courtly bed,
Like orient beauties in harem bred;
From the queen-like rose to the harebell small,
Gentle and simple she loved them all.

She loved whatever was lovely here;
And flowers, sweet flowers, to her heart were dear.
She knew their ways, and her joy and pride,
Was to gather them round her from every side,
To give them the site which themselves would
choose,
To trim their leaves, and to match their hues;
A staff in the weak one's hand to place,
And lift to the sun its small pale face;
To bring the diffident out to view,
The bold to check, and the proud subdue.
Not one of them all but had its share
Of her watchful love and judicious care.
She flitted among them as if on wings,
And talked to them all as to living things.
And they as conscious how great their bliss,
Held up their cheeks for a passing kiss;
Flung in her pathway their sweetest scent.
And smiled and nodded as on she went.

❧❧❧

They wander down to the broad seashore,
But not in his once dark spirit of yore.
Now, not a wild wing that across them flies,
Not a light shell in their path that lies,
Nothing in ocean, or earth, or sky,

111

Fails to awaken their sympathy.
Or, if the sun with his fiercer rays,
Drives their steps to the woodland ways,
The squirrel is there with his chattering glee,
And the jay glad shouting from tree to tree;
And the rabbit stirring the ferns among,
And the pheasant sunning her speckled young,
O! Nature a golden harvest yields
To all who will glean in her varied fields;
But their brightest tints her objects wear,
When those that we love are nigh to share!

❧❧❧ ❧❧❧ ❧❧❧

And O! she was rich in each social wile,
The night of its weariness to beguile!
She spoke, and mute attention hung,
Persuasion dwelt on her silver tongue;
Sweet fancies, clad in sweetest words,
Held the charmed ear with magic chords,
And judgment clear, and taste refined,
Brought food alike to the heart and mind.
And when her favourite songs she sung,
The birds stayed theirs; — the soft winds hung
Entranced around her to catch the ton,
And by her music to mend their own.

❧❧❧ ❧❧❧ ❧❧❧

Each lived for each, one will, one heart,
Without a thought or a wish apart.
As streams, from opposite hills that run,
But meet in the valley, and blend in one,
Their murmurs hushed, and their wanderings past,
Glide on together in peace at last!

SONG

Weep on! weep on! 'tis a world of woe;
'Tis vain to expect aught else below.
The life of man has but one true tone.
From its infantile cry, to its dying groan.
Each step he takes through a land of gloom,
But carries him onward to the tomb;
And all that he meets with as he goes,
Talks to his heart of the solemn close.

Weep on; there are many with man to weep,
The murmuring winds, and the moaning deep;
The fading flower, and the falling dews,
And the year expiring in dolphin hues.
What says the rainbow's beautiful dream?
Or the sunset's brief but gorgeous gleam?
Or the summer lightning, now come, now gone?-
We shine but to fade! Weep on! weep on!

Weep on! it is good on this earth to weep:
If we sow in tears, we in joy may reap.
While the hopes that we madly cherish there,
But pave the way to some new despair.
Pale is the young cheek's richest bloom,
When it strews the path to an early tomb;
And dim the fire of the brightest eye,
When a beacon that points to mortality.
Weep on! weep on!

THE COMPLAINT OF MARY MAGDALENE

She sat far off, — she sat and wept,
Heart-broken Magdalene!
  Her dark and silent watch she kept,
  Throughout the awful scene.
No power had she to soothe or aid,
  No hope to interpose;
Yet love and grief her heart upstayed,
  To watch Him to the close.

'Twas He, 'twas He, who first the way
  Of life to her had shown;
Had freed her soul from Satan's sway,
  And made it all His own.
'Twas He she soon had hoped to see,
  In kingly glory rise, —
And now, upon the fatal tree,
  He bleeds. He faints, He dies!

And she has followed Him through all
  His wrongs and griefs to-day;
Stood with Him in the Judgment hall,
  Trod o'er the public way.
The scourge, the cords, the savage thorns,
  She shared them to the close;
Scorned in her outraged Master's scorns,
  And bleeding in His woes.

The ponderous cross she saw Him bear,
  All fainting up the hill;
She saw them nail Him on it there,
  With unrelenting skill;
She heard their wild and withering cry,
  As He aloft was swung,
The gaze of every flashing eye,
  The scoff of every tongue!

No angel comes, on wings of love,
  His sinking soul to cheer;

The very heavens seem shut above,
    And mercy fails to hear;
Despised, deserted, crushed, and awed,
    He hangs upon the tree,
And cries in vain, 'My God, My God,
    Hast Thou forsaken Me?'

O trying scene for woman's eye!
    And yet she braved it all;
The struggle and the agony,
    The wormwood and the gall —
Though earth beneath in horror shook,
    Though heaven its light withdrew,
And sterner hearts the awe partook,
    Yet woman braved it through.

She sat far off — she sat and wept,
    Heart-broken Magdalene!
Her dark and silent watch she kept,
    Throughout the trying scene!
She sank not when His head He bowed
    She bore His dying groan —
Till passed away the sated crowd,
    And left her there alone!

The shades of evening round her head,
    Now gathered thick and fast;
And forth her burthened spirit fled,
    In louder woe at last.
Upon the ear of silent night,
    Her plaintive murmurs broke,
And sorrow seemed to grow more light,
    As thus she wept and spoke:

'And is all over? Can it be
    That they have had their will?
Thou hanging. Lord, on yonder tree,
    And we surviving still?
Is this to be the course and close,
    Of all Thy conflicts past?
A brief, dark path through wrongs and woes,
    To such a death at last?

'Yes, past all reach of ill Thou art, —
    I see no living sign;
And O, that this sad struggling heart,
    Were now as still as Thine!
I groan — Thou canst not heed my groan,
    Nor answer when I 'plain —
Ah! I shall never hear the tone
    Of that blest voice again.

'O hallowed head! compelled to bow
    Beneath unnumbered scorns;
O dear, dishonoured, glorious brow,
    Now crushed beneath the thorns;
O eyes, where heaven seemed once to reign
    Can ye grow glazed and dim?
O Death, by Him for others slain,
    Canst thou have power o'er Him?

'How couldst thou, brutal soldier, dare
    To pierce that breast Divine? —
There never dwelt a feeling there,
    But love to thee and thine.
How could ye harm one tender limb
    Of His, ye murderous crew,
And know, that while ye tortured Him,
    He prayed for you, for you?

'It must be right, I feel it must,
    Though all is darkness now; —
Lord, teach my trembling heart to trust
    And help my will to bow!
'Tis hard upon that cross to gaze,
    Nor feel the Tempter's power.
O God! sustain me through the maze
    Of this mysterious hour!

'Yes! mystery o'er the whole doth hang,
    To be unraveled still.
Who could on Him inflict a pang,
    Without the sufferer's will?

He, whom the slumbering dead have heard,
    Whose voice the winds could tame,
Could not He crush them with a word,
    If such had been His aim?

'But I remember well, when hope
    Seemed most our hearts to cheer,
What hints and warnings He would drop,
    Of pain and trial near.
He, doubtless, was intent to give
    A lesson here from high;
And asHe taught us how to live,
    Would teach us now to die!
'Yet surely 'twas a loftier task,
    That drew Him from the skies,
And ne'er could mere example ask,
    So dire a sacrifice; —
And surely these were all to tend
    At last to brighter bliss,
Not prematurely here to end,
    In double night like this.

'All prophecy proclaims a time
    When Satan's rule shall cease,
When earth shall pass from woe and crime,
    To endless love and peace, —
When death and hell, with all their hosts,
    Shall quail before their Lord,
And more than was in Adam lost
    Shall be in Christ restored.

'Yes, Lord of lords and King of kings,
    For such Thou art to me,
My soul through doubt and darkness clings
    With trembling faith to Thee, —
I feel some brighter morn shall yet
    Our shattered hopes surprise,
And glory's sun, that now is set,
    Again in glory rise.

'The great Messiah still Thou art,
    Confirmed by every sign;

117

And this may all be but a part,
    Of some sublime design.
What God ordains must needs be best, —
    What He permits is right;
On Him, on Him my soul I rest,
    And wait for further light.

'One mournful task is left me too, —
    Thy dear remains to tend;
With honours due Thy bier to strew,
    And watch Thee to the end.
Then let me to Thy lifeless clay
    Still sadly, fondly cling,
And wait, and weep, and hope, and pray,
    For what the day may bring.' —

She said, and seemed to ease her breast,
    In these complaints and prayers;
Then rose, and went to seek the rest,
    And mingle tears with theirs.
She went the spices to provide,
    His last sad rites to pay, —
Then by the tomb sat down and sighed,
    'Oh, when will it be day?'

THE DYING CHRISTIAN TO HIS SOUL

Bird of my breast, away!
    The long-wished hour is come!
        On to the realms of cloudless day,
    On to thy glorious home!

Long has been thine to mourn,
    In banishment and pain.
Return, thou wand 'ring dove, return,
    And find thy ark again!

Away, on joyous wing,
    Immensity to range;
Around the throne to soar and sing,
    And faith for sight exchange.

Lo! to the golden gate
    What shining thousands come!
My trembling soul, for thee they wait,
    To guard and guide thee home.

Hark! from on high they speak,
    That bright and blessed train,
'Rise, Heaven-born spirit, rise, and seek
    Thy rest in heavenly gain.
'Sweet are the songs above,
    Where hearts are all in tune;
They feed upon unfailing love,
    And bask in glory's noon.

'Their struggles all are still,
    Their days of darkness o'er;
At rapture's fount they drink at will,
    And drink for evermore.

'Flee, then, from sin and woe;
    To joys immortal flee;
Quit thy dark prison-house below,
    And be for ever free!'

I come, ye blessed throng,
    Your tasks and joys to share;
O, fill my lips with holy song,
    My drooping wing upbear.

Friends of my heart, adieu!
    I cannot weep to-day;

The tears that Nature prompts for you
   Are dried in glory's ray.

I see the King of kings,
   His glorious voice I hear.
O, who can dwell on earthly things
   With Heaven so bright and near?

❦❦❦

JANUARY 1, 1847

What solemn footfall smote my startled ear?
Heard I the step of the departing year?
Saw I her shadowy form flit slowly by,
To join her sisters in eternity? —
Sweeping down thither, as the autumn's blast
Sweeps summer's leaves, the records of the past,
The joys and griefs, the bustle and the strife,
The shadows and realities of life?
Hear me, stem daughter of old Time, O hear! —
Is there no plea may stay thy strong career?
pause in pity! pause and to my prayer
Grant a brief converse with the things that were —
I know the retrospect has much to pain,
Much to be mended could all come again;
Still, without one last look we must not sever,
Sad is the word that bids us part for ever!
Beam, then, again on me, dear, kindly faces,
And smile your best, old times and well-known places;
Bright looks, soft tones, high thoughts, and fancies fair,
Return, return, and be what once you were!
All that was precious in the year that's past, —
Too sweet to lose, too beautiful to last —
Sunshine, and song, and fragrance, things that threw
O'er life's dull path a brighter tint and hue;

Hopes realized, desires fulfilled; — success
Crowning long toils; the burthens of distress
Lightened, will subjugated, self-denied,
Ills overcome by long endurance, pride
Taught to be greatly humble, — all that wakes
The approving voice of conscience, all that makes
Heaven's windows open o'er us, converse sweet,
And sweeter meditation; all, — all fleet
Back into being. — Burst oblivion's chain,
And be awhile realities again! —
Blest be the powers that can the past restore; —
They come, they come, warm breathing as of yore!
I hear remembered voices, seem to dwell
Once more with forms I've known and loved so well,
Distinct, beyond my fondest hopes, they rise,
The shadows dimming the realities.
Beautiful witcheries! O would I might
Hold them thus ever, durable as bright!
But, like the splendours of a sunset sky,
E'en while I gaze their glories wane and die.
And, as they fade, uprising in their rear
A host of darker verities appear;
Sorrows and sins of various shades and hues,
That claim their notice in the year's review.
And shall they be rejected? shall my eyes
Be shut to life's too stern realities?
And shall the records of the past be seen,
Not as they were, but as they should have been?
No! small the gain and brief the joy that lives,
In the poor dreams such self-delusion gives;
And honest conscience scorns to take a tone,
Or speak a flattering language not her own;
And wherefore seek to bribe her, wherefore fear
Her rough but salutary voice to hear,
When every morning, now rejected, grows
To overwhelming thunder at the close?

The close! the close! How like a death-knell seems
That solemn word to wake me from my dreams!
One little year; yea, less than one like this,
May bring me to the close of all that is.
Far down Time's chequered stream I've voyaged on,

121

And seen my fellows drop off, one by one;
And now the widening waters seem to near.
Eternity's dark ocean; on my ear
Sound the deep heavings of that shoreless sea,
And awe my soul into solemnity!
Darkling I hover round the world to come,
And voices thence are heard to call me home;
And stretching on into the dread expanse,
I fain would lift the curtain, and advance.
One little step, I know, would bear me through,
And give the secrets of the dead to view;
But till that step is taken, mortal sense,
Ask as it may, gets no response from thence.
Thought may at times, when all around me sleep.
Launch sounding forth into that silent deep;
But without star to guide or light to cheer,
Soon back to land my trembling course I steer.
E'en bold conjecture onward fears to fare,
And reason shrinks to find no footing there;
Till conscious Nature, baffled and o'erawed,
Sinks suppliant on the mercy of her God,
Turns from self-confidence to faith and prayer,
Clings to His Word, and finds her refuge there.

Thrice happy we, not left to grope our way
From truth to truth, by Nature's feeble ray,
Where one false step were ruin. Happier still
Our wills conforming to the Heavenly Will;
Ready, as God may prompt, to think, and feel,
And take His impress, as the wax the seal;
At His blest feet content to sit and learn.
Or walk by faith, till faith to sight shall turn;
Beneath the Saviour's cross to stand and scan
All He has done, and all He claims for man;
Learn from His life, and on His death repose,
And grow in love and duty to the close.

On the year's threshold, on the narrow strand
That parts the past and future, here I stand,
Without control o'er either: one is flown
Beyond recall; — a dark and dread unknown,
The other stretches onward, — what to be,

Seen but by Him who fills eternity.
The present, and scarce that, is still my own; —
Oh, be it consecrate to Heaven alone!
Be mine, while all things shift and change around,
To cleave to Him in whom no change is found,
To rest on the Immutable, to cling
Closer and closer 'neath the almighty wing;
His voice in all its varied tones to hear,
And in all aspects feel Him ever near;
Be mine with Him to walk, on Him depend, —
Then, come what may, it all to good must tend!

TO A FIELD FLOWER FOUND BESIDE
A FAVOURITE ARBOUR EARLY IN SPRING

Hail, lovely harbinger of spring!
Hail, little modest flower!
 Fanned by the tempest's icy wing,
 Dashed by the hoary shower.
Thy balmy breath, thy softened bloom,
 Was ever welcome here;
But at this hour of wintry gloom,
 Thy smile is doubly dear.

The storm that o'er thy mossy bed,
 Subdues the towering tree,
Flies harmless o'er thy sheltered head,
 And wears no scowl for thee;
But resting in security,
 Thou teachest haughty souls.
The blessings of obscurity,
 Where ruin's whirlwind rolls.

The tulip flaunts in rich array;
 The rose is passing sweet;

123

But, ah! with summer's golden day,
   Their gaudy charms retreat:
But while the lingering winter lowers,
   And saddens all the green,
Thou, herald mild of brighter hours,
   Thy soothing smiles are seen.

Thy gems are strewed in every place,
   On every bank they fling
An early wreath, with artless grace,
   Around the brows of spring;
In woodland wilds, in gardens gay,
   In vale, on mountain drear;
The first to meet the sunny ray,
   And hail the waking year.

O! thou art Nature's fondest care,
   The foster-child of spring!
The virgin twines thee in her hair,
   To dance at village ring.
The bee, in thy soft bosom, stays
   His winglet's wild career;
The lark his morning song of praise
   Pours in thy dewy ear!

Dear little timorous, gentle flower,
   Sweet pilgrim of the storm,
Still, still beneath my sheltering bower,
   Recline thy paly form!
No plundering grasp, no heedless bruise,
   Shall harm one bud of thine:
And gaudier sweets while others choose,
   The primrose shall be mine.

MAY FLOWERS

Sweet babes, dressed out in flowers of May,
And fair and innocent as they;
A lovely type in them we see,
Of what you are, and what must be.
Like them you rise, like them you bloom,
Like them you hasten to the tomb.
Ye human flowers, smile on, smile on!
Your hours of bliss will soon be gone.

Soon manhood with its cares and crimes,
Shall cloud these early sunny times,
And call you from your sports and flowers,
To passions and pursuits like ours.
And what are all that men pursue,
But flowerets, gathered flowerets, too?
Howe'er they tempt, however they please
More fleeting and less fair than these.

Enjoyments, honours, talents, sway,
Wealth, beauty, all must pass away;
A cloud must come across their sky,
A frost but nips them, and they die.
One flower alone, when all are gone,
Shall bloom for aye unfading on —
'Tis Grace — the treasure seek and prize;
It grows to glory in the skies.

125

SONG

Sweetest daughter of the year,
Smiling June, I hail thee here.
Hail thee with thy skies of blue,
Days of sunshine, nights of dew.
Hail thee with thy songs and flowers,
Balmy air and leafy bowers,
Bright and fragrant, fresh and clear,
Smiling June, I hail thee here.

Yet, sweet June, it is not these,
Perfumed gales and whispering trees,
Blossoms shed with liberal hand,
Like a star-shower o'er the land,
Waves at rest and woods in tune;
'Tis not these, delicious June,
Give thee such a charm for me,
Move me thus to welcome thee.

'Tis that Agnes on thy skies
Opened first her brighter eyes;
That the flower of all thy flowers
Woke to life within thy bowers;
Gave thy charms a higher tone,
Lent thee honours not thy own;
And for this, thy brightest boon,
Take thy tribute, lovely June.

THOU, WHOSE NEVER-FAILING ARM

Thou, Whose never-failing arm
Led me all my earthly way,
   Brought me out of every harm
Safely to my closing day –
Thou, in Whom I now believe,
  Jesus, Lord, my soul receive.

From this state of sin and pain,
  From this world of grief and strife.
From this body's mortal chain,
  From this weak, imperfect life, --
Thou, in Whom I now believe,
  Jesus, Lord, my soul receive.

To the mansions of Thy love,
  To the spirits of the just,
To the angel host above,
  To Thyself my only trust, --
Thou in Whom I now believe,
  Jesus, Lord, my soul receive.

✿✿ ✿✿ ✿✿

A. M. M. L.

Died February 1821, aged One Month

A few bright moons the babe who slumbers here
Smiled on her parents, and that innocent smile
Was daylight to their eyes. They thought her fair,
And gentle, and intelligent, and dared
To lean their hearts upon her. There are ways
And looks of hers that long will dwell with them,
And there are bright anticipations held,
How fondly and feelingly resigned!
Her very helplessness endeared her to them,
And made her more their own. — But this is done; —
The wintry wind passed o'er the opening flower,
And nipped it in the bud — and it is gone.

Still there is comfort left. It still is joy
That they can lift their weeping eyes to Heaven,
And think that one of theirs is settled there;
Can know, beyond the shadow of a doubt,
That she is safe with Him who bears the lambs
Within His bosom, and, no longer babe
But angel, now beholds her Father's face,
And shares the fullness of eternal joy.

Sweet spirit, since now the ministry of love
From God to erring man is thine, O draw
The souls of those who loved thee to the place
Where thou art gone before them; make them feel
That earth is not their home; O fix their thoughts
On Heaven, on Him who once on earth took up
Babes such as thou, and blessed them, and bade all
Who looked for Heaven become like babes, like thee-
Pure, innocent, lowly, loving, and new-born.

THE SPIRIT
OF THE
PSALMS

PSALM 1 (First Version)

How blest are they who fear to walk,
Where sinners tempt, and scorners talk,
Who in the Word of God delight,
And feed upon it day and night!

Like trees with water at their root,
They spread their leaves, and bear their fruit:
And thus may we unwithering rise,
And ripen daily for the skies!

Thrice happy he whom God approves;
From strength to strength he onward moves;
While from His face the scoffer flees,
Like chaff before the driving breeze.

The good and bad are mingled here;
But ah, the sifting time is near!
The good shall then to glory go;
The sinner sink to endless woe.

PSALM 1 (Second Version)

Blest is the man who fears and flies,
The broad and downward way,
Where impious scorn its God defies,
And vice allures to slay.

Blest, who in God's unerring law,
Finds guidance and delight;
Walks by His Word with daily awe,
And ponders it by night.
Like trees with water at their root,
The heirs of glory rise;

Their boughs are hung with holy fruit,
Their verdure never dies.

Beneath the wings of heavenly love,
On earth they safely dwell;
And soar to endless joys above,
When sinners sink to hell.

PSALM 1 (Third Version)

Uphold me, Lord, too prone to stray,
Uphold me in Thy narrow way;
From sin and sorrow bid me flee,
And turn from all who turn from Thee.

The cloud and pillar of Thy Word,
My comfort be, my guide, O Lord;
By day, by night, at hand to bless,
And lead me through the wilderness!

So shall I flourish like a tree,
Planted, and watched, and nursed by Thee,
With streams of grace around its roots,
And bending low with holy fruits.

So shall I go from light to light,
Till prayer is praise, and faith is sight;
And while the sinner's doom I see,
Adore the grace that rescued me!

PSALM 2 (First Version)

Why do the people rage,
   Devising frantic things?
     Why do the kings of earth engage,
  Against the King of kings?
'Come, let us burst His yoke,' they say,
  'And cast His hateful bonds away!'

God on His heavenly throne,
  Laughs at their impious aims;
He made the nations for His own,
  And thus His will proclaims,
On Zion's hill My King shall sit;
  Perish, ye rebels, or submit!'

Ere time its course began,
  I issued My decree,
This day, My Son, the Son of Man,
  Have I begotten Thee.
To Thee the world and all that live,
  Thy blood-bought heritage, I give!'

Hear, then, ye monarchs, hear!
  Ye great, a greater own!
Bow down with holy joy and fear,
  Before Messiah's throne!
Upon Him life and death depend;
  O blest who find in Christ a friend!

PSALM 2 (Second Version)

The powers of earth and hell combine,
  With Jesus war to wage;
    God laughs to scorn their mad design,
And foils their impious rage.

Vain are the brutal pains they spend,
  His purpose to defeat;
Their wrongs and insults only tend,
  His conquests to complete.

He triumphed on the accursed tree,
  He burst the guarded grave;
Then rose on high, by God's decree,
  The world to sway and save.

Kings of the earth, your Monarch learn;
  O kiss the Son of God;
Nor bid His golden sceptre turn,
  Into an iron rod.

PSALM 3

Thy promise, Lord, is perfect peace,
  And yet my trials still increase;
  Till fears at times my soul assail,
  That Satan's rage must yet prevail.

Then, Saviour, then I fly to Thee,
And in Thy grace my refuge see;
Thou heardst me from Thy holy hill,
And Thou wilt hear and help me still.

Beneath Thy wings secure I sleep;
What foe can harm while Thou dost keep?
I wake and find Thee at my side,
My Omnipresent Guard and Guide!

O, why should earth or hell distress,
With God so strong, so nigh to bless?
From Him alone salvation flows;
On Him alone, my soul, repose!

PSALM 4 (First Version)

God of all my righteousness,
Guide through every past distress,
Show Thy mercy, hear my cry,
Save, O save me, ere I die.
Hark, the awful voice Divine!
'Flee from sin and thou art Mine;
Godly men to God are dear!
Serve Thou Him, and He will hear.

'Stand in awe, nor dare to sin,
Commune much with self within,
Wake at night with God to talk,
Rise at morn with Him to walk;
On His grace thy soul recline,
Bring thy offering to His shrine,
Plead thy Saviour's righteousness,
God will hear, and God will bless.'

Many cry, in fretful mood,
'Who will show us any good?'
Lord, Thy face lift up on me,
I have every good in Thee.
Worldlings, take your corn and wine;
I am blest, the Lord is mine;
Glad I wake, and safe I sleep,
Lord, with Thee my soul to keep.

PSALM 4 (Second Version)

O God of my righteousness, Hearer of prayer,
  Almighty to help and defend,
    Thine arm has upborne me through foe and
through snare,
  O bear me up still to the end!

I heard the poor worldling in trouble exclaim,
  'This earth is a desert to me!'
But, Father of Mercies, be Thou but the same,
  I'm rich, amid ruin, with Thee.

I look through the clouds, as they gather on high!
  I know there is sunshine above;
And earth and its joys cannot cost me a sigh,
  While heir of Thy heavenly love.

I lie down on this for my pillow at night,
  And slumber unharmed and unawed:
Afflictions are blessings, and darkness is light,
  While I have a friend in my God.

PSALM 4 (Third Version)

Lord of my life, my hopes, my joys,
  My never-failing Friend,
Thou hast been all my help till now,
  O help me to the end!

While worldly minds impatient grow,
  More prosperous times to see,
O let the glories of Thy face,
  Shine brighter, Lord, on me!

So shall my heart o'erflow with joy,
    More lasting and more true
Than theirs, possessed of all that they,
    So eagerly pursue.

Then down in peace I'll lay my head,
    And take my needful rest;
No other guard I ask or need,
    Of Thee, O Lord, possessed.

PSALM 5 (First Version)

Lord, in our hearts the feelings read,
    Which words can ill express:
O, 'tis a pleasant task to plead,
    With one so prompt to bless!

To Thee, O Lord, our voice shall rise,
    Each morn with homage due:
To Thee we lift our waking eyes;
    Lift Thou our spirits too!

Into Thy house 'tis good to come,
    And muse on all Thy love,
And look on to a better home,
    In Thy fair house above.

O by a safe and easy path
    Thy pilgrims thither lead!
For stubborn foes reserve Thy wrath,
    Thy people guard and feed.

PSALM 5 (Second Version)

Lord, hear our Sabbath song of praise,
    Accept our Sabbath prayer;
Again before Thy gracious throne,
    For mercy we repair.

How pleasant to Thy courts to come,
    Our sacred debt to pay!
O may we ever meet Thee here,
    On this Thy holy day!

Make plain Thy way before us, Lord,
    And guide us safe along:
'Tis sweet to trust our all to Thee,
    While dangers round us throng.

God never will desert the soul,
    That on His grace depends:
But with His favour all His saints,
    As with a shield, defends.

PSALM 6 (First Version)

Correct us, Lord, we know it good;
Correct, but not in angry mood;
A Father's chastening let us prove,
And temper discipline with love.

Remember man is but a worm,
And smooth Thy wave and stay Thy storm;
Amid the clouds Thy bow display,
And interchange our night with day.

Thy name is mercy; hear our prayer,
And send us comfort for despair;
Behold us trembling o'er the grave,
And come to succour, come to save.

He comes! new light around us springs;
He comes with healing in His wings!
The needful cross no more we shun,
But bow, and say, 'Thy will be done.'

PSALM 6 (Second Version)

Gently, gently lay Thy rod,
On my sinful head, O God.
Stay Thy wrath, in mercy stay,
Lest I sink before its sway.

Heal me, for my flesh is weak;
Heal me, for Thy grace I seek;
This my only plea I make,
Heal me for Thy mercy's sake.

139

Who within the silent grave,
Shall proclaim Thy power to save?
Lord, my trembling soul reprieve,
Speak, and I shall rise and live.

Lo! He comes! He heeds my plea!
Lo! He comes! the shadows flee!
Glory round me dawns once more;
Rise, my spirit, and adore!

PSALM 7

Lord, my God, in Thee I trust;
Save, O save, Thy trembling dust,
From the roaring lion's power,
Seeking whom he may devour;
From a thousand waves that roll,
Shipwreck o'er my sinking soul;
God Omnipotent, I flee
From them all to Thee, to Thee.

Thou my inmost wish canst read,
Thou canst help my utmost need;
Let the world Thy goodness see,
Let them mark Thy grace in me.
Lay the wicked in the dust,
Raise the feeble, guide the just; —
Searcher of the heart, I flee
From myself to Thee, to Thee.

God is righteous, God is strong;
Much abused, He suffers long;
Yet if still His love we spurn,
Love at last to wrath will turn.
O, the frown of the I AM!
O, the fury of the Lamb! —
God of grace and hope, I flee
From all else to Thee, to Thee.

PSALM 8 (First Version)

O Lord, how good, how great art Thou,
     In heaven and earth the same!
There angels at Thy footstool bow,
     Here babes Thy grace proclaim.

When glorious in the mighty sky,
     Thy countless worlds I see,
'O what is man,' I wondering cry,
     'To be so loved by Thee?'

To him Thou hourly deign'st to give,
     New mercies from on high;
Didst quit Thy throne with him to live,
     For him in pain to die.

Close to Thy own bright Seraphim,
     His favoured path is trod,
And all beside are serving him,
     That he may serve his God.

O Lord, how good, how great art Thou,
   In heaven and earth the same!
There angels at Thy footstool bow,
   Here babes Thy grace proclaim.

PSALM 8 (Second Version)

Exalted Jesus, Heavenly King,
Angels to Thee their offerings bring;
And yet Thou scornest not the praise,
The simple song that children raise.

(When in the nightly sky I see,
The worlds upheld and formed by Thee,
How wondrous seems the love Divine,
That condescends to me and mine.)

And hast Thou deigned from high to come,
And make this fallen world Thy home?
Yea, bow Thee to the cross and grave,
And die a sinful worm to save?

Crown Him with praises, all that live,
To Him your ceaseless homage giye;
Praises and homage well are due,
To Him who gave Himself for you.

Exalted Saviour, risen Lord,
Jesus, by all in heaven adored,
Set up with man Thy fallen throne,
And make all hearts on earth Thy own.

PSALM 8 (Third Version)

O Thou to whom all creatures bow,
　Whom all Thy works proclaim,
Through heaven and earth how great art Thou,
　How glorious is Thy name!

In heaven Thy praise is ever sung,
　Nor fully uttered there:
On earth Thou makst the infant tongue,
　Thy love and truth declare.

Lord, when Thy glorious works on high,
　Employ our wondering sight,
The moon that nightly rules the sky,
　The stars of feebler light, —

Lord, what is man, that Thou shouldst love,
　And hold him in such worth,
Next to Thy angel hosts above,
　And high o'er all on earth?

O Thou to whom all creatures bow,
　Whom all Thy works proclaim,
In heaven and earth how great art Thou,
　How glorious is Thy name!

❧❧❧

143

PSALM 9 (First Version)

Our hearts shall bless Thee, O Most High,
In Thee rejoice, on Thee rely.
O, how unequal all our aims,
To utter half our Saviour's claims!

High on Thy glorious throne above,
Thou sitt'st, the God of might and love,
The meet to raise, the proud to tame,
And save the souls that know Thy name.

That name of love, how sweet it sounds!
It drops like balm in sorrow's wounds;
It puts to shame each guilty fear;
And says, 'Be strong, thy God is near!'

O Refuge of the poor and weak,
More prompt to hear than we to seek,
Still be Thine arm our souls beneath,
Still lift us from the gates of death!

(The wicked soon shall sink to hell,
Thy servants rise with Thee to dwell;
Till then, O Lord, our succour be,
And lead us safe to heaven and Thee.)

PSALM 9 (Second Version)

Lord, I will praise Thee; all my heart,
Thy wonders shall proclaim:
My lips shall tell how good Thou art,
While they can speak Thy name.

When countless foes against me rose,
    Thy word dispersed them all:
My soul, upon thy God repose,
    He will not let thee fall!

O Refuge of the poor and weak,
    A Light of the distrest,
Thou hearest still when sinners seek,
    And givest still the best.

Here on Thy grace my soul shall dwell,
    And trust for all to Thee.
O when the wicked sink to hell,
    Arise and rescue me!

PSALM 10

O Lord, why hidest Thou Thy face,
    While dangers round me close?
Return in all Thy power and grace,
And save me from my foes.

The haters of Thy Word and name,
My firmness fiercely prove;
And through Thy servant's fall would aim,
A wound at Him I love.

Arise, O Lord, their rage control,
Awe down the swelling wave:
Arise to help the poor in soul,
And snatch him from the grave.

145

Thy grace prepares the heart to pray,
And hears its humble plea:
Arise to be the trembler's stay,
Arise to rescue me!

PSALM 11

My trust is in the Lord;
   What foe can injure me?
Why bid me like a bird,
  Before the fowler flee?
The Lord is on His heavenly throne,
  Omnipotent to save His own.

The wicked may assail,
  The tempter sorely try,
All earth's foundations fail,
  All Nature's springs be dry;
Yet God is in His holy shrine,
  And I am strong while He is mine.

His flock to Him is dear.
  He watches them from high;
He sends them trials here,
  To fit them for the sky:
But safely will He tend and keep,
  The humblest, feeblest of His sheep.

His foes a season here,
    May triumph and prevail;
But, ah! the hour is near,
    When all their hopes must fail:
While like the sun His saints shall rise,
    And shine with Him above the skies.

PSALM 12

Help, Lord, the godly fail!
    Help, Lord, the faithful flee!
And double hearts and tongues prevail,
    That taunt Thy saints and Thee.

With sophistries and lies,
    They cheat the simple soul,
Teach men Thy Gospel to despise,
    And spurn Thy mild control.

But ah! there is a voice,
    In this dark growth of crimes,
That bids prophetic hearts rejoice,
    In hope of brighter times.

The Word these fools oppose,
    Can well their scoffs endure,
As silver from the furnace flows,
    More precious and more pure.

147

Their rage but sooner brings,
   The Lord to earth again;
And safe beneath almighty wings,
   His Church shall rest till then.

PSALM 13 (First Version)

How long, O God of grace,
   Wilt Thou refuse my prayer?
How long withdraw Thy glorious face,
   And leave me to despair?

Without a smile, a word,
   Of Thy supporting breath,
My soul must sink, must perish. Lord,
   And sleep the sleep of death.

Shall foes of Thine exclaim,
   We have at length prevailed?
And must Thy servants own with shame.
   That prayer with Thee has failed?

No, I will trust Thy love,
   And hope for brighter days: —
And lo! e'en now the clouds remove,
   And prayer bursts into praise.

PSALM 13 (Second Version)

How long, my God, the God of grace,
Wilt Thou withdraw Thy shining face?
How long shall I Thy Word explore,
Nor gather thence one comfort more?

O hear me, send me life and light,
Before I sink in endless night!
Nor let my foes my ruin see,
And triumph o'er my God in me.

Shall any such have room to say,
Thou dost not hear when sinners pray?
Shall any penitent complain,
That he has sought Thy face in vain?

No! weak and prostrate in the dust,
Thy mercy still shall be my trust:
And lo! I have not sued in vain,
Salvation's morning breaks again.

Light dawns upon my soul's despair,
I feel, I feel the power of prayer;
My heart again its praise can pour;
O shall I ever doubt Thee more?

❧❧ ❧❧ ❧❧

PSALM 13 (Third Version)

How long wilt Thou forget me, Lord?
   Must I for ever mourn?
For ever weep an absent God,
   And sigh for His return?

How long shall darkness cloud my soul,
   And fears my heart oppress?
How long shall enemies insult,
   And I have no redress?

O hear, and to my longing eyes,
   Restore Thy wonted light;
Nor let my sun of comfort set,
   In everlasting night.

O come, and change my sighs to songs,
   My grief to lasting joy;
O save my life, and bid me still,
   That life for Thee employ.

PSALM 14 (First Version)

No God for me!' the fool exclaims,
And half believes the wish he frames.
'Twere well there was no God for them,
Whom God exists but to condemn.

Plunged in the desperate depths of sin,
Debased without, corrupt within,
What wonder men should wish to fly,
An awful omnipresent eye?

Yet Jesus from His throne above,
Holds out the sceptre of His love,
And offers peace to them, to all
That contrite at His feet will fall.

Rise, Sun of Righteousness, and fling,
A brighter morning from Thy wing;
The mourner cheer, the captive free,
And win Thy wanderers all to Thee.

PSALM 14 (Second Version)

O that the Lord's salvation
　Were out of Zion come,
To heal His ancient nation,
　To lead His outcasts home!

How long the holy city
　Shall heathen feet profane?
Return, O Lord, in pity,
　Rebuild her walls again.

Let fall Thy rod of terror,
　Thy saving grace impart;
Roll back the veil of error,
　Release the fettered heart.

Let Israel home returning,
　Her lost Messiah see;
Give oil of joy for mourning,
　And bind Thy Church to Thee.

PSALM 15

Within Thy courts, before Thy face,
　Lord, who shall find a dwelling-place?
Thy choicest converse who shall prove,
And feed most largely on Thy love?

That man alone whose upright walk,
Whose righteous aims and hallowed talk,
Bespeak a soul by grace renewed,
And quick to all of right and good.

That man alone whose hand nor tongue
Will do a fellow-creature wrong;
Who by his Saviour's precept moves,
And loved by Him, his brother loves.

That man who sinners hold abhorred,
And honours those that feared the Lord;
Who bow not down to power or pelf,
And lives for others more than self.

This man the power of grace displays;
The Christian shines in all his ways;
He walks with Christ on earth below,
And on from light to light shall go.

PSALM 16 (First Version)

O Lord, I am but sinful dust,
   Yet humbly hope in Thee:
Their idol gods let others trust;
   The God of gods for me!

A thousand varied gifts of His,
   Around me daily shine;
Yet richer still my portion is,
   The Lord Himself is mine!

His counsel is my faithful guide,
   His arm my strong defence.
Whom should I fear, when at my side
   I feel Omnipotence?

Through Him my heart with joy o'erflows,
    In this dark vale of tears;
On Him my flesh shall calm repose,
    When death itself appears.

He, by a new and living way,
    Shall bear me safe above;
To share with Him eternal day,
    And sing eternal love.

PSALM 16 (Second Version)

Pilgrims here on earth and strangers,
    'Neath a weary load we bend:
O how sweet, 'mid toils and dangers,
    Still to have a heavenly Friend!
      Christ has suffered,
    And to sufferers grace will send.

By as deadly foes assaulted,
    By as strong temptations tried,
Still His footsteps never halted,
    On from strength to strength He hied. [5]
      What could move Him,
    With Jehovah at His side?

To the shameful cross they nailed Him,
    And that cross became His throne:
In the tomb they laid and sealed Him;
    Lo, the Godhead bursts the stone,

---

[5] To go quickly; hasten.

And, ascending,
Claims all empire as His own.

Saviour, from Thy heavenly glories,
Here an eye of mercy cast;
Make our pathway plain before us,
Smooth the wave, and still the blast.
Thou hast helped us;
Bear us safely home at last.

PSALM 17

Support me. Lord; my hope Thou art,
Imperfect though my prayer:
But Thou hast searched and tried my heart;
O read my wishes there!

Fain would I walk in paths of Thine,
But Thou my Help must be.
How soon would Nature's powers decline,
If not sustained by Thee!

New dangers now upon me press,
New tempters seek my fall;
Arise, Almighty God of grace,
And bear me safe through all!

O give me to behold Thy face,
Exempt from sin's control;
And, waking, all Thine image trace,
Reflected in my soul!

PSALM 18 (First Version)

Whom should we love like Thee,
  Our God, our Guide, our King,
    The Tower to which we flee,
  The Rock to which we cling?
O for a thousand tongues to show,
  The debt that we to mercy owe!

The storm upon us fell,
  The floods around us rose,
The depths of death and hell,
  Seemed on our souls to close:
To God we cried in strong despair;
  And God was nigh to help our prayer.

He came, the King of kings,
  He bowed the sable sky,
And on the tempest's wings,
  Rode glorious down from high;
The earth before her Maker shook,
  The mountains quaked at His rebuke

Above the storm He stood,
  And awed it to repose;
He drew us from the flood,
  And scattered all our foes:
He set us in a spacious place,
  And there upholds us by His grace.

Whom should we love like Thee,
  Our God, our Guide, our King,
The Tower to which we flee,
  The Rock to which we cling?
O for a thousand tongues to show.
  The debt that we to mercy owe!

PSALM 18 (Second Version)

O God of truth and grace,
  My Saviour and my Guide,
Be with me on my earthly race,
  And lead me to Thy side.

Strength to the weak Thou art;
  O send me health Divine;
And arm my sinful, sinking heart,
  With righteousness of Thine.

Thy way is good and just;
  Thy word is tried and true:
Ye tremblers, in your Saviour trust;
  His arm will bear you through.

He lives; for ever blest,
  My Rock and Refuge be!
He lives to give His people rest,
  He lives to rescue me.

PSALM 18 (Third Version)

No change of times shall ever shock,
  My firm dependence, Lord, on Thee;
In danger Thou hast been a Rock,
  A Fortress in distress to me.

And still the same Thou art, my God,
  Supreme in wisdom, love, and power;
My Refuge still from foes abroad,
  At home my Safeguard and my Tower.

Praise to the Lord! He heareth prayer,
    I seek with joy His mercy-seat.
Thou wilt not leave me to despair,
    Nor spurn Thy suppliant from Thy feet.

Through Thee my darkness shall be light,
    Through Thee my weakness shall be strong;
O guide my wandering steps aright,
    And be Thy grace my daily song.

PSALM 19 (First Version)

Lord, the heaven Thy glory speaks;
From ten thousand orbs it breaks;
Day to day Thy wonders tells,
Night to night the chorus swells.

Silent though they seem to be,
Yet they find a voice for Thee;
And to all throughout the earth,
Talk of Him who gave them birth.

Monarch-like, the morning sun,
Toys his daily course to run,
Flinging from his mighty wings,
Glory to the King of kings.

Duly as his tributes fail,
Moon and stars take up the tale:
O how blind those hearts must be,
Who in all find nought of Thee!

PSALM 19 (Second Version)

Well Thy works proclaim Thee, Lord;
Better still Thy living Word:
All of God that man can bear,
Shines in softened glory there.

There Thy holy will we read,
There upon Thy grace we feed,
There find guidance for our way,
And correction when we stray.

Full, and free, and deep, and wide,
Flows the glorious Gospel tide,
And appropriate balm bestows,
For all human wants and woes.

Let it flow, O Lord, for me;
Let it fit my soul for Thee;
Try me, prove me, and reveal,
Him who came to wound and heal.

Cleanse me, change me, Lord, within!
Keep me from presumptuous sin!
Till Thy spirit dwell and shine,
In each thought and word of mine.

PSALM 19 (Third Version)

Heaven speaks Thy glory, Lord;
Sun, moon, and stars display Thy skill:
Yet in Thy pure and perfect Word,
We read Thee clearer still.

O let that Word go forth,
    As freely as the circling sun,
Till all that walk this fallen earth,
    Are to their Saviour won.

Sun of the soul, arise!
    Arise! and bid our darkness flee;
Make everywhere the simple wise,
    And draw all hearts to Thee!

The shadows deeper fall,
    The night of error, sense, and sin:
Rise, Sun of Glory, rise o'er all,
    And bid the day begin!

PSALM 19 (Fourth Version)

The heavens declare Thy glories. Lord,
    From every star they blaze;
And day to day, and night to night,
    Roll on their Maker's praise.

Their sacred lesson to no realm
    Or people is confined;
'Tis Nature's language, and addressed
    Alike to all mankind.

But where Thy Gospel, Lord, is heard,
    It spreads a clearer light:
It warms the heart, converts the soul,
    And brings the blind their sight.

Lord, let Thy guiding, cleansing grace,
   To us be freely given;
Till every thought and word of ours,
   Is tuned to Thee and heaven.

⚜ ⚜ ⚜

PSALM 20

The Lord in trouble hear thee,
   And help from Zion send;
The God of grace be near thee,
   To comfort and befriend!
Thy human weakness strengthen,
   Thy earthly wants supply,
Thy span of nature lengthen,
   To endless life on high!

Above His own anointed,
   His banner bright shall wave:
Their times are all appointed;
   The Lord His flock will save:
Through life's deceitful mazes
   Their steps will safely bear;
Accept their feeble praises,
   And hear their every prayer.
Go on, thou heir of glory!
   No ill can thee betide;
The prize is full before thee,
   Thy Guardian at thy side.
Who trust in mortal forces,
   Shall disappointed be;

But God a sure Resource is,
    And God shall succour thee.

✿✿✿ ✿✿✿ ✿✿✿

PSALM 21 (First Version)

Lord, Thy best blessings shed,
    On our loved monarch's head;
        Round her abide:
Teach her Thy holy will,
Shield her from every ill,
Guard, guide, and speed her still,
        Safe to Thy side.

Grant her, O Lord, to be,
Wise, just, and good, like Thee,
        Blessing and blest.
With every virtue crowned,
Honoured by nations round,
Midst earthly monarchs found,
        Greatest and best.

Long let her people share,
Here her maternal care,
        Long 'neath her smile.
May every good increase,
May every evil cease,
And freedom, health, and peace,
        Dance round our isle.

Under Thy mighty wings,
Keep her, O King of kings!
      Answer her prayer:
Till she shall hence remove,
Up to Thy courts above,
To dwell in light and love,
      Evermore there.

PSALM 21 (Second Version)

The Lord who died on earth for men,
  Now fills His Father's throne;
He loves us as He loved us then,
   And watches o'er His own.

For them He offers daily prayer,
   And all His prayers are heard;
He tends them with unceasing care,
   And feeds them from His Word.

Their every wish, and want, and woe,
   To Him are fully known;
They share His trials here below,
   Aid soon shall share His throne.

He guards and blesses them from high,
   While they are toiling here.
With such a Friend above the sky,
   What have His flock to fear?

PSALM 22 (First Version)

My Saviour, how Thy soul was awed,
   When, hanging on the tree,
Thou criedst aloud, 'My God, my God,
   Hast Thou forsaken Me?'

When angry foes around Thee strove,
   And faithless friends forsook;
And earth below, and heaven above,
   Wore one dark threatening look.

Beneath Thy cross. Lord, let me lie,
   Thy bleeding love to view;
And weep, and watch, and pray that I
   May ne'er those wounds renew.

Beneath Thy cross O let me lie,
   And mark what Thou hast won,
And hear Thy last triumphant cry,
   'Tis done! the work is done!'

Lord, let my soul that triumph share;
   I look to Thee to save.
Where is thy sting, O Death? and where
   Thy victory, O Grave?

PSALM 22 (Second Version)

O what a conquest Jesus won,
  When, on the fatal tree,
His great atoning work was done,
  And earth from guilt set free!

'Tis finished!' He exulting cried,
  The mighty Slayer slain;
The wrath of God is pacified,
  And man may hope again!

O rich reward for every groan!
  O victory complete!
To call a ransomed world His own.
  And hail it to His feet.

Yes, the great work shall onward go;
  The sure decree is past;
The nations to their Lord shall flow,
  And all be Christ's at last.

O hasten. Lord, those blessed times!
  Lead all Thy wanderers home!
Convert this world of woes and crimes,
  And bid Thy kingdom come!

❦❦❦

PSALM 22 (Third Version)

L ord, I am Thine; brought into life,
   By Thy creative word:
And when upon the breast I hung,
   I was Thy care, O Lord.

Thy guardian mercy watched and kept,
   My giddy youthful days;
And hither hast Thou led me on,
   Through life's bewildering ways.

Withdraw not, then, Thy grace from me,
   When foes and snares are nigh:
O send me help, Thy help, on which
   My soul can best rely.

O Thou who hitherto hast kept,
   Still keep me to the end!
With Thee my Guide, with Thee my Guard,
   I ask no other Friend.

PSALM 23 (First Version)

T he living Lord my Shepherd is;
   What can I want while I am His?
In greenest fields my soul He feeds,
My steps by stillest waters leads.

He guides me in His holy way,
He brings me back whene'er I stray;
The vale of death without a fear
I walk, for He is kind and near.

Yes, Thou art with me night and day,
Thy rod my guide. Thy staff my stay:
By Thee my table still is spread,
Thy oil of joy anoints my head.

Where'er I rest, where'er I go,
I meet Thy mercies here below.
When to Thy presence shall I soar,
To see and praise Thee evermore?

PSALM 23 (Second Version)

Glorious Shepherd of the sheep,
　May I dare to call me Thine,
One whom Thou wilt tend and keep,
　Safe beneath Thy wings Divine?
Ah! with Thee so kind, and near,
What have I to wish or fear?

Where the heavenly pastures grow,
　Where the living waters glide,
Led and fed by Thee below,
　I have nought to ask beside;
Nought but thankfulness of heart,
To proclaim how good Thou art.

Keep me in Thy righteous ways,
　Guide me with Thy holy wand,
Through this life's perplexing maze,
　Through the vale of death beyond;
Gracious Thou, and happy I,
With so great a Friend so nigh.

In the desert then I'm fed,
   Manna round me rains from high;
Holy oil anoints my head,
   And my cruse is never dry;
Then from grace I pass to grace,
Soon to meet Thee face to face.

PSALM 23 (Third Version)

The Lord Himself, the mighty Lord,
   Vouchsafes to be my Guide;
The great Good Shepherd tends my soul;
   My wants are all supplied.

In pastures green He makes me feed,
   Recalls me when I stray,
Refreshes me with streams of grace,
   And leads me in His way.

I pass with Him the vale of death,
   From fear and danger free;
His friendly rod and staff are there,
   To guide and succour me.

My cup is full, my table spread,
   His mercy crowns my days:
His house shall ever be my home,
   And all my life be praise.

PSALM 24 (First Version)

The earth is all Thy own, O Lord;
Called into being at Thy word,
At Thy command the waters fled,
And the young world rose fair instead.

Who in Thy courts shall find a place?
Who but the subjects of Thy grace?
The humble faithful souls, "that flee,
For all their righteousness to Thee.

Lift up your heads, ye heavenly gates:
Behold the King of Glory waits!
Rich with the spoils of earth He comes,
And leads His people to their homes.

Lift up your heads, yea, lift them high!
The King of Glory mounts the sky.
What King of Glory? Christ the Lord!
He comes to triumph, and reward!

PSALM 24 (Second Version)

Judgment's awful hour is past,
    Sinners have received their doom,
And the sons of God at last,
    Rise to their eternal home.
Lift your heads, ye heavenly gates!
    He that conquered death and sin,
With His ransomed thousands waits;
    Open and receive Him in!

Long for Him they bore below
    Grief, temptation, toil, and pain;
Now they rise from scorn and woe,
    With their risen Lord to reign.
Endless joys await them now,
    Angels on their steps attend,
Crowns of glory on their brow,
    God their Omnipresent Friend.

Lift, ye heavenly gates, your heads,
    Let the heirs of glory in!
Christ on high His people leads;
    Let their welcome song begin!
Lord, we walk the desert here;
    Nought but gloom around we see;
O vouchsafe our course to cheer,
    With a glimpse of heaven and Thee!

PSALM 24 (Third Version)

This spacious earth is all the Lord's,
    The Lord its maker is;
And every heart and hand therein,
    By sovereign right are His.
But who shall take their station, who,
    The nearest to His throne?
They, they whose nature grace has changed,
    Whom Christ has made His own.

Lift up your heads, eternal gates!
    Unfold to entertain
The King of Glory; lo. He comes,
    With all His ransomed train!

Who is the King of Glory, who?
   The Lord for strength renowned;
In battle mighty o'er His foes,
   Eternal Victor crowned!

Lift up your heads, ye heavenly gates;
   Unfold to entertain
The King of Glory; lo, He comes,
   O'er heaven and earth to reign!
Who is the King of Glory, who?
   The Lord who died for men,
And from His conquests now returns,
   To claim His throne again.

PSALM 25 (First Version)

O God, we lift our souls to Thee;
From all our foes a Refuge be,
O leave not us, leave none to shame,
Whose trust is in Thy saving name.

Direct our blindness in Thy way,
Our weakness let Thine arm upstay:
Thy grace in Christ can never fail;
Let that, and not our sins, prevail.

The Lord is good; the Lord is strong;
He leads the humble safe along;
To them His secret love reveals,
And on their hearts His covenant seals.

Our eyes are ever, Lord, to Thee;
Our Saviour and Supporter be!
O, heal our wounds, our sins forgive,
And bid us now arise and live.

PSALM 25 (Second Version)

Thy goodness and Thy truth,
   O Lord, recall to mind;
And graciously continue still,
   As Thou wert ever, kind.

Let all my former sins,
   Be blotted out by Thee,
And for a dying Saviour's sake,
   In mercy think of me.

The riches of His grace,
   The righteous Lord displays,
In bringing wandering sinners home,
   And teaching them His ways.

He never those deserts,
   Who His direction seek,
But in His paths securely leads,
   The humble and the meek.

PSALM 26

J udge me, O Lord, and try my heart,
   For Thou that heart canst see;
And bid each idol thence depart,
   That dares compete with Thee.

Though weak and cleaving to the dust,
   My soul adores Thee still;
Thy grace and truth are all my trust;
   O mould me to Thy will!

Thy altar. Lord, I would embrace,
   With hands by Christ made clean.
I love Thy house, I love the place,
   Where Thy bright face is seen.

O guide me in Thy love and fear;
   My soul on Thee I cast:
I would not walk with sinners here,
   To share their doom at last.

PSALM 27 (First Version)

T he Lord my strong Salvation is,
   My Helper ever near;
While He is mine and I am His,
   What has my soul to fear?

One wish, one ardent wish, is mine;
   Lord, grant my humble plea!
To dwell for ever near Thy shrine,
   And find my all in Thee.

O give me at Thy side a place,
 Secure from every harm;
Where I may daily view Thy face,
 And feel Thy helping arm.

From light to light, from strength to strength,
 My soul enlarge and raise;
Till from all bonds I burst at length,
 To endless joy and praise.

PSALM 27 (Second Version)

Father, we hail the word of grace,
 That issues from Thy throne on high.
'Seek ye,' it cries, 'your Saviour's face';
 'We seek it. Lord,' our hearts reply.

Our Help through trials past Thou wert,
 Our Hope through dangers yet unknown;
Though father, mother, all desert,
 They still are ours in Thee alone.

Shine on our path and make it plain;
 Conduct us safe through all our foes;
Their wiles defeat, their rage restrain,
 And lead us, feed us, to the close.

Our burthened souls would often faint,
 Without a glimpse of Thee and home;
But Christ supports His trembling saint:
 O wait on Him, and joy will come!

PSALM 27 (Third Version)

Whom shall I fear? The living God,
    My strong Salvation is!
I smile on all my foes around,
    And tell them I am His.

My face in need, ye tremblers, seek,
    The Lord in mercy cries.
Thy glorious face I'll always seek,
    My willing heart replies.

That face from me, O, hide not now,
    Nor forth Thy suppliant cast;
Thou hast been all my Help before,
    O leave me not at last!

Thou wilt not, Lord, Thou never wilt;
    Thy love is all-divine.
Father and mother may forsake,
    The Lord is ever mine.

O wait on God, in patience wait,
    And He will make Thee strong:
The heart that humbly waits on Him,
    Shall never want Him long.

❧❧❧

PSALM 27 (Fourth Version)

Whom should I fear, since God to me,
　　Is saving health and light?
Since strongly He my life supports,
　　What can my soul affright?

Continue, Lord, to hear my voice,
　　Whene'er to Thee I cry:
In mercy all my prayer receive,
　　Nor my requests deny.

When us to seek Thy glorious face,
　　Thou kindly dost advise,
Thy glorious face I'll always seek,
　　My grateful heart replies.

Then, hide not Thou Thy face, O Lord,
　　Nor me in wrath reject.
My God and Saviour, leave not him,
　　Thou didst so oft protect!

PSALM 28

Lord, I pray with confidence,
　　Since I pray to Thee;
Thou, the sufferer's sure Defence,
　　Thou wilt succour me.
See me trembling o'er the grave;
　　Come to comfort, come to save!

To Thy throne I lift mine eyes,
　　Lift my hands and heart.

Hear, O hear, my feeble cries;
   Health and hope impart:
Leave me not to sink with those,
   Who my God and me oppose.

Ah, He hears, my Saviour hears,
   Blessed be His name!
In His love I dry my tears,
   And His grace proclaim.
Saints, with mine your thanks record;
Look at me, and praise the Lord.

O what blessedness is theirs,
   Who on Him rely!
Who like Him can answer prayers,
   And all wants supply?
Lord, Thy people tend and feed,
   And at last to glory lead.

PSALM 29 (First Version)

Glory and praise to Jehovah on high:
   Glory from all thro' the earth and the sky!
Angels, approach Him in homage and duty,
   Fall at the feet of your heavenly King;
Saints, to His presence O throng in the beauty,
   Of holy devotion. His mercies to sing!
Glory and praise to Jehovah on high!
Glory from all through the earth and the sky!

The voice of Jehovah, majestic and loud,
In thunder comes forth from His palace of cloud.
That voice o'er the silence of ocean is breaking;

177

It rolls o'er the waters, it bursts on the shore;
The forests are bending, the mountains are quaking,
     And earth and her creatures stand still and adore.
Glory and praise to Jehovah on high!
Glory from all through the earth and the sky!

The voice of Jehovah more sweetly is heard,
By saints in His temple attending His word.
He speaks not to them in the whirlwind or thunder;
     He comes not to threaten, denounce, or reprove;
He comes with glad tidings of joy and of wonder,
     He bids them be blest in Immanuel's love.
Glory and praise to Jehovah on high!
Glory from all through the earth and the sky!

PSALM 29 (Second Version)

Give glory to the Lord,
     His holy name revere;
The wonders of His voice record,
     That all who live may hear.

The voice of God is strong,
     The voice of God is grand;
It rolls the sounding deep along,
     It breaks upon the land.

The voice of God can shake,
     This solid earth around:
The voice of God the rock can break,
     That in the heart is found.

Around His heavenly throne,
　　Ten thousand thousand sing;
O'er the vast flood He sits alone,
　　The world's Eternal King.

Omnipotent His arm,
　　Unchangeable His love,
He keeps His people here from harm,
　　And bears them safe above.

PSALM 29 (Third Version)

Awful is Thy voice, O God,
Terrible Thy lifted rod.
Trembling Nature sinks before Thee,
Souls are humbled and adore Thee.

At a word of Thine this earth,
Started beauteous into birth,
Seas have opened, rocks have shaken,
And the dead shall hear and waken.

Let that quick arid powerful word,
That dread voice, to-day be heard,
Rocks within our bosom breaking,
Souls from death to life awaking.

Yet before the sound shall cease,
Let it melt to love and peace;
Sweetly soothing every terror,
Gently winning back from error.

Saviour, make us, keep us Thine,
Crown us with Thy grace Divine;
From Thy fullness here provide us,
And at last to glory, guide us.

PSALM 30

Lord, Thou hast heard my prayer, and Thou
Shalt hear in turn my praises now;
Thy grace hath healed and set me free:
Whom should I now adore but Thee?

Thine anger for a moment burns,
Then wrath relents, and life returns;
Distress may through the night endure,
But joy at morn comes bright and sure.

Thy smile is life; Thy frown is death;
Eternity hangs on Thy breath;
I stand or fall by Thy decree,
And am just what Thou makest me.

'My rock stands strong,' I proudly cried;
Thou hidd'st Thy face, my comforts died:
Again I sought Thee from the grave,
And Thou wert prompt to help and save.

Thou spak'st; my terrors passed away;
My night became a glorious day;
My heart was full, my tongue was free:
Whom should they now adore but Thee?

PSALM 31 (First Version)

Lord, I look for all to Thee,
Thou hast been a Rock to me:
Still Thy wonted aid afford,
Still be near, my Shield and Sword;
I to Thee my soul commit,
Ah! Thy blood has ransomed it.

Faint and sinking on my road,
Still I cling to Thee, my God;
Bending 'neath a weight of woes,
Harassed by a thousand foes,
Hope still chides my rising fears,
Joy still mingles with my tears.

On Thy word I take my stand,
All my times are in Thy hand;
Make Thy face upon me shine,
Take me 'neath Thy wings Divine:
Lord, Thy grace is all my trust,
Save, O save, Thy trembling dust.

O what mercies still attend,
Those who make the Lord their Friend;
Sweetly, safely, shall they bide,
'Neath His eye, and at His side.
Lord, may this my station be!
Seek it, all ye saints, with me.

❧❧❧

PSALM 31 (Second Version)

M y spirit on Thy care,
  Blest Spirit, I recline;
Thou wilt not leave me to despair,
For Thou art love Divine.

In Thee I place my trust,
   On Thee I calmly rest;
I know Thee good, I know Thee just,
   And count Thy choice the best.

Whate'er events betide,
   Thy will they all perform;
Safe in Thy breast my head I hide,
   Nor fear the coming storm.

Let good or ill befall,
   It must be good for me,
Secure of having Thee in all,
   Of having all in Thee.

PSALM 32 (First Version)

B lest is the penitent who feels,
  His sins are all forgiven;
Thrice blest the soul whom Jesus heals,
   And fills with hopes of heaven.

Before His feet in dumb despair,
   A culprit long I lay;
But when I prayed He heard my prayer,
   And turned my night to day.

O seek Him, all ye sinners round,
    Fall low before His face!
O seek Him while He may be found,
    And share like me His grace!

'Tis ours to pray, 'tis His to bless;
    The Lord is ever nigh,
To guide us through the wilderness,
    And land us safe on high.

PSALM 32 (Second Version)

Blest is the man, how blest,
    Ye ransomed sinners say,
Whose guilt to Christ is all confessed,
    And washed by Him away.

Faith in a risen Lord,
    Has conquered death and sin;
The spirit on his heart is poured,
    And hallows all within.

O happy hour when I
    Was thus to Jesus brought,
Confessed my guilt, and found Him nigh,
    To grant the peace I sought.

Thy work, O Lord, complete;
    O set me fully free;
And lead up many to Thy feet,
    To sing Thy grace with me.

PSALM 33 (First Version)

Ye righteous, in the Lord rejoice;
　　To Him your songs are due.
Well may you give Him heart and voice,
　　Who gave Himself for you.

His word how faithful, how profound!
　　His works how good and right!
O praise the Lord, till all around,
　　Shall in His praise unite.

He spread the starry sky abroad,
　　He forth the ocean poured;
Tremble, thou earth, before thy God,
　　Who made thee with a word.

His counsels ever constant stand;
　　On Him, my soul, depend.
How blest the people of His hand,
　　How blest in such a Friend!

PSALM 33 (Second Version)

Ye righteous, in the Lord rejoice.
　　To Him your best returns are due;
Well may you give Him heart and voice,
　　While He vouchsafes His grace to you.
O sing His wondrous works and ways,
And emulate His gifts with praise!

His acts are mighty, true His word;
　　Creation with His love overflows;

He spake, and heaven her Maker heard,
    He called, and lo, the earth arose.
Let them, let all that live, be awed,
Be still, before one look from God.

But ye, blest souls, rejoice, rejoice,
    Whom God vouchsafes to make His own,
O happy in His love and choice,
    Who sees and tends you from His throne.
Who can support and rescue, who
Like Him whose eye is over you?

When mortal powers grow vain and weak,
    When earthly hopes are low and dim;
There still is one who heeds the meek,
    And bids them rest for all on Him.
O Lord, our Lord for ever be;
O bless the souls that trust in Thee.

PSALM 34 (First Version)

At every time, in every place,
    The Lord my song shall be;
Ye mourners, mark my altered case,
    And sing His praise with me.

I sought Him in my hour of grief,
    And found Him good and true.
He gave my troubled soul relief;
    He holds the same for you.

Angelic guards His saints embrace;
   O taste, and sweetly prove,
The riches of redeeming grace,
   The depths of heavenly love.

O fear the Lord, all other fears,
   Will quickly then subside.
He who the hungry lion hears,
   Will for His flock provide.

PSALM 34 (Second Version)

The praises of the Lord,
   My tongue shall ever pour;
My soul His mercies shall record,
   Till all that hear adore:
Till every sinking heart around,
Shall wake and gladden at the sound.

O praise the Lord with me,
   With me His grace proclaim;
He heard my fainting, trembling plea,
   And to my rescue came:
He snatched me from the jaws of hell,
And bade His angels round me dwell.

Ye sinners, taste and see,
   What grace the Lord can send;
O come and learn how blest is he,
   Who calls Jehovah Friend!
O fear the Lord, ye saints, and ne'er
Have aught on earth beside to fear.

Who walk with Him shall find,
    Of good a rich supply;
He lives the broken heart to bind,
    He hears His people's cry;
Though trials may their course attend,
The Lord will save them in the end.

PSALM 34 (Third Version)

Through all the changing scenes of life,
    In trouble and in joy,
The praises of my God shall still,
    My heart and tongue employ.

Of His deliverance I will boast,
    Till all that are distressed.
From my example comfort take,
    And charm their griefs to rest.

O magnify the Lord with me,
    With me exalt His name;
When in distress on Him I called,
    He to my rescue came.

O make but trial of His love,
    Experience will decide,
How blest are they, and only they,
    Who in His truth confide.

Fear Him, ye saints, and you will then,
    Have nothing else to fear:
Make you His service your delight,
    He'll make your wants His care.

187

PSALM 35

O plead my cause, blest Saviour, plead,
    I trust it all to Thee.
Thou who didst once for sinners bleed,
    A sinner save in me.

Assure my weak desponding heart,
    My threatening foes restrain;
O tell me Thou my helper art,
    And all their rage is vain.

When round Thy cross they rushed to kill,
    How was their fury foiled:
Their madness only wrought Thy will,
    And on themselves recoiled.

The great salvation there achieved,
    My hope shall ever be;
My soul has in her Lord believed,
    And He will rescue me.

PSALM 36 (First Version)

O Thou whom thoughtless men contemn,
    And yet who ne'er neglectest them,
      My soul would Thee adore.
Thy love the heaven of heaven transcends,
Thy faithfulness, Thy truth extends,
      Beyond where thought can soar.

Thy justice like the mountains stands,
Vast are the wonders of Thy hands,

Thy judgments deep and broad;
And all Thy creatures, man and beast,
Down from the loftiest to the least,
Thy bounty share, O God.

But blest o'er all the heirs of grace,
The favoured souls that find a place,
Beneath a Saviour's wing.
How from Thy table are they fed,
How drink they from the fountain head,
The mercies of their King!

The springs of life are all with Thee;
Light in Thy light alone we see,
Creator, Father, Friend.
Still on our souls Thy graces shed,
Still feed us with Thy living bread,
And keep us to the end.

PSALM 36 (Second Version)

My God, what monuments I see,
In all around of Thine and Thee!
I view Thee in the heavens above;
More high than these is heavenly love.

I mark the strong eternal hill,
Thy faithfulness is stronger still.
I gaze on ocean deep and broad,
More deep Thy counsels are, O God.

O give me 'neath Thy wings to rest,
To lean on Thy parental breast,

To feed on Thee, the living Bread,
And drink at mercy's fountain-head.

The springs of life are all Thine own,
They flow from Thine eternal throne:
Light in Thy light alone we see.
O save us, for we rest on Thee!

PSALM 36 (Third Version)

Thy mercy, Lord, the sinner's hope,
    The highest orb of heaven transcends:
The sacred truth's unmeasured scope,
    Through all eternity extends.

Thy justice like the hills remains,
    Unfathomed depths Thy judgments are,
Thy providence the world sustains,
    The whole creation is Thy care.

Thy saints shall to Thy courts be led,
    To banquet on Thy love's repast,
And drink as from a fountain-head,
    Of joys that shall for ever last.

The streams of life with Thee abound;
    Thy presence is eternal day,
O shower Thy gifts the world around,
    Thy glorious face to all display!

PSALM 37 (First Version)

Why should I fret though sinners thrive?
  Their doom will, ah, too soon arrive;
And one bright glimpse of heavenly day,
Thy servants' sufferings well repay.

O trust the Lord, my soul, and He,
In darkest hours will comfort thee.
Thy way to Him in faith commit,
His grace will shape and prosper it.

Clad in His righteousness Divine,
Thou soon shalt as the noonday shine;
Shalt in His favour bask below,
And on from grace to glory go.

The meek, O Lord, the meek shall prove,
The sweetness of Thy saving love: —
With them to me a place be given,
Near Thee on earth, near Thee in heaven.

PSALM 37 (Second Version)

O God of love, how blest are they,
  Who in Thy ways delight!
Thy presence guides them all the day,
  And cheers them all the night.

Whene'er they faint, a mighty arm,
  Is nigh them to uphold;
And sin or Satan cannot harm,
  The feeblest of Thy fold.

191

The Lord is wise, the Lord is just,
  The Lord is good and true;
And they who on His promise trust,
  Will find it bear them through.

His word will stay their sinking hearts;
  Their feet shall never slide:
The heavens dissolve, the earth departs;
  They safe in God abide.

PSALM 38

Rebuke us. Father, but in love:
Let all Thy chastenings mercies prove;
With every stroke Thy grace impart,
And let them move, not break, the heart.

Thy hand is heavy, but our sin,
Is heavier still our souls within:
It whelms, it sinks us to the grave;
Arise, Redeemer, help and save!

Our hearts are open. Lord, to Thee;
Our inmost wish Thine eye can see:
Thou know'st our dangers, foes, and snares,
And will not scorn our humble prayers.

In Thee we hope, on Thee we rest;
O give us what Thou seest the best!
Our guide through every trial past,
O lead us safely home at last!

PSALM 39 (First Version)

Teach us, O Lord, how brief our date,
　How few our fleeting years;
How worthless is our best estate,
　In this poor vale of tears.

Our life indeed is but a span,
　Dependent on Thy breath:
And all the pomps and gains of man,
　But gild the road to death.

We turn from these, we turn from all,
　That binds our hearts to dust:
Down at Thy footstool, Lord, we fall;
　Thy grace is all our trust.

O free our souls from guilt and fear,
　Let fall Thy angry rod.
We are, Thou know'st, but strangers here;
　Be Thou our home, O God.

PSALM 39 (Second Version)

Lord, at Thy feet I bow;
　In Thee I live, to Thee I die.
How great, how changeless. Lord, art Thou!
　How weak and sinful I!

This life, this eager life,
　What is it, but a fleeting breath?
A little hour of toil and strife,
　That hurries on to death.

Remove the veil, O God;
   My true condition make me see;
That I may spurn this earthly clod,
   And soar to heaven and Thee.

Shall this poor passing show,
   These shadowy joys, detain my soul?
Shall these be all my portion? No!
   I quit for Thee the whole.

With Thee to bless and cheer,
   The wilderness I safely roam,
A pilgrim and a stranger here,
   But hastening on to home.

PSALM 39 (Third Version)

Lord, let me know my term of days,
   How soon my life must end;
And all the train of ills disclose,
   Which this frail state attend.

My life, Thou know'st, is but a span,
   A cipher sums my years;
And every man in best estate,
   But vanity appears.

Then why should I on worthless toys,
   With anxious care attend?
On Thee alone my steadfast trust,
   Shall ever, Lord, depend.

Lord, hear my cry, accept my tears,
   Regard my humble prayer,
Who sojourn like a stranger here,
   As all my fathers were.

PSALM 40 (First Version)

In deep distress to God I prayed,
My soul upon His promise stayed.
And, O His grace! He heard my prayer,
And came and snatched me from despair.

He drew me from the fearful pit,
Upon a rock He set my feet,
Upholds my goings in His ways,
And fills my mouth with thankful praise.

Ye sinners round, my rescue see,
And to His footstool throng like me,
And prove, by sweet experience prove,
The freeness, fulness of His love.

O God of grace, to all below,
How large, how rich. Thy mercies flow!
And this the crown of all beside,
That Thy dear Son for sinners died.

He came Thy counsels to fulfil,
He came to do and teach Thy will:
On Him I rest my hope and plea;
Lord, for His sake deliver me!

PSALM 40 (Second Version)

I waited suppliant on the Lord,
  He heard at last my soul's desire,
He raised me from the pit abhorred,
  He freed me from the clogging mire.

Upon a rock He set my feet,
  He taught me in His ways to go,
He filled my mouth with praises meet,
  And bade my heart with love overflow.

My happy change, ye wanderers, see,
  And quit the paths you long have trod;
And turn to Him, and find with me,
  How sweet it is to hope in God.

Ill can my groveling powers sustain,
  The tribute that to Thee belongs;
But when Thy holy face I gain,
  I hope to give Thee worthier songs.

PSALM 40 (Third Version)

'I come, I come,' the Saviour cries,
  'The wrath of God to brave.'
My sinful soul, awake, arise,
  And fly to Christ to save.

'I come,' he cries, 'to you, to all,
  New righteousness to give.'
My soul, before Him contrite fall;
  Believe, adore, and live.

196

'Tis Thine, O Lamb of God, 'tis Thine,
    For sinners to atone;
O touch with grace this soul of mine,
    O break this heart of stone!

Beneath Thy cross O let me sit,
    Thy dying love to see!
And make me feel, while sharing it,
    The same strong love to Thee.

PSALM 41 (First Version)

Blest is the man whose spirit shares,
A suffering brother's wants and cares:
The Lord will visit him in grief,
And bring his trials sweet relief.

The sinners' Friend delights to see,
His people kind and good as He;
And bids them each with each unite,
To make their common burthen light.

That burden well the Saviour knows;
He bore on earth our sins and woes;
By friends betrayed, by foes assailed,
Yet love Divine o'er all prevailed.

That love, O Lord, still let us share,
Still lead us on through foe and snare,
Till we Thy face unclouded see,
And lose ourselves and earth in Thee.

PSALM 41 (Second Version)

Happy the man whose tender care,
Relieves the poor distressed;
When troubles compass him around,
The Lord will give him rest.

His heart with blessings God will crown,
His life in peace prolong,
And disappoint the will of those,
Who seek to do him wrong.

If he in languishing estate,
Through pain and sickness lie,
The Lord will easy make his bed,
And inward health supply.

The Lord will give him grace to pray,
And answer his request;
And through a Saviour's merits bless,
The man who others blest.

PSALM 42 (First Version)

As thirsts the wild deer in the chase,
So thirst I, Lord, to see Thy face.
For God, the living God, I pine;
When shall His smile again be mine?

Tears are my portion night and day;
'Where is thy God?' my tempters say.
The taunt would drive me to despair,
Could I not ease my soul in prayer.

I turn to brighter days gone by,
When I was blest, and God was nigh,
When 'mid His servants I could raise,
The loudest, gladdest song of praise.

Then why, my soul, mistrust Him now?
The Lord is good, be faithful thou:
His nature changes not like thine;
Believe, and soon His face will shine.

PSALM 42 (Second Version)

God, my spirit sinks again,
I founder 'midst a stormy main;
Deep calls to deep, and wave to wave,
And none at hand to help and save.

To Thee, O Lord of life, to Thee,
Through waves and storms I trembling flee.
Without Thee morning brings no day,
And night no rest with Thee away.

Why do I seek Thee, Lord, in vain?
Thy saving grace O why restrain?
Why still that question of despair,
'Where is thy God, vain boaster, where?'

Be calm, my soul, and meekly bow:
The Lord is good, be faithful thou.
He shifts and changes not like thee;
Believe, and thou His face shalt see.

PSALM 42 (Third Version)

L one amidst the dead and dying,
　Lord, my spirit faints for Thee;
Longing, thirsting, drooping, sighing,
　　When shall I Thy presence see?

O how altered my condition!
　　Late I led the joyous throng;
Beat my heart with full fruition,
　　Flowed my lips with grateful song.

Now the storm goes wildly o'er me,
　　Waves on waves my soul confound:
Nought but boding fears before me,
　　Nought but threatening foes around.

Save me, save me, O my Father!
　　To Thy faithful word I cling.
Thence, my soul, thy comfort gather,
　　Hope, and thou again shalt sing.

PSALM 42 (Fourth Version)

A s pants the hart for cooling streams,
　When heated in the chase,
So pants my soul, O Lord, for Thee,
　　Aid Thy refreshing grace.

For Thee, the Lord, the living Lord,
　　My thirsty soul doth pine.
when shall I behold Thy face,
　　Thou Majesty Divine?

I sigh to think of happier days,
    When Thou, O Lord, wert nigh;
When every heart was tuned to praise,
    And none so blest as I.

Why restless, why cast down, my soul?
    Trust God, and thou shalt sing
His praise again, and find Him still
    Thy health's eternal spring!

PSALM 43

Judge me, O Lord; to Thee I fly;
Few foes and fears my spirit try;
    Plead Thou my cause, my soul sustain,
    And let the wicked rage in vain.

The mourner's refuge, Lord, Thou art;
Wilt Thou not take Thy suppliant's part?
Wilt Thou desert, and lay me low,
The scorn of each insulting foe?

Send forth Thy light and truth once more;
To Thy blest house my steps restore:
Again Thy presence let me see,
And find my joy in praising Thee.

Arise, my soul, and praise Him now:
The Lord is good, be faithful thou.
His nature changes not like thine;
Believe, and soon His face will shine.

PSALM 44

L ord, we have heard our fathers tell,
The wonders of Thy hand;
How all their foes before Thee fell,
    And they possessed the land.

They conquered not by spear or sword,
    Or aught that was their own;
And we, like them. Almighty Lord,
    Would rest on Thee alone.

But ah, Thou seem'st to cast us off,
    And put our hopes to shame:
And yet amidst defeat and scoff,
    We trust Thee still the same.

Arise, great God, no longer sleep;
    Thy grace no more withhold.
Redeem, restore Thy scattered sheep,
    And save us as of old.

PSALM 45 (First Version)

I n loftier mood of loftier things
I speak: anointed King of kings,
    Thy glories shall the theme supply;
Fairer than all of mortal race,
Rich in the plentitude of grace,
    And crowned with honours from on high;
Gird on, great Prince, Thy conquering sword;
Send forth Thy soul-subduing word.

202

Ride on; in truth and meekness ride!
What foe Thy terrors may abide,
   What friend Thy love and power mistrust?
Thy throne, O God, for ever stands;
A righteous sceptre fills Thy hands;
   O'er all Thou reignest good and just,
How fair art Thou, how fair Thy bride,
In golden vesture at Thy side!

Thy queen, the Church, O still may she,
Forsake all else and follow Thee,
   Trampling o'er earth, and self, and sin;
Holy, and great, and good, and wise,
Like morning let her spread and rise,
   Glorious alike without, within.
Let her fill earth with praise and love,
To praise Thee better soon above!

PSALM 45 (Second Version)

Lord of the realms above,
   Our Saviour and our King,
How shall our souls return Thy love,
   And all Thy glories sing?

O love Divine indeed,
   O rich surpassing grace,
Which brought the Godhead down to bleed,
   For man's apostate race!

Great King of Glory, gird
   Thy sword upon Thy thigh!
Speed on, speed on Thy conquering word,
   Till all that live comply!

The world is all Thine own;
   O spread Thy sway abroad,
Till every heart becomes Thy throne,
   And owns a present God!

PSALM 46 (First Version)

God is our Refuge, tried and proved,
   Amid a stormy world;
We will not fear though earth be moved,
   And hills in ocean hurled.

The waves may roar, the mountains shake,
   Our comforts shall not cease:
The Lord His saints will not forsake;
   The Lord will give us peace.

A gentle stream of hope and love,
   To us shall ever flow;
It issues from His throne above,
   It cheers His Church below.

When earth and hell against us came,
   He spake, and quelled their powers;
The Lord of Hosts is still the same,
   The God of grace is ours.

PSALM 46 (Second Version)

The Lord is our Refuge, the Lord is our Guide;
We smile upon danger with Him at our side:
The billows may blacken, the tempest increase,
Though earth may be shaken. His saints shall have
peace.

A voice still and small by His people is heard,
A whisper of peace from His life-giving word.
A stream in the desert, a river of love,
Flows down to their hearts from the fountain above.

Be near us, Redeemer, to shield us from ill;
Speak Thou but the word, and the tempest is still.
Thy presence to cheer us, Thine arm to defend,
A worm grows almighty with Thee for a Friend!

The Lord is our Helper; ye scorners, be awed!
Ye earthlings, be still, and acknowledge your God.
The proud He will humble, the lowly defend;
O happy the people with God for a Friend!

PSALM 47 (First Version)

Shout, ye people, clap your hands,
To the Saviour's glory sing;
Wake, ye dark and distant lands,
Wake to hail your God and King.

Lo, His Church shall flourish on,
Till the world shall own His sway.

Forth to conquest Christ is gone;
　Who His glorious course shall stay?

Praise, then, to the mighty Lord,
　Praise to our triumphant King!
All that live, with glad accord
　To His feet your honours bring.

Princes, humbly bow the knee;
　Nations, to His footstool flow.
Lord He is in heaven, and He
　Shall be Lord of all below!

PSALM 47 (Second Version)

Ye that love the Saviour's name,
　Shout, your King is on His throne,
Terrible His foes to tame,
　Mighty to protect His own.
He hath triumphed o'er the grave,
He is risen strong to save.

Onward shall His empire flow,
　Over all that live and move,
Till His will is done below,
　As within His courts above,
Satan, sense, and sin subdued,
Evil all reduced to good.

Shout, ye people of the Lord,
　Ye shall rise with Him to reign;
Christ His servants shall reward,
　Dry their tears, and burst their chain.

All that live, your homage bring,
Praise, O praise, your Saviour King.

PSALM 48 (First Version)

Great is the Lord; His praise be great!
Ye lands, your tributes bring:
And, Britain, thou, His chosen seat,
Be first to praise thy King.

God in thy borders well is known,
A strong and faithful Friend:
O rest thou still on Him alone,
And He will still defend.

Here in Thy courts again we stand,
Thy grace, O Lord, to see:
Soon let it shine on every land,
And win all hearts to Thee.

But, Lord, be Britain still Thy choice;
Still walk around her towers:
Still let her sons in Thee rejoice,
And cry 'The Lord is ours!'

PSALM 48 (Second Version)

Fair, O Lord, Thy dwellings are,
All beside excelling far,
Bright abodes of peace and love,
Types on earth of those above.

Here Thy Gospel voice is heard,
Here we feed upon Thy word,
Here Thy grace is shed abroad,
Here we feel a present God.

Here Thy mysteries are known,
Here is reared Thy earthly throne,
Hence our prayers accepted rise,
And our praises reach the skies.

Lord, Thy Church shall onward flow,
Till it fills the world below;
Undisturbed by countless foes,
Prospering in the midst of woes.

Still to us propitious be;
Shine on those who trust in Thee:
Living, dying, be our Guide,
Till we safely reach Thy side.

PSALM 49

J ehovah speaks; let earth be awed,
    And deep attention give.
Ye sinners, hear the way to God!
    Ye dead, arise and live!

Trust not in earthly wealth and show —
    Vain, vain their power to save:
Gold cannot buy release from woe,
    Or ransom from the grave.

Worlds cannot reach the mighty price,
    Of one immortal soul.
No, Lord; Thy blood and sacrifice,
    Alone can make us whole.

In Thee be our salvation sure,
    No other wealth we seek:
We're rich in Thee, however poor;
    And strong, however weak.

PSALM 50 (First Version)

'Tis He! 'tis He! the Son of God!
He sends His awful voice abroad:
    Let earth her Lord revere!
With thousand saints behold Him come;
The world before her Judge is dumb,
    And waits her doom to hear.

He calls to heaven. He calls to earth;
The nations from their tombs come forth,
    And throng before His face.
'Approach, ye, first,' the Saviour cries,
'Whose boast is in My sacrifice,
    And covenant of grace.'

'My people, hear!' your God will speak:
'No empty rites and forms I seek,
    No specious act or word:
Mine eye is on the heart within,
And there the service must begin,
    That satisfies the Lord.

209

'Where secret wickedness I see,
The fawning lips or bending knee,
   But move My scorn and hate!'
Lord, on our souls this truth impress,
And make us all that we profess.
   Ere yet it be too late!

PSALM 50 (Second Version)

O that day of dread and wonder,
   When to judgment Christ shall come!
When a voice of more than thunder,
   Sounding through the silent tomb,
      Shall awaken,
   All to their eternal doom!

Midst the crowds who then assemble,
   Naked at their Judge's throne,
Who of all the most shall tremble?
   They that now among His own,
      Dwell and worship,
   But whom Christ has never known.

Empty forms and loud profession,
   Offerings heaped upon His shrine,
Where there is no heart impression,
   Cannot please the eye Divine.
      All is worthless,
   Till the spirit, Lord, is Thine.

Light a flame of love within us;
   Tune our souls to prayer and praise;
To Thine own blest image win us;

Guide us in Thy righteous ways.
　　Here convert us,
And at last to glory raise.

PSALM 51 (First Version)

Have mercy on me, Lord!
　　My countless sins forgive!
I cast me on Thy plighted word;
　　O bid me rise and live!

Upon my guilt I dwell;
　　It haunts me day and night,
And shouldst Thou send me straight to hell,
　　I here must own it right.

In sin I was brought forth,
　　Defiled in every part;
And Thou requirest spotless worth,
　　And perfectness of heart.

O let the precious blood,
　　That on the cross was spilt,
Pour on my soul its healing flood,
　　And wash out all my guilt.

Renew my fallen heart,
　　My broken peace restore;
And inward light and strength impart,
　　That I may fall no more.

PSALM 51 (Second Version)

Lord, I have sinned; but, O forgive,
Nor cast me quite away.
Restore my soul, and bid me live,
And be my future stay.

O let me from my fall arise,
More watchful and more strong;
Light up my dim and tearful eyes,
And fill my mouth with song.

On Christ's prevailing sacrifice,
I all my hopes recline.
A broken spirit Thou dost prize;
And such, O Lord, be mine!

Give me a meek, dependent heart,
For all my days to come;
Nor let Thy Spirit e'er depart,
Till I am safe at home.

PSALM 51 (Third Version)

Have mercy. Lord, on me,
As Thou wert ever kind.
I cast my guilty soul on Thee;
Let me Thy mercy find!

O let me hear once more,
Thy kind, forgiving voice!
A word of Thine can life restore,
And bid despair rejoice.

Blot out my deadly sin;
   Bid all my fears be still;
Create my soul anew within,
   And mould me to Thy will.

O do not quite forsake,
   Nor cast me from Thy sight;
Nor let Thy injured Spirit take,
   His everlasting flight.

PSALM 52

In vain the powers of darkness try,
   To work the Church's ill.
The Friend of sinners reigns on high,
   And foils them at His will.

Though mischief in their hearts may dwell,
   And on their tongues deceit;
A word of His their pride can quell,
   And all their rage defeat.

Let worldlings pant for worldly wealth;
   Its worth His people see.
The Lord is their desire and health;
   The Lord will strengthen me.

My trust is in His grace alone;
   His mercy is my home.
How sweet His blessings past to own,
   And hope for more to come!

213

PSALM 53

Lord, what a world of sense and sin,
I find around me and within!
And in Thy breast what thoughts must rise,
When Thou look'st hither from the skies!

Thy glorious work so overthrown,
Thy children all rebellious grown,
Thy followers faint and few, and those
Encompassed by unnumbered foes.

O that Thy Gospel were gone forth,
From East to West, from South to North!
Thy people back to Zion come,
And all Thy outcasts gathered home!

Arise, great Sun of Righteousness!
Arise, the world to light and bless!
From realm to realm advance and shine,
Till every heart and hand are Thine!

PSALM 54

Save me by Thy glorious name;
Lord, that name is Love!
Help through Christ I humbly claim,
    Help from Thee above.
Hear, O hear, my suppliant voice;
Hear, and bid my heart rejoice.

Foes to Christ and every good,
    Fiercely throng on me:

Soon my soul must be subdued,
    Without aid from Thee.
But with Thee to make me strong,
Lord, they shall not triumph long.

Lo, He comes. He takes my part!
    All my struggles cease.
Rise in praise, my grateful heart,
    Bless the Prince of Peace.
God Himself has set me free;
God my worship ever be!

PSALM 55 (First Version)

O God of mercy, hear my cry,
    Behold me in the dust.
What should I be, or whither fly,
    If Thou wert not my trust?

O that my weary soul had wings;
    How swiftly would I flee,
From earthly men and earthly things,
    To dwell, my God, with Thee!

I look within, I look abroad;
    The blight on all has passed:
E'en friends, that seemed the friends of God,
    Prove foes too oft at last.

How sweet it is to turn from all,
    Thy converse, Lord, to claim!
At morn and noon and eve to call,
    And find Thee still the same!

Ye saints, to God your burthens bring,
    And He your strength will be.
To earthly props let others cling;
    The Lord, the Lord for me!

PSALM 55 (Second Version)

O Had I, my Saviour, the wings of a dove,
How soon would I soar to Thy presence above!
How soon would I flee where the weary have rest,
And hide all my cares in Thy sheltering breast!

I flutter, I struggle, I pant to get free;
I feel me a captive while banished from Thee:
A pilgrim and stranger the desert I roam,
And look on to heaven, and long to be home.

Ah, there the wild tempest for ever shall cease;
No billow shall ruffle that haven of peace;
Temptation and trouble alike shall depart,
All tears from the eye, and all sin from the heart.

Soon, soon may this Eden of promise be mine;
Rise, bright Sun of Glory, no more to decline,
Thy light, yet unrisen, the wilderness cheers;
O what will it be when the fullness appears!

PSALM 56

Lord, be merciful to me,
To Thy sheltering side I flee;
Foes around me fiercely throng,
Faith is weak, and fear is strong.
Whither shall Thy trembler fly?
Whither, but to Thee, Most High?

Yes, to Thee my soul shall turn;
Thou wilt not my pleadings spurn.
On Thy word my hopes abide;
I before its strength have tried:
Trusting, yielding all to Thee,
What can shake or injure me?

Foes my faltering steps may view;
Thou, O Lord, wilt note them too.
Thou wilt number all my tears,
Check my wanderings, calm my fears.
Tended and sustained by Thee,
What can shake or injure me?

Here to Thee myself I give;
Thou hast called, and bade me live,
Ah, the work of grace complete;
Guide, support my failing feet:
Lead me on from strength to strength,
Till I reach Thy face at length.

✤✤✤ ✤✤✤ ✤✤✤

PSALM 57 (First Version)

Show mercy, mercy, King of kings!
 On Thee our souls we cast.
Protect us 'neath Thy sheltering wings,
 Till life's dark storm is passed.

O be the same Almighty Arm,
 That held us up till now,
Outstretched to keep us still from harm;
 For who can save but Thou?

Reign, glorious God, through earth and sky,
 Let all Thy grace adore;
Win every heart, fix every eye,
 On Thee for evermore.

Awake, awake, my slumbering powers,
 Be first the song to raise!
While God on me such mercy showers,
I well may give Him praise.

PSALM 57 (Second Version)

Be glorified, O God!
 Above the heavens exalted high;
By men throughout the earth adored,
 By angels in the sky!

My heart, my thankful heart,
 Thy mercies. Lord, would fain proclaim;
Would tell the world how good Thou art,
 And bid them sing the same.

218

Awake, my slumbering powers,
  My tenderest thoughts, awake, arise!
Say what a glorious God is ours,
  How holy, kind, and wise!

O let Thy praises. Lord,
  As widely as Thy bounties flow!
In heaven by angels be adored,
  By all mankind below!

PSALM 57 (Third Version)

Thy mercy, Lord, to us extend,
  On Thee alone our hopes depend;
  Thy sheltering wings around us cast,
  Till life's rude storm be overpast.

  Our hearts, O God, our hearts are fixed;
  Our fears with holy joy are mixed;
  And with our hearts our voice we raise,
  To Thee in grateful songs of praise.

  Thy praises, Lord, we will resound,
  To all the listening nations round:
  Thy truth beyond the clouds extends,
  Thy love the highest heaven transcends.

  Be Thou, O God, exalted high;
  And as Thy glory fills the sky,
  So let it be on earth displayed,
  Till Thou art here as there obeyed!

PSALM 58

Christians, are the words you speak,
Like your Master's, kind and meek?
Do you judge your fellow-men,
As you would be judged again?

Do you in your conduct prove,
Children of a God of love,
Good and gentle, just and true,
As your Lord has been to you?

Ah, the bitterness of sin,
Lurks the fallen heart within,
And from thence unceasing flows,
Poisoning, blighting as it goes!

Lord, the slanderer's malice blast:
Let it come to nought at last,
Let Thy rescued people cry,
'Yea, there is a God on high!'

PSALM 59

Lord, a thousand foes surround us:
Come to succour and defend.
Hell's dark hosts cannot confound us,
While our souls have such a Friend.
Let their legions round us gather;
Be but Thou us nigh to aid;
Strong in Thee, Almighty Father,
We can meet them undismayed.

Holiest, greatest, best, and wisest,
  Who shall dare to cope with Thee?
When to conflict Thou arisest,
  Ah, how soon the boldest flee!
Thou Thy people's wrongs resentest;
  On Thy saving arm we rest:
Thou with grace our prayers preventest;
  Thou wilt choose and give the best.

To our help, then, rise and hasten;
  Check, if not destroy, the foe.
If he must be left to chasten,
  Let him not our hopes o'erthrow.
Safe through suffering and temptation,
  Lead us to Thy fold at last,
To adore Thy full salvation,
  And our crowns before Thee cast.

PSALM 60 (First Version)

Why hast Thou cast us off, O Lord?
  Return, return, Thy Church to aid;
We sink beneath Thy chastening rod!
O heal the breaches Thou hast made!

How long wilt Thou Thy people prove?
How long the cup of trembling give?
Unfurl the banner of Thy love;
Proclaim Thy grace, and bid us live.

'Tis sweet in trouble's gathering night,
To muse on Thy unfailing word,
To think of all Thy love and might,
And, trembling, trust in Thee, O Lord.

Vain is the help that earth affords,
Vain all that human hands bestow:
But Thou be with us. Lord of lords,
And soon we rise o'er every foe.

PSALM 60 (Second Version)

Through foes and dangers, sin and death,
  A pilgrim band we move,
To Canaan's promised land, beneath
  The flag of heavenly love.

Almighty, omnipresent grace,
  Goes with us all the way;
And nothing; can impede our race,
  With Christ to guide and stay.

The empire of the world is His;
  By Him from Satan won.
He speaks the word, and, lo, it is;
  He wills, and all is done!

Though we are weak, the Lord is strong;
  On Him our hopes depend.
We cannot dwell in darkness long,
  While blest with such a Friend!

PSALM 61 (First Version)

Lord, to our prayer attend;
　Our Help and Refuge be,
Remote and reft of every friend,
　　We turn for all to Thee.

O, lead us to the Rock,
　Where we may safe remain:
Our Shield from many a former shock,
　　Defend us now again.

Within Thy shrine we rest;
　Beneath Thy wings we flee;
Among the holy and the blest,
　　Our place and portion be.

O let us there be found,
　Through all our future days:
Let mercy, Lord, to us abound,
　　To Thee redoubled praise!

PSALM 61 (Second Version)

When sinks my heart in gloom and grief,
　And earth no aid supplies,
One hope remains, one sure relief —
　　To heaven I lift my eyes.

The Lord omnipotent is there,
　The Rock no power can move,
The Ear that thrills to every prayer,
　　The Heart that flows with love.

223

My Shield, my Tower, Thou, Lord, hast been,
    My Refuge still Thou art:
Thy spreading wings shall be my screen,
    When all beside depart.

My soul on Thee would calm repose,
    In Thee her portion claim;
And choose her heritage with those,
    Who fear Thy holy name.

O on my cold and barren heart,
    Thy graces largely pour;
And daily more of zeal impart,
    To love and praise Thee more.

PSALM 62

On God, on God my soul relies;
From Him shall my salvation rise;
He is my Rock, my Strong Defence;
What power shall ever hurl me thence!

My foes may rage, my foes may hate:
On God, thy God, my spirit, wait!
He is thy Rock, thy Sure Defence:
Believe, and none shall hurl thee thence!

Let all that live on God depend,
And find Him an Almighty Friend;
Pour out their hearts before His throne,
And rest for all on Him alone.

How poor are all in heaven and earth,
When matched with Him who gave them birth!
Friends, yea, and foes alike must own,
That might and love are God's alone.

PSALM 63 (First Version)

O my God, the God of grace,
Early will I seek Thy face,
In this weary waste of woe,
Where no healing waters flow!

O to stand before Thy shrine,
Basking in Thy light Divine!
O to feed upon Thy love,
As Thy angels feed above!

Better, Lord, than life to me,
Is one quickening smile from Thee,
Life indeed is all a void,
In Thy service unemployed.

Blest with Thee my spirit glows,
And my heart with song o'erflows.
Thoughts of Thee at dead of night,
Turn my darkness into light.

Thou till now my help hast been;
Still Thy wings shall be my screen:
Hard Thy footsteps I pursue;
Send me grace, and bear me through.

PSALM 63 (Second Version)

God of love, my God Thou art;
   To Thee I early cry:
Refresh with grace my thirsty heart,
   For earthly springs are dry.

Thy power. Thy glory let me see,
   As seen by saints above.
'Tis sweeter, Lord, than life to me,
   To share and sing Thy love.

I freely yield Thee all my powers,
   Yet ne'er my debt can pay;
The thought of Thee at midnight hours
   Turns darkness into day.

Lord, Thou hast been my Help, and Thou
   My Refuge still shalt be.
I follow hard Thy footsteps now —
   O when Thy face to see?

PSALM 63 (Third Version)

O God, my gracious God, to Thee
   My morning prayer shall offered be:
   For Thee my thirsty soul doth pant.
My fainting flesh implores Thy grace,
Within this dry and barren place,
   Where souls refreshing waters want.

When down I lie sweet sleep to find,
Thou, Lord, art present to my mind,

And when I wake at dead of night,
Because Thou still dost succour bring,
Beneath the shadow of Thy wing,
   I rest with safety and delight.

O to my longing eyes once more,
That view of glorious power restore,
   Which Thy majestic house displays.
Because to me Thy wondrous love,
Than life itself doth dearer prove,
   My lips shall always speak Thy praise.

My life, while I that life enjoy,
In blessing God I will employ,
   In pouring out my soul on high;
And feel the while, that they who share,
Earth's richest gains or proudest fare,
   Have no such happy lot as I.

PSALM 64

Hear, O Lord, our supplication;
   Let our souls on Thee repose!
Be our Hope, our Strong Salvation,
   'Mid ten thousand threatening foes.

Lord, Thy saints have many troubles,
   In their path lies many a snare:
But before Thy breath, like bubbles,
   Melt they soon in idle air.

Cunning are the foe's devices,
    Bitter are his words of gall;
Sin on every side entices;
    Lord, conduct us safe through all.

Be our foes by Thee confounded,
    Let the world Thy goodness see;
"While, by might and love surrounded,
    We rejoice, and trust in Thee.

PSALM 65 (First Version)

Praise for Thee, Lord, in Zion waits;
    Prayer shall besiege Thy temple gates;
    All flesh shall to Thy throne repair,
    And find through Christ salvation there.

    Our spirits faint; our sins prevail;
    Leave not our trembling hearts to fail.
    O Thou that hearest prayer, descend,
    And still be found the sinner's Friend.

    How blest Thy saints! how safely led,
    How surely kept, how richly fed!
    Saviour of all in earth and sea,
    How happy they who rest in Thee.

    Thy hand sets fast the mighty hills,
    Thy voice the troubled ocean stills;
    Evening and morning hymn Thy praise,
    And earth Thy bounty wide displays.

The year is with Thy goodness crowned,
Thy clouds drop wealth the world around;
Through Thee the deserts laugh and sing,
And Nature smiles and owns her King.

Lord, on our souls Thy influence pour;
The moral waste within restore.
O let Thy love our springtide be,
And make us all bear fruit to Thee.

PSALM 65 (Second Version)

God of the seasons, come again
To bless the circling year!
Give us clear shining after rain,
    And bid the spring appear!

Breathe on this fallen world of ours,
    And wake it into life;
And send us genial suns and showers,
    For winter's stormy strife.

'Tis Thine to rear the tender crop,
    Thy wandering flocks to feed;
And plenteous in Thy footsteps drop,
    Supplies for every need.

The year is with Thy goodness crowned,
    The valleys laugh and sing,
The little hills rejoice around,
    And earth adores her King.

God of the year, while thus the rest,
   Thy genial influence share,
Shine into every wintry breast,
   And make a springtide there.

PSALM 65 (Third Version)

For Thee, O Lord, our constant praise,
   In Zion waits. Thy chosen seat;
Thy promised altars there we'll raise,
   And all our zealous vows complete.

O Thou, that to our humble prayer,
   Didst ever bend a listening ear,
To Thee shall all mankind repair,
   And at Thy gracious throne appear.

Our sins, though numberless, in vain
   To stop Thy flowing mercy try;
While Thou o'erlook'st the guilty stain,
   And washest out the crimson dye.

Blest is the man who, near Thee placed,
   Shall in Thy heavenly presence live!
And blest are we, allowed to taste,
   The joys Thy earthly temples give.

From light to light, from grace to grace,
   Vouchsafe our faltering steps to bear,
And lead us up before Thy face,
   To know and praise Thee better there.

PSALM 66 (First Version)

Ye distant lands, in God rejoice,
   Approach, adore, and sing!
Revere His name, obey His voice,
   And own Him for your King.

O God of mercy, God of might,
   Soon, soon let all that be,
Around Thy glorious throne unite,
   And yield their hearts to Thee!

Thy wondrous acts to us of old,
   Surpass our power to tell;
Approach, ye nations, and behold,
   He is your God as well.

O bless the Lord, ye people, bless;
   With us His love proclaim,
He brought us help m our distress,
   He offers you the same.

PSALM 66 (Second Version)

'Tis Thine, O Father, to assign
   To each his needful cross;
Our souls by trials to refine,
   And purge away the dross.

We know Thee only good, whate'er
   May be withheld or given;
And dare not call the lot severe,
   That helps us on to heaven.

231

It is not ill, it is not woe,
    That comes from such a Friend.
Through toils and dangers on we go,
    To gladness in the end.

O ye that doubt and suffer, come
    Our bettered state to view;
He raised the rod, and drove us home;
    He means the same to you!

PSALM 66 (Third Version)

L ow in Thy holy house,
    Before Thee, Lord, I fall:
Well may I pay Thee thankful vows,
    To whom I owe my all.

O ye that love the Lord,
    Come, see His grace to me:
Before His throne my plaint I poured;
    He spake, and I was free.

Great Hearer of my prayer,
    My praise Thou now shalt hear.
guard me still through every snare!
    O guide me in Thy fear!

I yield my all to Thee,
    Though poor the best I bring.
Ye saints around, O join with me,
    To glorify our King!

PSALM 67 (First Version)

Be merciful to us, O God;
　　Upon Thy people shine;
And spread Thy saving truth abroad,
　　Till all that live are Thine.

Give light and comfort to Thy own;
　　And O that light extend,
Till Thy prevailing name is known,
　　To earth's remotest end.

Let all the nations praise thee, Lord;
　　Let all their homage bring.
From sea to sea be Thou adored,
　　Redeemer, Judge, and King.

Let all the nations praise Thee, Lord;
　　Then earth her fruits shall give:
Thy blessing shall on all be poured,
　　And all to Thee shall live.

PSALM 67 (Second Version)

God of mercy, God of grace,
Show the brightness of Thy face:
Shine upon us, Saviour, shine,
Fill Thy church with light Divine;
And Thy saving health extend,
Unto earth's remotest end.

Let Thy people praise Thee, Lord;
Be by all that live adored;
Let the nations shout and sing,
Glory to their Saviour King;
At Thy feet their tributes pay,
And Thy holy will obey.

Let the people praise Thee, Lord;
Earth shall then her fruits afford;
God to man His blessing give,
Man to God devoted live;
All below, and all above,
One in joy, and light, and love.

PSALM 67 (Third Version)

To bless. Thy chosen race,
  In mercy. Lord, incline;
And cause the brightness of Thy face,
  On all Thy saints to shine.

That so Thy wondrous way,
  May through the earth be known;
Till all that live their tributes pay,
  And Thy salvation own.

O let the nations join,
  Their Saviour to proclaim;
Let all the world, O Lord, combine
  To praise Thy glorious name.

O let them shout and sing,
  In awe and holy mirth,

Till heaven repeat that God is King,
    And join the hymns of earth.

PSALM 68 (First Version)

Arise, O God: let all Thy foes,
    Be scattered and overthrown:
Arise, O God, and interpose,
    To shield and save Thine own.

O Thou, the widow's, orphan's Friend,
    The contrite sinner's Plea;
To Thee we pray, on Thee depend,
    For who can help like Thee?

In Sinai's wilderness of yore,
    How strong to save wert Thou!
Protector of our sires before,
    Protect their children now.

The same Thou art in every age,
    As faithful, strong, and true;
And we are on our pilgrimage;
    O bear us safely through!

❧❧ ❧❧ ❧❧

PSALM 68 (Second Version)

The Son of Man is gone on high;
  He fills His Father's throne again;
He captive leads captivity,
  And wields the gifts of God for men.

O Holy Spirit, Heavenly Dove,
  Of gifts Divine the first and best,
Descend on wings of peace and love,
  And fix Thy home m every breast.

Health, light, and comfort, every good,
  That man can wish or God can lend,
Are all the purchase of Thy blood.
  Our dying, ever-living Friend!

In life, in death, to Thee we cling;
  To Thee with all our wants we come.
O keep us here beneath Thy wing!
  O guide us soon and safely home!

PSALM 68 (Third Version)

Rise, King of Glory, rise!
  Resume Thy heavenly throne;
The vaunting sinner to chastise,
  And bless and save Thy own,
      Halleluiah!
Shout, ye dumb; ye tremblers, sing;
Christ, the sinner's Friend, is King.

Through Sinai's wilderness,
　　He led our sires of old;
And He is still as prompt to bless,
　　As strong to guard His fold.
　　　　Halleluiah!
We are in the desert too:
Saviour, bear us safely through.

For us He came to die;
　　For us He rose again;
And freely offers now from high,
　　The gifts He won for men.
　　　　Halleluiah!
Jesus here was might and love;
Jesus is the same above.

O praise our Saviour King;
　　Before Him humbly fall.
To Him let all their tributes bring,
　　Whose bounty flows to all.
　　　　Halleluiah!
Mighty Thou, and happy we,
Blest and shielded. Lord, by Thee!

PSALM 69 (First Version)

Save me, Lord, the waters roll,
Loud and threatening on my soul.
Foes without, and fears within,
Doubt, temptation, sense, and sin,
Rush at once on helpless me,
And I have no friend but Thee.

Lord, I look to Thee alone;
All my heart to Thee is known.
O behold me where I wait,
Knocking at Thy mercy's gate.
Let no foe of Thine maintain.
That Thou mayst be sought in vain.

Keen reproach for Thee I bear,
Still I yield not to despair;
Still to Thee my spirit flies;
Still on Thee my hope relies.
Blest with Thee, whatever befall,
Thou art still my All-in-all.

Poor and feeble though I be,
Yet how rich, O Lord, in Thee!
O Thy great salvation give,
Send Thy grace, and bid me live.
Send Thy grace, that all may own,
Thou art God, and Thou alone!

PSALM 69 (Second Version)

Lord, I would stand with thoughtful eye,
  Beneath Thy fatal tree,
And see Thee bleed, and see Thee die,
    And think 'what love to me!'

Dwell on the sight, my stony heart,
    Till every pulse within,
Shall into contrite sorrow start,
    And hate the thought of sin.

Didst Thou for me, my Saviour, brave,
    The scoff, the scourge, the gall,
The nails, the thorns, the spear, the grave,
    While I deserved them all?

O help me some return to make,
    To yield my heart to Thee,
And do and suffer for Thy sake,
    As Thou didst then for me!

PSALM 70

Haste, O Lord, my spirit faints;
    Hear my weak, but earnest plea:
Saviour of Thy trembling saints,
    Haste, O haste, to rescue me!

Fierce and many on my soul,
    Rush the threatening powers of hell.
Roll them back, Redeemer, roll,
    As the rock the ocean's swell.

Shame, confusion, fear, and grief,
    Visit, Lord, Thy foes alone!
Light, and comfort, and relief,
    Beam for ever on Thine own!

Help the weak, the fallen raise;
    Fill the meek with joy and love:
Guide us through this earthly maze;
    Land us safe at last above.

PSALM 71 (First Version)

I n Thee, O Lord, my trust I place;
   They cannot fail who rest on Thee.
Thou hast upheld me by Thy grace,
   O to the close my Refuge be!

Brought into life by Thee at first.
   My childhood's Guide, my manhood's Friend;
By Thee till now sustained and nursed, —
   Why should I doubt Thee to the end?

The Guardian of my earliest hours,
   The Strengthener of my feeble frame,
   Will not desert my sinking powers,
But love and tend me still the same.

Strong in Thy righteousness I stand;
   On in Thy might I hope to move;
And each new blessing from Thy hand,
   Shall wake from me new praise and love.

PSALM 71 (Second Version)

W hile foes on me with envy gaze,
   The Lord supports me still.
His honour, therefore, and His praise,
   My mouth shall always fill.

His righteous acts and saving health,
   My tongue shall still declare,

Unable to recount them all,
   Though summed with utmost care.

While God vouchsafes me His support,
   I'll in His strength go on:
All other righteousness disclaim,
   And mention His alone.

Then joy shall fill my mouth, and songs
   Employ my cheerful voice.
My grateful heart, by God redeemed,
   Shall in His light rejoice.

PSALM 72

Exalt, O God, Thy glorious Son!
Throughout the world His will be done;
Set up on earth His promised throne;
And make all hearts and hands His own!

Soft as the dews from heaven descend,
He comes, He comes, the sinner's Friend!
The fall'n to raise, the meek to bless,
And reign o'er all in righteousness!

As bright and lasting as the sun,
From sea to sea His sway shall run;
Kings to His footstool shall repair;
And nations find their refuge there.

Prayer to His throne shall daily rise,
His praises sound through earth and skies;
His grace on all that live be poured,
And all but live to serve the Lord.

Thrice welcome to the King of kings,
Who comes with healing in His wings!
From age to age, from shore to shore,
His name be praised for evermore!

PSALM 73 (First Version)

Yes, God is righteous, God is good;
My soul this truth too long withstood;
But ah, I see my error now,
And at His feet submissive bow.

I saw the vile in triumph drest,
The good by countless ills oppressed.
'Is this,' I said, 'Thy saint's reward?
Is this to serve and trust the Lord?'

But when the end of each I viewed,
It checked at once my murmuring mood;
And taught how light all ills must be,
That lead us, Lord, at last to Thee!

My God, around me ever stand!
O guide my steps! O hold my hand!
O let Thy grace my wants relieve,
Thy glory then my soul receive!

Whom have I, Lord, in heaven but Thee?
On earth is none so dear to me.
When faints my flesh, when fails my heart,
Thou, Thou my strength and portion art.

PSALM 73 (Second Version)

Great Source of my being, my Guardian and Guide,
Through guilt and neglect still the same at my side,
My soul on Thy mercy through life would depend,
And love Thee and trust Thee the same to the end.

The hand that has borne me so well through the past,
Can lead me on safely to glory at last;
Through Life's daily changes on Thee I repose,
For Thou art unchanging in love to the close.

O what is in heaven with Thee to compare?
'Twould lose all its brightness if Thou wert not there.
Or what were this earth with its fairest and best,
If Thou didst not lend them a relish and zest?

My spirit all weakness, my nature all sin,
With little to rest on without and within;
'Tis sweet to look up to a Helper Divine,
O what can I want, while the Saviour is mine?

PSALM 73 (Third Version)

L ord, Thou art good: I know it well.
To Thee alone the praise is due.
If I have stood while others fell,
    It is Thy grace has borne me through.

Thy presence still my strength supplied,
    Thy hand did every want relieve.
Thy counsel to the end will guide,
    Thy glory then my soul receive.

Whom, Lord, in heaven, but Thee alone,
    Have I whose favour I require?
Throughout the wide world there is none,
    That I before Thee could desire.

My trembling flesh, and aching heart,
    May often fail to succour me;
But Thou wilt inward strength impart,
    And my eternal portion be.

PSALM 74 (First Version)

C ast not, O Lord, Thy Church away!
Cease not Thy people to befriend!
Thou hast been Britain's Guide and Stay;
    O bless and shield her to the end.

The walls wherein Thou long hast dwelt,
    The hallowed house of praise and prayer,
Still let Thy presence there be felt,
Still shed Thy choicest blessings there.

Unnumbered foes upon us press;
    But, Lord, we look through all to Thee.
We think of Sinai's wilderness,
    We think of Egypt's traversed sea.

Thy wonders round us daily stand,
    The world Thy glory wide displays:
Suns rise and set by Thy command,
    And seasons roll Thy varying praise.

O Saviour of Thy Church of old,
    Our Guide through every former ill,
Forsake not now Thy suffering fold,
    But guard, and guide, and save us still.

PSALM 74 (Second Version)

Of every earthly stay bereft,
    Beset by many an ill,
One hope, one precious hope, is left,
    The Lord is faithful still.

His Church through every past alarm,
    In Him has found a Friend.
And, Lord, on Thine almighty arm,
We now for all depend.

Thy mercies hourly round us shine,
    The world Thy power displays;
The day is Thine, the night is Thine,
    The seasons roll Thy praise.

Thy holy covenant shall stand,
    For ages bright and sure.
And tell us God is still at hand,
    To shield, to save, to cure.

On Thee, O Lord, our hopes recline;
    O still Thy comforts give.
Defeat our enemies and Thine,
    And bid Thy tremblers live!

PSALM 75

Lord, at Thy feet our thanks we pay,
    For all Thy love has borne and done,
For all Thy mercies day by day,
    And most of all for Christ Thy Son.

The world beneath her load of sin,
    In hopeless, helpless ruin lay;
When He, the Lord of life, stepped in,
    And snatched from death and hell the prey.

Be humbled, then, ye sons of pride;
    Rest in His merits, not your own:
Cast every feebler prop aside,
    And look for all to Christ alone.

Tis Thine, O Lord, to judge and save;
    We live or die by Thy decree;
Whatever beside we want or have,
    Lord, we are rich, if found in Thee.

PSALM 76

God in His Church is known,
His name is glorious there;
He there sets up His earthly throne.
And hears His people's prayer.

The powers of death and hell,
In vain her peace oppose;
A word of His the storm can quell,
And scatter all her foes.

The Lord to judgment came;
Earth trembled and was still.
'Tis His, 'tis His, the proud to tame.
And shield the meek from ill.

The fury of His foes,
Fulfils but His decree.
Ye saints, on Him your hopes repose,
And He your strength will be.

PSALM 77 (First Version)

Hear, O Lord, our supplications,
Look upon our soul's distress;
On through trials and temptations,
To Thy sheltering side we press.
Friend of sinners,
Hear our prayer, O hear and bless!

Musing on Thy grace and favour,
    Through so many years gone by,
Can the Lord cast off for ever?
    Can His mercies fail? we cry.
            He hath blessed us!
    Can the fount of love run dry?

No! it is our own delusion;
    God must still the same abide.
Contradiction or confusion,
    Cannot, Lord, in Thee reside.
            Thou hast promised!
    In that promise we confide.

By Thy many ancient wonders,
    By Thy deeds in Egypt's sea,
Canaan's conquest, Sinai's thunders,
    Lord, our God, we trust in Thee.
            Israel's Shepherd,
    Still Thy people's Guardian be!

PSALM 77 (Second Version)

Lord, Thou hast ever heard my cry;
To Thee in trouble now I fly:
To Thee pour out my secret pain;
O shall I seek Thee, Lord, in vain?

For Thee I sigh the livelong night,
For Thee I look at morning light;
Ah, morning dawns not. Lord, on me,
Till blest by one bright smile from Thee.

Can sovereign mercy cease to love?
Can truth eternal faithless prove?
No, Lord, it is my faithless heart,
That cannot read Thee as Thou art.

O help my musing eye to trace,
Thy works of providence and grace!
What to Thy Israel once wert Thou!
What to Thy suffering people now!

The waters saw Thee then, and fled;
Earth heard Thy voice, and shook with dread:
And still Thou walk'st the troubled wave,
As prompt to help, as strong to save.

PSALM 78

How good, how faithful. Lord, art Thou!
How false and stubborn we!
O teach us at Thy feet to bow,
    And yield our all to Thee.

Our fathers at their darkest hours,
    From Thee found strong relief;
O let their mercies, Lord, be ours,
    But not their unbelief!

The rocks were cleft their thirst to slake,
    The skies rained down their food;
And still Thy word they daily brake,
    And still Thy will withstood.

The same kind Father, Lord, Thou art;
   The same dark rebels we;
O touch with grace each erring heart,
   And win us all to Thee.

PSALM 79

Low in the dust, O Lord, we lie,
   O'erwhelmed beneath Thy chastening rod;
Yet to Thy throne we humbly cry,
   Yet look for all to God, our God!

How long shall we Thy succour crave,
   And Thou refuse Thy grace Divine?
Arise, Thy suffering Church to save,
   And scatter all her foes and Thine!

Our past neglect no more reprove,
   Our countiess sins forget, forgive;
Shine forth once more a God of love;
   Break off our bonds, and bid us live.

Accept the captive's lonely plea;
   The contrite sinner's hopes restore.
Be Thine to guide, to guard, to free;
   Be ours to praise Thee evermore.

PSALM 80 (First Version)

Shepherd of Israel, God of grace,
   Thy saving health display.
Shine from Thy holy dwelling-place,
   And turn our night to day!

Shine on our inward darkness, shine;
   Convert our hearts to Thee.
We cast us on Thy grace Divine;
   Arise, and set us free.

Beneath Thy chastening frown we pine,
   And seem to sue in vain.
Shine on our souls, blest Spirit, shine,
   And all will smile again.

From light to light, from grace to grace,
   O bid us onward move;
Till we behold Thy glorious face,
   Without a cloud above.

PSALM 80 (Second Version)

O Israel's Shepherd, Joseph's Guide,
   Our prayer to Thee vouchsafe to hear;
Thou that dost now Thy glory hide,
   Forth from Thy holy place appear.

Do Thou convert us. Lord: do Thou,
   The brightness of Thy face display;
And all the ills we suffer now,
   Like scattered clouds, shall pass away.

O Thou whom heavenly hosts obey,
 How long shall Thy fierce anger burn?
How long Thy suffering people pray;
 And to their prayers have no return?

Do Thou convert us, Lord; do Thou,
 The brightness of Thy face display;
And all the ills we suffer now,
 Like scattered clouds, shall pass away.

PSALM 81

Sing to the Lord our might;
 With holy fervour sing!
Let hearts and instruments unite,
 To praise our heavenly King.

This is His holy house,
 And this His festal day,
When He accepts the humblest vows,
 That we sincerely pay.

The Sabbath to our sires,
 In mercy first was given;
The Church her Sabbaths still requires
 To speed her on to heaven.

We still, like them of old,
 Are in the wilderness;
And God is still as near His fold,
 To pity and to bless.

Then let us open wide,
 Our hearts for Him to fill:
And He that Israel then supplied,
 Will help His Israel still.

PSALM 82

God is the Judge, and God alone;
He marks us from His heavenly throne;
He destines with unerring skill,
And works unmoved His sovereign will.

How long, frail man, wilt thou presume,
To place Thee in thy Maker's room?
And judge and doom without dismay,
The fellow-creatures of a day?

From God wouldst thou compassion claim,
To erring man show thou the same.
To mildest judgments still be prone,
And spare all errors but thine own.

Arise, O God; judge Thou the earth;
Assert the claims of injured worth:
Put down the boast of sinful men,
And make all hearts Thine own again.

PSALM 83

A ssert Thy claims, O God!
Arouse Thy slumbering powers!
And crush beneath Thy conquering rod.
Thine enemies and ours.

The crafty and the strong,
Conspire 'gainst Thee and Thine.
O shield Thy hidden ones from wrong,
And blast their foes' design.

O let the same right arm,
That helped our sires of yore,
Preserve Thy people still from harm,
And their faint hopes restore.

Let Thy prevailing name,
Throughout the earth be known;
Put Satan and his hosts to shame,
And glorify Thy own.

PSALM 84 (First Version)

T hy earthly dwellings. Lord, are fair,
More fair Thy courts above.
When shall I rise, and banquet there,
On Thy eternal love?

Happy the birds that round Thy shrine,
Can daily sing and roam!
I with their songs would mingle mine,
And choose with them my home.

'Tis sweet into Thy house to come,
   And all Thy mercies trace:
Within Thy arms to find a home,
   And see Thee face to face.

The spirit thus from strength to strength,
   From light to light, shall move;
Till earthly trials end at length,
   In joy and praise above.

O happy seasons, spent with Thee,
   Within Thy house of prayer!
I'd rather there a servant be,
   Than reign a king elsewhere.

The Lord will grace and glory give,
   A Sun and Shield is He.
How happy, Lord, how safe they live,
   Who trust their all to Thee!

PSALM 84 (Second Version)

Pleasant are Thy courts above,
In the land of light and love;
Pleasant are Thy courts below,
In this land of sin and woe:
O my spirit longs and faints,
For the converse of Thy saints,
For the brightness of Thy face,
For Thy fullness, God of grace.

Happy birds that sing and fly,
Round Thy altars, O Most High;
Happier souls that find a rest,
In a Heavenly Father's breast:
Like the wandering dove that found,
No repose on earth around,
They can to their ark repair,
And enjoy it ever there.

Happy souls! their praises flow,
Even in this vale of woe;
Waters in the desert rise,
Manna feeds them from the skies:
On they go from strength to strength,
Till they reach Thy throne at length,
At Thy feet adoring fall,
Who hast led them safe through all.

Lord, be mine this prize to win;
Guide me through a world of sin;
Keep me by Thy saving grace;
Give me at Thy side a place;
Sun and Shield alike Thou art,
Guide and guard my erring heart;
Grace and glory flow from Thee, —
Shower, O shower them. Lord, on me.

PSALM 84 (Third Version)

L ord, how lovely is the place,
  Where saints adore Thy name!
I long to stand before Thy face,
  And pay my vows with them.

I envy. Lord, the birds that can,
  To Thy blest shrine repair.
I envy more the favoured man,
  Who makes his dwelling there.

From grace to grace, from strength to strength,
  He on securely goes;
Till, gathered safe to Thee at length,
  No wish or want he knows.

Lord, give me in Thy house a place;
  My Sun and Buckler be:
And lead and feed me by Thy grace,
  Till I Thy glory see!

PSALM 84 (Fourth Version)

O God of Hosts, the mighty Lord,
  How lovely is the place,
Where Thou enthroned in glory show'st
  The brightness of Thy face!

My longing soul faints with desire.
  To view Thy blest abode;
My panting heart and flesh cry out,
  For Thee the living God.

257

For in Thy courts one single day,
    'Tis better to attend,
Than, Lord, in any court beside,
    A thousand days to spend.

O God, whom heavenly hosts obey,
    How highly blest is he,
Whose hope and trust, securely placed,
    Is still reposed on Thee!

PSALM 85 (First Version)

Lord, Thou hast set Thy people free;
    A brighter day begins;
And mercy, flowing full from Thee,
    Has covered all their sins.

Thy anger, Lord, is turned to love;
    O turn Thy people too!
A blest revival let us prove,
    And health and joy renew.

Thy full salvation bid us see;
    Thy perfect peace restore:
And bind our souls with love, that we
    May ne'er desert Thee more.

The Gospel sounds; the Lord descends;
    The sinner's fears may cease.
Mercy and Truth have met as friends,
    And Justice kisses Peace.

Beneath Messiah's golden reign,
    May all be soon restored;
The Lord with man abide again,
    And man adore the Lord.

PSALM 85 (Second Version)

LORD, Thou art love Divine!
    I yield my heart to Thee!
Fetters and darkness long were mine;
    But grace has set me free.

The Saviour's blood is spilt;
    The day of mercy come:
And to His cross from shame and guilt,
    I flee, and find a home.

Thy work, O Lord, complete;
    Thy daily grace impart.
Direct aright my wandering feet!
    Upstay my sinking heart.

Still let me onward move,
    Rejoicing more and more;
Till I behold Thy face above,
    And at Thy feet adore.

PSALM 85 (Third Version)

When hope is low, and faith is weak,
    And earthly comforts fail to move,
How good to hear a Father speak!
    How sweet to scan a Saviour's love!

It points me to the mighty plan,
    Matured through countless years on high,
Brought down by Christ to fallen man,
    And finished, when He deigned to die.

O rich resource! O plenteous grace!
    So sure, so constant, full, and free!
Here righteousness and peace embrace,
    And heavenly truth and love agree.

Here let me sit beneath the cross;
    Here lay my sins and sorrows down;
And think how light each earthly loss,
When poised with an eternal crown.

PSALM 86 (First Version)

Thy gracious ear, O Lord, incline;
    Our Help and Refuge be:
Preserve our souls, for they are Thine,
    And look for all to Thee.

To Thee we lift our daily prayer.
    O shall we pray in vain?
Thou hast redeemed us from despair;
    Descend and save again.

Who is like Thee, the wise, the just?
    Your King, ye nations, own!
All-good Thou art, and good Thou dost;
    Thou, Thou art God alone.

Our hearts to Thee in love unite;
    Our mouths with praises fill.
Direct our wandering steps aright,
    And form us to Thy will.

Plenteous in grace and truth Thou art;
    On us that grace outpour:
And seal and fix each erring heart,
    Thine own for evermore.

PSALM 86 (Second Version)

To my complaint, O Lord, my God,
    Thy gracious ear incline.
Hear me, distressed and destitute,
    Of all relief but Thine.

Teach me, O Lord, Thy way, and I
    From thence shall ne'er depart.
In reverence on Thy holy name,
Devoutly fix my heart.

261

Thee will I praise, my King, my God;
 O make that praise sincere.
And to Thyself within my heart,
 Eternal trophies rear.

Thy boundless mercies. Lord, to me,
 Surpass my power to tell;
Blest as I am, and crowned by Thee,
 And saved from depths of hell.

O still the same Almighty arm,
 To my assistance bring,
Of patience, mercy, truth, and grace,
 Thou everlasting Spring!

PSALM 87

The Church of God below,
 Is like His church above,
Safe shielded from her every foe,
 By heavenly power and love.

On high and holy ground,
 Her deep foundations rest;
And God within her courts is found,
 An omnipresent Guest.

God loves her sacred gates,
 Her solemn praise and prayer;
And none that humbly on Him waits,
 Shall fail to find Him there.

The Church of God below,
  Shall yet more honoured be;
The nations to her side shall flow,
  The world her glories see.

O blest and favoured men,
  That in her courts are born;
Their life but sets to rise again,
  In heaven's eternal morn.

PSALM 88

Lord God of my salvation,
  To Thee, to Thee, I cry;
O let my supplication,
  Arrest Thine ear on high.
Distresses round me thicken,
  My life draws nigh the grave;
Descend, O Lord, to quicken,
  Descend my soul to save.

Thy wrath lies hard upon me,
  Thy billows o'er me roll,
My friends all seem to shun me,
  And foes beset my soul.
Where'er on earth I turn me,
  No comforter is near.
Wilt Thou too. Father, spurn me?
  Wilt Thou refuse to hear?

No! banished and heart-broken,
　　My soul still clings to Thee;
The promise Thou hast spoken,
　　Shall still my refuge be.
So present ills and terrors,
　　May future joy increase,
And scourge me from my errors,
　　To duty, hope, and peace.

PSALM 89 (First Version)

The mercies of my God and King,
　　My tongue shall still pursue:
O happy they who, while they sing
　　Those mercies, share them too!

As bright and lasting as the sun,
　　As lofty as the sky,
From age to age Thy truth shall run,
　　And chance and change defy.

The covenant of the King of kings,
　　Shall stand for ever sure;
And 'neath the shadow of Thy wings,
　　Thy saints repose secure.

Thine is the earth, and Thine the skies,
　　Created at Thy will:
The waves at Thy command arise,
　　At Thy command are still.

In earth below, in heaven above,
    Who, who is Lord like Thee!
O spread the Gospel of Thy love,
    Till all Thy glories see.

PSALM 89 (Second Version)

O how blest the congregation,
    Who the Gospel know and prize,
Joyful tidings of salvation,
    Brought by Jesus from the skies!
        He is near them,
    Knows their wants, and hears their cries.

In His name rejoicing ever,
    Walking in His light and love,
And foretasting, in His favour,
    Something here of bliss above;
        Happy people!
    Who shall harm them? what shall move?

In His righteousness exalted,
    On from strength to strength they go;
By ten thousand ills assaulted,
    Yet preserved from every foe.
        On to glory,
    Safe they speed through all below.

God will keep His own anointed;
    Nought shall harm them, none condemn.
All their trials are appointed,
    All must work for good to them,
        All shall help them,
    To their heavenly diadem.

PSALM 89 (Third Version)

Thy mercies, Lord, shall be my song,
    My song on them shall ever dwell;
To ages yet unborn my tongue,
    Thy never-failing truth shall tell.

For such stupendous love as Thine,
    I ne'er can pay the half I owe.
Help me, ye angel choirs Divine!
    O help me, all ye saints below!

The heavens are Thine, the earth is Thine,
    The wonders of Thy mighty hand:
And all that round Thee breathe and shine,
    Obey Thine infinite command.

Thou dost the lawless sea control,
    And check and change the restless deep;
Thou mak'st the sleeping billows roll,
    Thou mak'st the rolling billows sleep.

Thy arm is strong. Thy hand is high:
    Justice and judgment round Thee wait,
And who can better tell than I,
    Thou art as good as Thou; art great!

PSALM 90 (First Version)

O God of glory, God of grace,
  From age to age our dwelling-place,
    Before Thy throne we bow.
Ere the vast mountains rose of yore,
When they and earth shall be no more,
    The same, O Lord, art Thou.

Man's generations rise and pass.
Like morning flowers, or summer grass,
    The creatures of Thy breath.
Our life runs onward like a stream;
We come and vanish as a dream,
    The prey of sin and death.

Unnumbered ills beset our path,
Our days are darkened 'neath Thy wrath;
    And yet how heedless we!
O touch with grace each erring heart,
True wisdom to each soul impart,
    And win us all to Thee.

We sink, we perish 'neath Thy frown:
O send Thy healing mercy down,
    To light our coming years!
Then be they many, be they few,
Thy grace will bear us safely through,
    Beyond the reach of tears.

PSALM 90 (Second Version)

Thou art, Thou wert, O Lord,
  Long ere the mountains had their birth;
Long ere at Thy creative word,
  Uprose this breathing earth.

Man, like a summer flower,
  Lives through his little varied day,
The slender creature of an hour,
  That blossoms to decay.

This truth O make us see!
  O bid us, Lord, be timely wise,
And seek a Saviour, seek from Thee,
  The life that never dies!

Forgive us every sin;
  Fill our dark souls with joy and light;
And let that glorious day begin,
  That never sinks in might.

PSALM 91 (First Version)

There is a safe and secret place,
  Beneath the Wings Divine,
Reserved for all the heirs of grace; —
  O be that refuge mine!

The least and feeblest there may bide,
  Uninjured and unawed;

While thousands fall on every side,
 He rests secure in God.

The angels watch him on his way,
 And aid with friendly arm;
And Satan roaring for his prey,
 May hate, but cannot harm.

He feeds in pastures large and fair,
 Of love and truth Divine.
O child of God, O glory's heir,
 How rich a lot is thine!

A hand almighty to defend,
 An ear for every call,
An honoured life, a peaceful end,
 And heaven to crown it all!

PSALM 91 (Second Version)

O how safe, how happy he,
Lord of Hosts, who dwells with Thee!
Sheltered 'neath almighty wings,
Guarded by the King of kings!
Thou my Hope, my Refuge art;
Touch with grace my rebel heart;
Draw me home unto Thy breast;
Give me there eternal rest!

Many are the ills and foes,
Which the child of God inclose;
Plagues that walk the sullen night,
Shafts that fly in noonday light,

269

Here his snares the fowler plies,
There the world's pollution tries.
Lord, while thousands round me fall,
Help, and I am safe from all.

How to him should evil come,
Who has found in Thee a home?
Angels round him take their stand,
Guide him with unerring hand!
Safe he speeds his conquering way,
Where the lion lurks to slay;
Treads the crested dragon down,
Hasting to his heavenly crown.

Hark the voice of Love Divine!
'Fear not, trembler, thou art Mine!
Fear not, I am at thy side,
Strong to succour, sure to guide.
Call on Me in want or woe,
I will keep thee here below;
And, thy day of conflict past.
Bear thee to Myself at last!'

PSALM 92 (First Version)

Lord, 'tis a pleasant thing to raise,
Our hearts to Thee above;
In morning's ear to sound Thy praise,
And tell the night Thy love.

Morning and night new mercies show;
O might our gratitude

To Thee as warmly, freely flow,
   As Thou to us art good.

Thy works are vast, Thy counsels high,
   Beyond our power to scan.
The summer grass, that springs to die,
   Is not more frail than man.

But Thou, Most High, art still the same;
   And worthless though we be,
We hope, when sinners sink to shame,
   To rise and reign with Thee.

PSALM 92 (Second Version)

Good it is to praise the Lord,
   Good His holy name to bless;
Morn His mercies shall record,
   Night shall hear His faithfulness:
Great has been His love to me;
O that mine might equal be!

Wake, my soul, with all thy powers,
   Speak His wondrous works and ways;
Say how great a God is ours,
   Fill creation with His praise;
Put the world around to shame,
Till they love and sing the same.

How should they their homage give,
   Who His grace have never known?
How should they before Him live,
   Who must live His foes alone?
But the children of our King,
They are blest, and they should sing.

Sinners in their pride should fall,
   Saints shall higher rise and shine,
Planted by the Lord of all,
   Watered by His grace Divine,
Monuments of truth and love
In His courts below, above!

PSALM 93 (First Version)

High above created things,
   Reigns the glorious King of kings,
Seated in approachless light,
Self-arrayed in awe and might.

Everlasting is His throne;
Heaven and earth are all His own,
Fashioned by His wondrous hand,
Subject to His strong command.

Ocean lifts his voice on high;
Angry waves assault the sky,
Calmly o'er them sits the Lord,
And controls them by His word.

Midst the roaring of the sea,
Sweet it is to Him to flee.
He is faithful. He is near;
Wherefore should His people fear?

PSALM 93 (Second Version)

The Lord is on His throne again,
The Lord who came to die for men,
His earthly scorns and trials past,
And heaven's full joy restored at last.

He clothes Himself with holy light,
Wields in His hands eternal might;
The nations tremble at His nod,
And conscious earth adores her God.

Hark, the deep winds lift up their voice,
Far 'neath His feet the waves rejoice;
The elements are in His hands,
And rest or rage as He commands.

More fierce and restless. Lord, than they,
Man's passions too Thy word obey:
'Tis Thine to temper and control,
The inward workings of the soul.

Breathe on this world of sin and sense,
O breathe Thy holiest influence:
Bid passion's angry tumults cease,
And reign o'er all the Prince of Peace.

PSALM 94

O God of glory, wake!
O Judge of earth, arise!
Our foes amidst their triumphs check,
    And hear Thy people's cries.

We know Thy chastening rod
    Is not upraised to slay;
And thank Thee for the strokes, O God,
    That keep us in Thy way.

Our hearts are wild and vain;
    But Thou art good and wise:
And all Thou givst of ill and pain,
    Is blessing in disguise.

Thou wilt not cast aside
The people of Thy love;
But through the waves Thine ark will guide,
And land us safe above.

Lord, Thou hast been our Stay,
    Through years of trial past;
And Thou wilt help us all the way,
    To Thee and heaven at last.

PSALM 95 (First Version)

Come, let us to Jehovah raise,
Our hearts and voices high;
Resounding back their love and praise,
To angels in the sky.

Before Him let us daily come,
Our daily debt to pay:
To look on to a heavenly home,
And serve Him by the way.

The God of gods Jehovah is,
Before Him let us fall.
The sea is His, the land is His;
He made and loves us all.

Come, let us to His voice attend,
And for His blessing pray.
He is our Father, Guide, and Friend,
O prove Him such to-day.

PSALM 95 (Second Version)

Come to His presence with song and with love,
Praise Him on earth as the angels above.
The King of salvation, O let us adore Him,
With hearts and with voices our gratitude show.

Ourselves and our all let us lay down before Him;
They cannot repay Him the half that we owe.
Come to His presence with song and with love,
Praise Him on earth as the angels above.

Come to His presence, Jehovah is great:
The armies of glory around Him await.
He speaks, and the universe trembles to hear Him;
The mighty creation arose at His call.

O come to His footstool; fall down and revere Him,
The Maker, Upholder, and Ruler of all.
Come to His presence with song and with love,
Praise Him on earth as the angels above.

Come to His presence, Jehovah is good,
His wing is our shelter, His word is our food.
O come where His Gospel still sweetly is flowing;
O come where His people are heard when they pray.

Approach Him with feelings all tender and glowing,
And taste the full joys of His temple to-day.
Come to His presence with song and with love;
Praise Him on earth as the angels above.

PSALM 95 (Third Version)

O come, loud anthems let us raise;
Tune every heart to thankful praise;
For heart and voice we well may bring,
To magnify salvation's King.

O let us to. His courts repair,
And humbly bow before Him there,
Upon His name devoutly call,
And yield to Him ourselves, our all.

Into His presence let us haste,
To thank Him for His mercies past.
To Him our joyful songs address,
And ask Him still our souls to bless.

He is our God; our Shepherd He,
His flock and pasture sheep are we.
O hear His word. His grace adore;
O praise Him, serve Hun evermore!

PSALM 96 (First Version)

Sing to the Lord, His praises sound;
Sing to the Lord in joyful strains;
Spread the triumphant tidings round,
    And tell the world her Saviour reigns.

Your worthless gods, vain men, forgo,
    And give the God of gods His due,
Your songs, your hearts, your all bestow,
    On Him, who gave Himself for you.

The Lord is good, the Lord is great:
    How good, how great, what tongue can tell?
Glorv and grandeur round Him wait,
    And lo! He comes with man to dwell.

Let heaven be glad, let earth rejoice;
    Let rocks make answer to the wave.
Woods, hills, and vales find all a voice,
    For Him, who comes to bless and save!

PSALM 96 (Second Version)

Sing to the risen Lord!
A new glad anthem sing!
Let earth to heaven her joy record,
And say that Christ is King.

Proclaim it wide around,
His saving grace proclaim,
That all who five may hear the sound,
And love and praise the same.

Come to His holy seat,
Before Him humbly fall:
Adore, ye nations, at His feet,
And own Him Lord of all.

O holy, good and great,
Beyond our power to scan,
Sublimer honours on Thee wait,
Than spring from dying man.

Let all in heaven rejoice,
Let all creation sing;
Seas, mountains, woods, find all a voice,
To say that Christ is King.

❧❧ ❧❧ ❧❧

PSALM 96 (Third Version)

Sing to the Lord a new-made song;
Let all in one assembled throng,
  The great Jehovah's might resound,
Sing to the Lord and bless His name:
From day to day His praise proclaim,
  And spread His glories wide around.
To heathen lands His works rehearse,
His wonders to the universe.

Tell the wide world Jehovah reigns,
Whose power alone that world sustains,
  Whose mercy will its fall restore.
Let heaven its lofty joy confess,
And heavenly mirth let earth express,
  Its loud applause let ocean roar.
Its mute inhabitants rejoice,
And for His triumphs find a voice.

For joy let fertile valleys sing,
And tuneful groves their tribute bring,
  Hills, rocks, and plains, all Nature, wake.
He comes. He comes, mankind to bless,
He comes in truth and righteousness,
  His empire o'er this earth to take.
Through Him we live, on Him we call:
Hail, glorious, gracious Lord of all!

PSALM 97 (First Version)

The Lord is King, let earth be glad;
He comes in heavenly glory clad,
To fix in human hearts His throne,
And make the mighty world His own.

Darkness and clouds around Him move,
Himself is everlasting love.
Ye heathen, at His footstool fall:
Ye gods, adore the God of all!

Rejoice, ye saints; the King of kings,
Appears with healing in His wings.
Rejoice, your Saviour God to view;
He brings but hope and peace to you.

O follow good, and evil flee;
His presence then your joy shall be.
Light for His people here is sown;
The full fruit reaped in heaven alone.

PSALM 97 (Second Version)

The Lord is on His throne on high;
    Let all the world adore Him!
The clouds and tempests of the sky,
    Frown dark and solemn o'er Him.
Wide from His hand the lightnings fly;
Earth trembling feels her Maker nigh,
    And bows in awe before Him.

Behold your God, behold and own,
    Ye dark and senseless nations,
That long to gods of wood and stone
    Have raised your supplications!
Ye gods, fall down like Dagon prone,
And to the God of gods alone
    Yield now your adorations!

He reigns His people's hearts to cheer,
    He reigns their bonds to sever.
Long have they sought to serve Him here,
    Though vain their best endeavour.
Now God, their Saviour God, is near,
To bear them high from toil and fear,
    To light and joy for ever.

PSALM 98 (First Version)

Sing to the Lord, His triumphs tell;
    Let all to Jesus sing.
Crushed are the powers of death and hell,
    And Christ alone is King.

Sound forth the glorious Gospel; sound
    His saving name abroad;
Till every sinking heart shall bound.
    And own a present God!

Sing to the Lord, thou fallen world,
    Be joyful and adore:
The curse from off thy head is hurled,
    Thy fields shall mourn no more.

Awake, ye saints; let every voice,
    And heart its tribute bring.
Seas, woods, and hills rejoice, rejoice,
And say that Christ is King!

PSALM 98 (Second Version)

The Lord of heaven to earth is come,
    The Lord expected long:
Let every heart prepare a home,
    And every voice a song.

He comes to free the fettered slaves,
    Their haughty foes to bind.
Salvation in His banner waves,
    And waves for all mankind.

The sinner finds a Saviour now,
    His trembling Church a King.
Ye heathen, at His footstool bow;
    Believe, adore, and sing!

Exult, ye lame! behold, ye blind!
    Break forth in song, ye dumb!
Seas, woods, and mountains voices find,
    And shout, 'The Lord is come!'

PSALM 99

Jehovah reigns, enthroned in state;
Ten thousand angels round Him wait,
To bless and scourge at His award,
Tremble, thou earth, before thy Lord!

High o'er this little world of sin,
He sits, and orders all therein.
Ye nations, own with one accord,
The holy, holy, holy Lord!

Jehovah reigns. He loves the right;
And sin with judgment will requite.
But ah. His people can declare,
How well He hears contrition's prayer.

O Wise and Good! Thou canst. Thou wilt,
The guilty spare, and slay the guilt.
Let heart and voice with one accord,
Adore the holy, holy Lord!

PSALM 100 (First Version)

With humble love, and holy fear,
Ye nations, to your God draw near:
Surround His throne in joyful throngs,
And give Him service, give Him songs!

The God of gods Jehovah is;
He made us all, and we are His:
His favoured flock. His pasture sheep,
Whom He has called, and He will keep.

Approach His courts with joy to-day;
Before His shrine your homage pay:
His Gospel hear. His grace entreat;
And lay your all down at His feet.

The Lord is good; His mercies flow,
As wide as human want and woe.
O might our grateful homage prove,
As large and lasting as His love.

PSALM 100 (Second Version)

Let all the world in joyful throngs,
Approach Jehovah's throne;
To Him pour out their hearts and songs,
And live to Him alone.

Come to His feet, ye nations, come!
Come, own your God and King!
Come, find a safe and happy home,
Beneath His spacious wing!

A word of His has made us all;
We are His constant care.
Down in His presence let us fall;
And praise Him daily there.

The Lord is good, the sinners' Friend;
Eternal is His word.
His grace and truth shall never end;
Let all adore the Lord.

PSALM 100 (Third Version)

With one consent let all the earth,
   To God their cheerful voices raise;
Glad homage pay with awful mirth,
   And sing before Him songs of praise.

Convinced that He is God alone,
   From whom both we and all proceed;
We whom He chooses for His own,
   The flock whom He vouchsafes to feed.

O enter then His temple gate!
   Thence to His courts devoutly press;
And still your grateful hymns repeat;
   And still His name with praises bless!

For He's the Lord supremely good;
   His mercy is for ever sure;
His truth, which still has firmly stood,
   To endless ages shall endure.

PSALM 100 (Fourth Version)

All people who on earth do dwell,
   Sing to the Lord with cheerful voice.
Him serve with fear; His praise forth tell;
   Come ye before Him and rejoice.

The Lord, ye know, is God indeed;
   Without our aid He did us make:
We are His flock: He doth us feed;
   And for His sheep He doth us take.

O enter, then. His gates with praise,
    Approach with joy His courts unto;
Praise, laud, and bless His name always,
    For it is seemly so to do.

For why? The Lord our God is good;
    His mercy is for ever sure:
His truth at all times firmly stood;
    And shall from age to age endure.

PSALM 100 (Fifth Version)

Before Jehovah's awful throne,
    Ye nations bow with sacred joy.
Know that the Lord is God alone;
    He can create, and He destroy.

His sovereign power, without our aid,
    Made us of clay and formed us men;
And when like wandering sheep we strayed,
    He brought us to His fold again.

We'll crowd Thy gates with thankful songs,
    High as the heavens our voices raise;
And earth with her ten thousand tongues,
    Shall fill Thy courts with sounding praise.

Wide as the world is Thy command;
    Vast as eternity Thy love;
Firm as a rock Thy truth shall stand,
    When rolling years shall cease to move.

PSALM 101

I sing of judgment and of grace,
And, Lord, to Thee my song address.
I tell Thee what I fain would be;
The change, I know, must spring from Thee.

Blest Spirit, in my heart abide!
O'er every thought and step preside!
And bid me walk in peace and love,
With men on earth, with God above.

O keep me safe from Satan's snare!
O make me of the world beware!
Nor let me choose my friends from those,
That are my kind Redeemer's foes.

The froward heart, the haughty eye,
The slanderous tongue, be mine to fly;
Those whom Thou lovest I would love,
And dwell with them below, above.

PSALM 102 (First Version)

When earthly joys glide fast away,
  When hopes and comforts flee,
When foes oppress, and friends betray,
  I turn, my God, to Thee.

Thy nature. Lord, no change can know,
  Thy promise still is sure;
And ills can ne'er so hopeless grow,
  But Thou canst find a cure.

Deliverance comes most bright and blest,
   At danger's darkest hour;
And man's extremity is best,
   To prove almighty power.

High as Thou art. Thou still art near,
   When suppliants succour crave:
And as Thine ear is swift to hear,
   Thine arm is strong to save.

PSALM 102 (Second Version)

I t comes, the awful hour,
   Of darkness and despair!
I feel, I feel the tempter's power,
   And flee for aid to prayer.

Frail nature sinks apace;
   My soul draws nigh the grave;
Arise, Almighty God of grace,
   Arise to help and save.

Before Thy feet I bow,
   Beneath Thy wings I fly,
All faint and desolate, but Thou,
   Wilt not disdain my cry.

Love is Thy holy name,
   The trembling sinner's plea;
And love, eternally the same,
   Shall raise and rescue me.

PSALM 103 (First Version)

A dore my soul, the Lord,
   Adore His holy name;
His love to Thee record,
   And try to love the same.
Life, health, and hope to thee He gave.
He lives to bless; He died to save.

The Lord His people loves;
   The Lord His people tries:
His anger slowly moves;
   His willing mercy flies.
He gives us, not what we might dread,
But what His grace suggests instead.

Survey yon spacious sky,
   Its silent glories scan;
So wide, so vast, so high,
   The love of God to man.
Far as the east from west appears.
He drives from us our sins and fears.

He sees with Father's eye;
   He knows His creature's frame;
He hears his feeble cry,
   And thinks from whence he came;
A child of dust, a summer flower,
That blooms and fades within an hour.

Ye angels, praise the Lord,
   For ye in strength excel:
Ye hear and do His word,
   And in His presence dwell.
Ye works of His below, above,
Join with my soul in praise and love.

PSALM 103 (Second Version)

Praise, my soul, the King of Heaven;
  To His feet Thy tribute bring!
Ransomed, healed, restored, forgiven,
   Who like me His praise should sing?
     Praise Him! praise Him!
  Praise the everlasting King!

Praise Him for His grace and favour,
   To our fathers in distress!
Praise Him still the same for ever,
   Slow to chide, and swift to bless!
     Praise Him! praise Him!
  Glorious in His faithfulness!

Father-like, He tends and spares us;
   Well our feeble frame He knows.
In His hands He gently bears us,
   Rescues us from all our foes,
     Praise Him! praise Him!
  Widely as His mercy flows!

Frail as summer's flower we flourish:
    Blows the wind, and it is gone.
But while mortals rise and perish,
    God endures unchanging on.
        Praise Him I praise Him!
    Praise the high eternal One!

Angels, help us to adore Him;
    Ye behold Him face to face:
Sun and moon, bow down before Him;
    Dwellers all in time and space,
        Praise Him! praise Him!
    Praise with us the God of grace!

PSALM 103 (Third Version)

Awake, my soul, awake and sing,
The praises of thy God and King:
His hourly benefits recall;
Awake, my soul, and sing them all!
My heart, my heart, begin the song;
My tongue resound it loud and long;
And all within me join the lays,
That speak my Benefactor's praise!

Awake, my soul, awake and sing,
The praises of thy God and King;
Who raised thee hopeless from the grave,
And freely all thy guilt forgave;

New health bestowed, new food supplies,
With daily bounty from the skies:
Lends more than eagle's eye and wing; —
Awake my soul. His praise to sing!

The Lord subdues the tyrant's arm,
And shields His own from every harm.
Long favoured Israel may declare,
How well He hears His people's prayer.
To melting mercy God is prone;
His wrath is slow, and quickly gone:
Our crimes he doth not strictly view:
Nor sternly bid us take our due.

High is yon azure heaven above;
But not so high as heavenly love.
'Tis far from east to yonder west;
Our sins from us are farther cast.
A father looks not half so mild,
As God upon His wayward child:
He knows His creature nought but dust;
And loves to show Him more than just.

Behold yon flower; it springs, it blooms,
And wide the morning air perfumes;
A sudden cloud comes o'er the skies;
The blast descends: the floweret dies.
Such, such is man; so bright his bloom;
So soon he hastens to the tomb;
The creature of a summer day,
That springs, and blows, and fades away.

Not so his God. Unmoved is He,
While worlds dissolve, and ages flee;
And as unmoved His promise stands,

To all that keep His high commands,
That build their hopes on grace alone,
And make almighty strength their own.
They, when all else shall fail or flee,
They, Lord, shall rise and reign with Thee.

Praise Him, ye angels, and sustain,
With your high notes my sinking strain.
Ye starry hosts that round Him shine,
Sun, moon, break forth in strains Divine.
With all thy offspring, earth, arise,
And join the chorus of the skies.
Nor thou, my soul, be last to sing,
The praises of thy God and King.

PSALM 104 (First Version)

My soul, bless the Lord,
 The glorious, the great,
By angels adored,
 And seated in state:
The broad ocean under,
 The sky o'er Him cast.
He speaks in the thunder,
 He walks on the blast!

All creatures on earth,
 Upon Him await;
He gave them their birth,
 He gives them their date.
To Him as a Father,
 For nurture they cry:

293

He gives, and they gather;
   Withholds, and they die.

His Spirit is food
   And life to the soul:
By Him 'tis renewed,
   By Him 'tis made whole.
As able to humble,
   As prompt to forgive;
He frowns, and we tremble,
   He smiles, and we live.

To God every day,
   My homage I'll bring:
His will I'll obey,
   His praises I'll sing.
In sweet meditation,
   His mercies I'll trace;
Enjoy His salvation,
   And hope for His face.

PSALM 104 (Second Version)

God of glory, God of might,
Seated in approachless light,
Dwelling where the skies surround,
Like a tent the blue profound,
Walking on the tempest loud,
Riding on the rolling cloud,
Seated on creation's throne. —
Thou art King, and Thou alone!

At the voice of Thy command,
Rose of old the breathing land,
And the murmuring waters fled,
Down to their appointed bed;
There to rage, and there to roar,
But to pass their bounds no more,
Save to feed the fruitful rills,
Leaping from ten thousand hills.

This wide world is in Thy hand;
Thine the sea, and Thine the land.
When Thou breathest on the earth,
Plant and flower awake to birth.
Living creatures, great and small,
Rose obedient to Thy call;
And dependent die or live,
As Thou dost withhold or give.

Thou art mighty Nature's Soul;
By Thy will the seasons roll:
Elements obey Thy nod:
Sun and moon confess Thee God.
Lord of providence and grace,
Filling, ruling time and space,
Praise from all that live is Thine;
With their hymns I mingle mine.

PSALM 105 (First Version)

Sing praises to the Lord,
  Adore His holy name;
His wondrous works, His saving word,
  To all the world proclaim.

The glories of our King,
  Let every lip record;
Let every heart rejoice and sing,
  That humbly seeks the Lord.

O seek Him for His grace!
  O seek Him for His might!
Seek evermore His glorious face,
  And in His love delight I

His mercies to our sires,
  To us shall be renewed.
His covenant, when time expires,
  Shall stand as it has stood.

PSALM 105 (Second Version)

O render thanks, and bless the Lord;
  Invoke His sacred name.
Acquaint the nations with His deeds;
  His matchless deeds proclaim.

Sing to His praise in lofty hymns;
  His wondrous works rehearse:
Make them the theme of your discourse,
  And subject of your verse.

Rejoice in His almighty name,
    Alone to be adored:
Let every heart overflow with joy,
    That humbly seeks the Lord.

Seek ye the Lord; His saving strength,
    Devoutly still implore:
And where He's ever present seek
    His face for evermore.

PSALM 106 (First Version)

O praise the Lord, for He is good:
    Let all that live His wonders know:
Proclaim His love, that like a flood,
    Has flowed, and shall for ever flow.

Who can His mighty works declare?
    Who can His honours duly raise?
Lord, for the task our hearts prepare,
    And bid our lives show forth Thy praise.

Enrol us 'midst Thy chosen race,
    Their choicest gifts to us impart;
And grant us. Lord, with them a place,
    Before Thy face, beside Thy heart.

Now in the wilderness we roam;
    O Lord, our guiding Pillar be;
So shall we reach our promised home,
    And raise a worthier song to Thee.

PSALM 106 (Second Version)

O render thanks to God above,
The Fountain of eternal love;
Whose mercy firm through ages past,
Has stood, and shall for ever last.

Who can His wondrous works express,
As vast as they are numberless?
What mortal eloquence can raise,
His tribute of immortal praise?

Extend to me that favour. Lord,
Thou to Thy chosen dost afford;
When Thou return'st to set them free,
Let Thy salvation visit me.

O while around Thy throne they prove,
The fullness of eternal love,
Their joyful chorus let me join,
And make Thy people's triumph mine!

PSALM 107 (First Version)

O praise the Lord, the God of grace,
The Saviour of our fallen race;
Who saw us in the desert roam,
And sought, and bore us safely home.

He found us hungry, and He fed
Our fainting souls with living bread;
The milk, the manna, of His word.
O that all hearts would praise the Lord!

The Lord the lonely captive cheers;
The Lord dries up the mourner's tears:
Binds every wound, bursts every chain,
And helps when other help is vain!

There lives no grief He cannot heal;
No curse His grace may not repeal.
The feeblest prayer by Him is heard —
O that all hearts would praise the Lord!

PSALM 107 (Second Version)

The seaman on the swelling sea,
Meets God in all His majesty;
He sees Him walk the wind and wave,
And finds Him daily strong to save.

The storm awakes; the billows rise;
The staggering ship ascends the skies.
Thence down they sink in deep despair;
And nought seems left them — nought but prayer.

They cry; and lo, their cry is heard!
Their God redeems them with a word.
He speaks, and instant at His will,
The tempest and their fears are still.

Swift o'er the main the vessel glides;
Soon in the promised haven hides:
Home, friends, and peace are now restored.
O that all hearts would praise the Lord!

PSALM 107 (Third Version)

Blest be the mighty Lord!
  The seas obey His will.
He called, and lo, the billows heard!
  He spake, the storm was still!

Fierce was the swelling flood,
  And weak and helpless I.
But God above the tempest stood,
  And made its rage comply.

Lord, still make bare Thine arm,
  When dangers on us press.
What fears can move, what foes can harm,
  With Thee at hand to bless?

My shattered bark O guide,
  O'er life's tempestuous sea;
And bring me safe through wind and tide,
  To heaven at last and Thee!

PSALM 108 (First Version)

My God, my King,
    Thy praise I'll sing;
My heart is all Thine own.
    My highest powers,
    My choicest hours,
I yield to Thee alone.

My voice, awake,
    Thy part to take;
My soul, the concert join;
    Till all around,
    Shall catch the sound,
And mix their hymns with mine.

But man is weak,
    Thy praise to speak;
Your God, ye angels, sing:
    Ye taste and see.
    More near than we,
The glories of our King.

His truth and grace,
    Fill time and space;
As large His honours be;
    Till all that live,
    Their homage give,
And praise my God with me.

PSALM 108 (Second Version)

My heart its God would sing,
    But ah, my powers are small.
Spirit of grace. Thy succour bring,
    And raise and claim them all.

At morn, at noon, at night,
    In secret and abroad,
O make it still my chief delight,
    To thank and praise my God!

301

Beyond the' spreading sky,
   Thy love and truth extend.
Set up Thy glory. Lord, on high,
   And reign the sinner's Friend.

Let earth her Monarch know;
   Set all Thy people free:
And while Thou healest others' woe,
   Be gracious. Lord, to me.

PSALM 109

Stranger and pilgrim here below,
   I turn for refuge, Lord, to Thee.
Thou knowst my every want and woe;
   O smite my foes, and rescue me!

Thy name is Love — for that name's sake,
   Sustain and cheer my sinking soul.
Thou seest me low, and poor, and weak:
   O speak the word, and make me whole.

Help, Lord! let all my foes perceive,
   'Tis Thine to comfort or condemn.
With Thee to bless me and relieve,
   I little heed reproach from them.

Arise, then, on my soul arise!
   Thy sheltering wings around me cast!
And all that now afflicts or tries,
   Shall work my peace, O Lord, at last.

PSALM 110 (First Version)

Jehovah to Messiah said,
  At my right hand exalted be,
Until Thine enemies are made
  Thy footstool, subjected to Thee;
In the midst among Thy foes,
Thou Shalt reign, and none oppose.

In Zion shall Thine empire be;
  Thy rod of strength Thy throne of grace.
And Zion's sons shall welcome Thee,
  And meet Thee in Thy holy place.
Like the dew from morning's womb;
Bright and countless shall they come.

I swore, and heaven's courts within,
  Declared and registered the vow,
For ever Priest, for ever King,
  The true Melchizedek art Thou.
Prince of Peace and Righteousness,
Thou shalt reign and Thou shalt bless.

Insulting kings shall own Thy sway,
  Opposing nations feel Thy wrath;
Destruction mark Thine onward way,
  And death and judgment strew Thy path.
He who drank and hastened on,
His the triumph, His the crown!

PSALM 110 (Second Version)

Redemption's holy work was done;
  The Saviour back from earth returned;
The Father hailed His conquering Son,
    And gave the crown He well had earned.
Ascend, He cried, and share My throne;
Ascend, and make all hearts Thy own!

Ascend, and fill Thy native seat,
    Eternal Prophet, Priest, and King;
While foes lie scattered 'neath Thy feet,
    And friends their free-will offerings bring,
And converts at Thy word are born,
As plenteous as the dews at morn!

Messiah hears, ascends His throne,
    Begins His mediatorial reign;
He claims the nations for His own;
    He calls the world to God again;
And pleads with Him His promise past,
That all shall be restored at last.

For this He sojourned long below,
    A Pilgrim in a world of sin,
And drained Himself the cup of woe,
    A better lot for man to win:
Upon His cross, upon His throne.
He died, He lives for man alone!

PSALM 111 (First Version)

Praise ye the Lord! My spirit glows,
To pay the grateful debt she owes:
With heart and tongue, at home, abroad,
Be mine to serve and praise my God.

His works are great. Let those declare
How great, who His salvation share.
Let age to age with joy record,
The might and mercy of the Lord.

His ways are just; His precepts pure;
They stand for ever fast and sure;
And, more than all, His grace is given,
To help His saints o'er earth to heaven.

Redemption is through Christ revealed,
By covenant ordained and sealed:
And wise are they who onward move,
Through holy fear to joy and love.

PSALM 111 (Second Version)

Praise ye the Lord! Her God to praise,
My soul her utmost powers shall raise:
'Mid private friends, and in the throng
Of saints. His praise shall be my song.

His bounty like a flowing tide,
Hath all His people's wants supplied;
His truth, confirmed through ages past,
Shall to eternal ages last.

Just are the dealings of His hands;
Immutable are His commands:
He sets His saints from bondage free.
O may His grace deliver me!

Who wisdom's sacred prize would win,
Must with the fear of God begin.
Thrice happy they to whom 'tis given,
To walk with Him o'er earth to heaven.

PSALM 112 (First Version)

Blest is the man who knows the Lord,
  Who joys to work His holy will;
He rests on God's unchanging word,
  And finds it food and counsel still.

In prosperous times, when Satan tries,
  His grace shall strengthen Nature's powers;
And light break in with sweet surprise,
  To cheer affliction's darkest hours.

God's image in His child we see;
  He feels for others' woe and pain;
And, loving all around him, he
  Is loved himself by God again.

His heart is fixed. He learns to rise,
  Above this little world of tears;
And, strong in One beyond the skies,
  He smiles at earthly foes and fears.

PSALM 112 (Second Version)

That man is blest who stands in awe
Of God, and loves His sacred law;
To pity the distressed inclined,
As well as just to all mankind.

If trials come, 'tis his to feel
That God who smites can also heal;
The soul that's filled with Gospel light
Shines brightest in affliction's night.

Beset with threatening dangers round,
Unmoved shall he maintain his ground;
The sweet remembrance of the just,
Shall flourish when he sleeps in dust.

Ill tidings never can surprise,
His heart that fixed on God relies;
On safety's Rock he sits, and sees
The shipwreck of his enemies.

PSALM 113 (First Version)

Praise ye the Lord! His servants, raise
Your hearts and voices in His praise:
His presence seek, His name adore;
O praise the Lord for evermore!

His praise begins. I hear it run,
From rising to the setting sun.
From clime to clime it rolls along;
And heaven to earth repeats the song.

307

Above the earth, beyond the sky,
The Lord in glory reigns on high.
The best is vile, the brightest dim,
The loftiest low, compared with Him.

Yet suppliant miser3r's faintest groan,
Can reach Him on His lofty throne;
And all the Godhead from above,
Flows down in melting grace and love.

Lord, to our feeble cry attend;
Be still the contrite sinner's Friend:
Still mark our wants, and hear our plea,
And bear us on to heaven and Thee.

PSALM 113 (Second Version)

Ye saints and servants of the Lord,
   The triumphs of His grace record;
   His sacred name for ever bless.
Where'er the circling sun displays,
His rising or his setting rays,
   To Him let all their praise address.

God through the world extends His sway;
The splendours of eternal day,
   But shadows of His glory are.
With Him supreme in love and might,
Who said, ' Be light,' and there was light,
   Let no created power compare.

Though 'tis beneath His state to view,
In highest heaven what angels do,
   Yet He to earth vouchsafes His care.
He takes the needy from his cell,
And gives him in His courts to dwell,
   Companion to the greatest there.

Thus, Lord, to us extend Thy grace,
Thus find us in Thy courts a place,
   Secure from earthly sin and pain.
And having walked awhile below,
With Christ our pilgrimage of woe,
   Then let us rise with Him to reign.

PSALM 114 (First Version)

When Israel forth from bondage passed,
   The Lord of Hosts before Him trod;
The sea beheld, and fled aghast;
   The mountains shook, and owned their God.

Why do ye shake, ye mountains? Why,
   Thou swelling deep, so fast retreat?
Earth, tremble on; thy God is nigh!
   And who shall dare His face to meet?

But ah, when Jesus came to earth,
   He left His royal pomps above;
Sweet strains of peace announced His birth,
   And fear was lost in joy and love.

His acts were acts of grace alone;
   He came Himself for man to give;
He stooped to raise us to His throne;
   He died that we might ever live.

O flee from Israel's God of awe,
   To Christ, the sinner's Hope and Plea;
Embrace the Gospel for the Law,
   And let the Judge thy Saviour be!

PSALM 114 (Second Version)

When bursts the soul its earthly chains,
   And dares be greatly free,
What hopes and terrors, joys and pains,
   Must long its portion be!

It launches on a weary road,
   Beset with ills and foes;
Yet leads that narrow way to God,
   And glory crowns its close.

When clouds frown o'er it wide and drear,
   When dangers round increase,
The Lord shall through the storm appear,
   And awe its rage to peace.

Our ills are soon turned all to good,
   With Jesus for our Friend;
And every trial by the road,
   Shall sweeter make the end.

PSALM 115

Not unto us. Almighty Lord,
But to Thyself, the glory be.
Created by Thine awful word,
We only live to honour Thee.

Where is their God? the heathen cry,
And bow to senseless wood and stone;
Our God, we tell them, fills the sky,
And calls ten thousand worlds His own.

Vain gods! vain men! The Lord alone,
Is Israel's worship, Israel's Friend.
O fear His power! His goodness own!
And love Him, trust Him to the end!

Who lean on Him from strength to strength,
From light to light, shall onward move!
Till through the grave they pass at length,
To sing on high His saving love.

PSALM 116 (First Version)

I love the Lord. I'll love Him now,
While life shall leave me power to love;
And call on Him, who deigned to bow.
And heed me from His throne above;
Who marked the tears, and heard the cry,
And helped the prayer, of such as I.

Long had I roamed secure and blind,
　But knew my sinful self at last;
And all the woes of sin assigned,
　In dark array before me past;
And death and hell rushed full on me,
My portion through eternity.

To God I turned in wild distress,
　And for my soul deliverance sought:
And He was prompt to hear and bless,
　Beyond what I had asked or thought.
He came to earth; He died for me;
And brought me life and liberty.

Rest then, my soul, securely rest!
　The Lord Himself will guard thee now.
Upon a Saviour's bleeding breast,
　Thy weary head in peace may bow.
He there invites thee to recline,
And call His strength and merits thine.

O blessed change for me forlorn!
　And blessed He through endless years,
Who thus my soul from death has borne,
　My feet from falling, eyes from tears!
To Him those feet, those eyes shall turn,
That soul for Him shall ever burn.

PSALM 116 (Second Version)

Dark was my lot; and long it spumed
  The poor reliefs that man could give;
Till God my wayward spirit turned,
  And bade me see, believe, and live.
Then flowed my tears; then woke my tongue;
And loud His grace to sinners sung.

O what return can I bestow,
  Bestow, my God, on mighty Thee?
What can I give, that will not flow,
  In tenfold blessings back on me?
How rich on earth Thy cup of love!
How richer still the fount above!

Be mine to own Thy gentle sway,
  To live, to die on Thee alone.
Whom should I love, and whom obey,
  But Him who made me twice His own?
Who formed me by His living breath?
Who rescued me from sin and death?

Him will I praise; heart, hand, and tongue,
  To Him shall daily offerings bring;
I'll dwell His ransomed train among,
  The Lamb's high song with them to sing:
Till I shall join a brighter choir,
And lend a theme to every lyre.

❧❧❧ ❧❧❧ ❧❧❧

313

PSALM 116 (Third Version)

I love the Lord, the gracious Lord,
  Who heard my humble prayer,
Who sent His bright consoling word,
  And snatched me from despair.

On Him my hopes secure shall dwell,
  Through every coming ill:
He saved me now from death and hell,
  And He can save me still.

Rest, then, my wandering spirit, rest
  Beneath Thy Saviour's wings.
No foe can reach thee in the breast,
  Of Him, the King of kings.

He stayed my feet when nigh to fall,
  He dried my tearful eyes;
And He will bear me safe through all.
  To glory in the skies.

PSALM 116 (Fourth Version)

Redeemed from guilt, redeemed from fears,
  My soul enlarged, and dried my tears,
What can I do, O Love Divine,
What, to repay such gifts as Thine?

What can I do, so poor, so weak,
But from Thy hands new blessings seek?
A heart to feel my mercies more,
A soul to know Thee, and adore?

O teach me at Thy feet to fall,
And yield Thee up myself, my all;
Before Thy saints my debt to own,
And live and die to Thee alone!

Thy Spirit, Lord, at large impart;
Expand, and raise, and fill my heart:
So may I hope my life shall be,
Some faint return, O Lord, to Thee.

PSALM 117

O praise the Lord! ye nations, pour
  Your praises at His shrine:
Around the world, from shore to shore,
  Roll on the strain Divine.

Let all that live their tributes bring;
  They live through Him alone;
Let every breeze upon its wing,
  Waft homage to His throne.

Ye angels that behold His face,
  His love to earth proclaim:
Ye earthly children of His grace,
  Resound it back to them.

How rich His mercy, how Divine!
  His truth how deep and broad!
From age to age the same they shine.
  Let all adore our God!

315

PSALM 118 (First Version)

O bless the Lord, the gracious Lord,
    Eternal is His love;
By all on, earth be Thou adored,
    And praised by all above.

To Thee I never raised mine eye,
    But Thou wert strong and near;
As poor and helpless still am I,
    And Thou as prompt to hear.

They hedged me in; they sought my fall;
    My soul they sorely thrust.
The Lord has borne me safe through all;
    The Lord is still my trust.

With Him I hope to rise and shine,
    Through many future days;
And while the mercies all are mine,
    To Him be all the praise.

PSALM 118 (Second Version)

Within Thy sacred gates again,
    O Lord, we now appear.
Help us to join the favoured train,
That meet and praise Thee here.

On Christ, that sure Foundation Stone,
    The builders cast aside,
Thy Church, we know, shall flourish on,
    Whatever ills betide.

Tis Thine to give us there a place,
  Our souls to raise and cheer:
And this is. Lord, Thy day of grace,
  When Thou art wont to hear.

Descend then. Lord; Thy people meet;
  Descend to bless and save:
Receive us bending at Thy feet,
  And take the best we have.

PSALM 119 (First Version)

Blest is the heart enlarged by grace,
  Enlightened by Thy word;
Deeply its hallowed truths impress,
  Upon my soul, O Lord.

A stranger 'mid a world of sin,
  From Thee I hourly fall.
O light Thy lamp my breast within;
  And guide me safe through all.

My soul cleaves to the dust. O burst
  My chains, and set me free.
Give my fall'n heart a nobler thirst,
  And bid me live to Thee.

Still let Thy precepts guide me right,
  While here on earth I rove.
And lead me on from faith to sight,
  To praise Thee more above.

317

PSALM 119 (Second Version)

Word of God, in mercy given,
  To the pilgrims of a day,
To conduct our steps to heaven,
  To console us by the way,
      Blessed Gospel,
  Be through life our guide and stay.

Thine it is the soul to quicken,
  Cleaving to this earthly clod;
Thine, when troubles round us thicken,
  To proclaim a present God;
      And remind us,
  Who it is that holds the rod.

What the steps of youth can order,
  Like the lamp of Truth Divine?
What can cheer life's gloomy border,
  But that still small voice of Thine,
      Sweetly whispering,
  Fear not, trembler, thou art Mine!

Thou, when Nature's powers are sinking,
  Heavenly health and hope canst give;
At Thy fount refreshment drinking,
  Dying souls arise and live.
      Bread of heaven,
  Let us all of Thee receive.

Shine on every clime and nation;
   Soothe all human wants and woes;
Bear us safe through all temptation;
   Shield us from all fears and foes.
     Glorious Gospel,
   Lead us, feed us, to the close!

PSALM 119 (Third Version)

My Hiding-Place, my Refuge-Tower,
  My Shield art Thou, O Lord!
I firmly anchor all my hopes,
   On Thy sustaining Word.

Secure, substantial peace have they,
   Who truly love Thy law:
No smiling mischief them shall tempt,
   No frowning danger awe.

Eternal and unerring rules
   Thy testimonies give:
O bid my weak and wavering soul
   To Thee for ever live.

According to Thy gracious Word,
   From danger set me free;
Nor make me of those hopes ashamed,
   That I repose on Thee.

PSALM 120

On God I've called in trouble's hour,
  And never called in vain.
Again afflictions round me lower;
  Lord, hear and help again.

A stranger's lot, a pilgrim's fare,
  Is all I meet below;
In every sweet I find a snare;
  In every smile a foe.

Ah, woe is me, that I must roam
  So long this land of tears!
When shall my spirit reach her home,
  Above all foes and fears?

There is a peace that none can break,
  A joy that ne'er shall flee.
When shall I lay me down to wake
  To these, O Lord, and Thee?

PSALM 121 (First Version)

My help comes down from God above,
  Who made the earth and skies:
His arm is might. His heart is love;
  To Him I lift mine eyes.

Preserved by Him I safe shall dwell,
  My footsteps shall not slide.
What should I fear from earth or hell,
  While God is at my side?

His eye is watchful o'er me still,
    And guards me day and night;
His hand is nigh to shield from ill,
    And guide my steps aright.

My soul with Him shall go and come,
    Secure through every snare,
Pass on to her eternal home,
    And serve Him better there.

PSALM 121 (Second Version)

To Zion's hill I lift mine eyes,
    From expecting thence aid;
From Zion's hill and Zion's God,
    Who heaven and earth has made.

Rest then, my soul, in safety rest!
    Thy Guardian will not sleep.
A powerful arm, a wakeful eye,
    Will Israel watch and keep.

Sheltered beneath almighty wings,
    Thou shalt securely rest;
Where neither sun nor moon shall thee
    By day or night molest.

At home, abroad, in peace and war,
    Thy God shall thee defend;
Conduct thee through Life's pilgrimage,
    And crown thy journey's end.

PSALM 122 (First Version)

Sweet is the solemn voice that calls,
  The Christian to the house of prayer;
I love to stand within its walls,
    For Thou, O Lord, art present there.

I love to tread the hallowed courts,
    Where two or three for worship meet;
For thither Christ Himself resorts,
And makes the little band complete.

'Tis sweet to raise the common song,
    To join in holy praise and love;
And imitate the blessed throng,
    That mingle hearts and songs above.

Within these walls may peace abound!
    May all our hearts in one agree!
Where brethren meet, where Christ is found,
    May peace and concord ever be.

PSALM 122 (Second Version)

O pray we all for Salem's peace;
  For they shall prosperous be,
Thou holy city of our God,
    Who bear true love to Thee.

May peace within thy sacred walls,
    A constant guest be found;
With plenty and prosperity
    Thy palaces be crowned!

For my dear brethren's sake, and friends
    No less than brethren dear,
I'll pray, may peace in Salem's towers
    A constant guest appear.

But most of all I'll seek thy good,
    And ever wish thee well,
For Zion and the Temple's sake,
    Where God vouchsafes to dwell.

PSALM 123

Unto Thee I lift my eyes,
Thou that dwellest in the skies;
At Thy throne I meekly bow,
Thou canst save, and only Thou.

As a servant marks his lord,
As a maid her mistress' word,
So I watch and wait on Thee,
Till Thy mercy visit me.

Let Thy face upon me shine,
Tell me, Lord, that Thou art mine;
Poor and little though I be,
I have all in having Thee.

Here to be despised, forgot,
Is Thy children's common lot:
But with Thee to make it up,
Lord, I ask no better cup.

PSALM 124

The Lord is on our side,
  We need not feel alarm;
With Him to guard, with Him to guide,
  What enemy can harm?

Before, when like a flood,
  Our foes upon us rose,
The Lord has o'er the tempest stood,
  And awed it to repose.

The Lord maintains our cause;
  His interposing care,
Has snatched us from the lion's jaws,
  And burst the fowler's snare.

Though poor and helpless we,
  The Almighty to defend;
The world is His, and He, yea. He,
  Will help us to the end.

PSALM 125 (First Version)

As firm as Zion's rock are they,
  Who trust in Zion's King;
They find a sure and lasting stay,
  Beneath His sheltering wing.

The hills do not Jerusalem
  More safely round enclose,
Than heavenly arms encircle them,
  And shield them from their foes.

324

The rod upon their lot may come,
    But shall not settle there,
'Twould scourge them to their heavenly home,
    Not drive them to despair.

Lord, by a safe and pleasant path,
    Thy flock to Zion lead;
And while the froward feel Thy wrath,
    Thy people bless and feed.

PSALM 125 (Second Version)

Who place on Zion's God their trust,
    Like Zion's rock shall stand,
Fixed and upheld immovably,
    By an almighty hand.

Look, how the hills on every side
    Jerusalem enclose;
So stands the Lord around His saints,
    To guard them from their foes.

Affictions may be theirs awhile,
    But cannot long oppress;
His smile shall turn them now to good,
    And all at last redress.

The wicked shall not prosper long,
    Beneath their Maker's frown;
And the same hour that wrecks their hopes,
    Shall bring His saints their crown.

PSALM 126 (First Version)

When Jesus to our rescue came,
    And set our spirits free,
It seemed at first some happy dream,
    Of all we longed to see.

Our hearts with raptures sweet and strange,
    Our lips with song o'erflowed;
And all around beheld the change,
    And owned the hand of God.

'The Lord,' they said, 'great things hath done.'
    'Yea, things,' we cried, 'Divine.'
Then perfect, Lord, Thy work begun,
    And make us wholly Thine.

Thrice happy they in tears that sow,
    To reap in joy and love;
That drop their' seed on earth below,
    And find their sheaves above.

PSALM 126 (Second Version)

A captive long 'neath sense and sin,
    In dark despair I lay;
The Lord upon my soul looked in,
And turned my night to day.

I saw the glory round me break;
    I felt the darkness flee;
I seemed as from a dream to wake,
    And cried, 'It cannot be.'

God's glorious ways I judged by mine,
   Nor half His goodness knew;
But (O the depth of love Divine!)
   I found the whole was true.

My heart was full, my tongue was fain,
   My praises flowed apace;
And many round me joined the strain,
   And sang with me His grace.

Behold, I cried, what God has wrought,
   Beyond my hope or claim;
Ye mourners, mark my altered lot,
   He offers you the same.

O holy sighs! O happy tears!
   By contrite spirits poured.
O sacred salutary fears,
   That drive us to the Lord!

The praying lip, the weeping eye,
   Point on to better days;
When tears to smiles shall change on high.
And prayer be turned to praise.

PSALM 127

O let the people of the Lord,
   On Him alone depend;
His mercies past with joy record,
   And trust Him to the end.

When He assists the house to build,
   Secure and strong it stands.
The city He vouchsafes to shield,
   Is safe from hostile hands.

To late retire, and early rise,
   Cannot ensure success;
And thrift his labours vainly plies,
   Without the Lord to bless.

Children and friends, yea, every good
   We hold, are all the Lord's.
O happy were our gratitude
   As large as His rewards!

PSALM 128

How blest the man who fears the Lord,
Who walks by His unerring word;
His labours find a full increase,
His days are crowned with health and peace.

Domestic comfort builds her nest,
Beneath his roof, within his breast;
And earth's best blessings hourly rise,
To cheer his pathway to the skies.

But earth's best gifts are poor to those,
The Spirit on his soul bestows;
The earnest here of joys above,
The foretaste of eternal love.

Onward he goes from strength to strength,
Till heaven's bright morning breaks at length,
And calls him to his full reward —
How blest the man who fears the Lord!

PSALM 129

How many. Lord, my fall have sought,
    And tried me from my birth!
The heir of heaven, I see, must not
    Expect his home on earth.

Yet foes and snares have joined in vain,
    My steadfastness to move;
A monument I still remain,
    Of Thine unchanging love.

The Lord is strong, the Lord is good:
    Though human powers may fail,
The wicked in their fiercest mood,
    'Gainst Him cannot prevail.

On Zion, Lord, arise and shine;
    Bid all her sufferings cease;
Blight with one look her foes and Thine,
    And give Thy people peace!

PSALM 130 (First Version)

From deep distress to Thee I cry;
O Lord, vouchsafe me a reply!
Where should a trembling sinner turn,
Shouldst Thou remain unmoved and stern?

But there is mercy, Lord, with Thee;
Yea, mercy e'en for guilty me.
To Thee I fly, on Thee depend,
Nor dare distrust the sinner's Friend.

The shipwrecked sailor does not watch,
More wistfully the dawn to catch,
Than waits my soul, O Lord, to trace,
The opening daylight of Thy face.

O to Thy trembling suppliant prove,
A God of hope, a God of love!
I know Thy grace is large and free,
Lord, pour it largely now on me!

PSALM 130 (Second Version)

From depths of woe to God I cry,
    And God my cry will hear:
The Friend of sinners reigns on high,
    And suppliants need not fear.

I cast me on Thy plighted word,
    I knock at mercy's gate;
O hear my supplication, Lord,
    Receive me ere too late!

As seamen on the stormy main,
    As pilgrims on their road,
Look out by night for morn again,
    So looks my soul for God.

Sweet are the dawnings of His grace,
    More sweet the perfect day.
Rise, Sun of Righteousness, and chase
    Each lingering cloud away!

PSALM 130 (Third Version)

My soul with patience waits,
    On Thee, the living Lord:
My hopes are on Thy promise built,
    Thy never-failing word.

My longing hopes look out,
    For Thy enlivening ray,
More than the eyes that watch all night,
    To spy the dawning day.

Let Israel trust in God!
    No bounds His mercy knows;
The plenteous source and spring, from whence
    Eternal succour flows.

His grace for all our wants,
    Can full supplies convey;
A healing spring, a spring to cleanse,
    And wash our guilt away.

PSALM 131

Humble, Lord, my haughty spirit;
  Bid my swelling thoughts subside;
Strip me of my fancied merit:
  What have I to do with pride?
Was my Saviour meek and lowly?
  And shall such a worm as I,
Weak, and earthly, and unholy,
  Dare to lift my head on high!

Teach me. Lord, my true condition;
  Bring me childlike to Thy knee,
Stripped of every low ambition,
  Willing to be led by Thee.
Guide me by Thy Holy Spirit;
  Feed me from Thy blessed Word:
All my wisdom, all my merit,
  Borrowed from Thyself, O Lord!

Like a little babe, confiding,
  Simple, docile, let me be;
Trusting still to Thy providing,
  Casting every care on Thee.
Thus my all to Thee submitting,
  I am Thine, and not my own;
And, when earthly hopes are flitting,
  Rest secure on God alone.

PSALM 132

In this wide, weary world of care,
How kindly God to man hath given,
A Sabbath-day, a house of prayer,
Fair emblems of approaching heaven!

Here pilgrims view their future home;
Here find refreshment by the way;
And here we to Thy footstool come,
And seek Thy favour, Lord, to-day!

Arise, O Lord, Thy Church to bless;
Shower down Thy graces from above.
O clothe Thy priests in righteousness!
O crown Thy saints with light and love!

Thy chosen flock, blest Saviour, lead;
In every heart set up Thy shrine:
The naked clothe, the hungry feed,
And make us all for ever Thine.

PSALM 133

'Tis a pleasant thing to see,
Brethren in the Lord agree,
Children of a God of love,
Live as they shall live above;
Acting each a Christian part,
One in lip, and one in heart.

As the precious ointment shed,
Upon Aaron's hallowed head,
Downward through his garments stole,
Spreading odour o'er the whole;
So from our High Priest above,
To His Church flows heavenly love.

Gently as the dews distil,
Down on Zion's holy hill,
Dropping gladness where they fall,
Brightening and refreshing all;
Such is Christian union, shed
Through the members from the Head.

Where Divine affection lives,
There the Lord His blessing gives;
There His will on earth is done;
There His heaven is half begun.
Lord, our great Example prove,
Teach us all like Thee to love!

PSALM 134

Praise to God on high be given.
Praise from all in earth and heaven.
Ye that in His presence stand,
Ye that walk by His command,
Saints below, and hosts above.
Praise, O praise, the God of love!

Praise Him at the dawn of light,
Praise Him at returning night;
Strings and voices, hands and hearts.
In His praises bear your parts.
Thou that madest earth and sky,
Bless us in return from high!

PSALM 135

O praise the Lord, ye saints of His!
   For ye His goodness know;
And sweet to grateful hearts it is,
   To pay the debt they owe.

O praise the Lord, the Strong, the Wise!
   He watches o'er His sheep,
His will is law through earth and skies:
   And He His flock will keep.

The elements His word obey,
   The world is in His hand!
And ills and blessings go or stay,
   As He may give command.

His love to Israel's froward race,
   His Church may still assure;
And all who trust His saving grace,
   Shall find their trust secure.

PSALM 136 (First Version)

O lift your hearts! O tune your tongues!
The God of glory claims your songs:
The Lord of lords, the lung of kings,
Who life to all and comfort brings;
The Strong, the Wonderful, the Wise,
Who filled the seas, who spread the skies.
Sing, saints below; sing, hosts above;
Tell earth and heaven that God is love.

Thou God of Israel, Thou of old,
From Egypt ledd'st Thy captive fold;
The sea at Thy command withdrew,
And gave Thy flock a passage through.
The skies rained manna on their road;
Streams in the burning desert flowed;
And all around, and all above,
Proclaimed a present God of love.

O God of providence and grace,
The same in every time and place,
Thy flock on earth are wanderers now,
And who can guide or save but Thou?
Through Thee refreshment round us flows,
The desert blossoms as the rose;
And earth is heaven, while here we prove
An omnipresent God of love.

PSALM 136 (Second Version)

Sing praises to the Lord,
The Wise, the Good, the Grand,
Who formed us by His word,
Who leads us with His hand.
The Lord will prove
A faithful Friend;
His might and love
Will never end.

Sing praises to our God,
Who bade the world to be,
Who spread the skies abroad,
And filled the sounding sea.
The Lord will prove
A faithful Friend;
His might and love
Will never end.

Sing praise to Him whose eye,
Beheld us near the grave:
And sent His Son from high,
To succour and to save.
The Lord will prove
A faithful Friend;
His might and love
Will never end.

Sing, creatures all below!
  Sing, angels in the height!
Ye all your tributes owe;
  Let all in praise unite.
    The Lord will prove
    A faithful Friend;
    His might and love
    Will never end.

PSALM 137 (First Version)

By Babel's waters, dark and wide,
A lonely band we sat and sighed:
Our harps upon the willows slept;
We thought of Zion — thought, and wept.

Our foes the while, with taunting tongues,
Cried, 'Sing us one of Zion's songs!'
Yea, they who held us captive there,
Demanded mirth from our despair.

Where should we find a heart to sing,
On hostile ground to God our King?
How should our souls forgetful be,
O Zion, of our home, and thee.

No! let my hand forget her skill,
My tongue in death be mute and still,
Wien thou shalt cease my joy to be,
When aught beside I match with thee!

Soon, Lord, the blessed season bring,
When Zion from the dust shall spring;
Her captive children burst their chain,
And find their long-lost home again.

PSALM 137 (Second Version)

Far from my heavenly home,
  Far from my Father's breast,
Fainting I cry, blest Spirit, come,
  And speed me to my rest.

Upon the willows long,
  My harp has silent hung;
How should I sing a cheerful song,
  Till thou inspire my tongue?

My spirit homeward turns,
  And fain would thither flee.
My heart, O Zion, droops and yearns,
  When I remember thee.

To thee, to thee, I press,
  A dark and toilsome road.
When shall I pass the wilderness,
  And reach the saint's abode?

God of my life, be near!
  On Thee my hopes I cast.
O guide me through the desert here,
  And bring me home at last!

PSALM 137 (Third Version)

When we, our wearied limbs to rest,
   Sat down by proud Euphrates stream,
We wept with heavy thoughts oppressed,
   And Zion was our mournful theme.
Our harps, that, when with joy we sung,
   Were wont with tuneful parts to bear,
With silent strings neglected hung,
   On willow-trees that withered there.

Meanwhile our foes, who all conspired,
   To triumph in our slavish wrongs,
Music and mirth of us required,
   'Come, sing us one of Zion's songs.'
How shall we tune our voice to sing,
   Or touch our harps with skilful hands?
Shall hymns of joy to God our King
   Be sung by slaves in foreign lands?

O Salem, once our happy seat,
   When I of thee forgetful prove,
Let then my trembling hand forget,
   The speaking strings with art to move.
If I to mention thee forbear,
   Eternal silence seize my tongue;
Or if I sing one cheerful air,
   Till thy deliverance is my song.

PSALM 138 (First Version)

Our hearts shall praise Thee, God of love,
  Here in Thy courts below;
Praise Thee, as angels praise above,
  For more than they we owe.

When did Thy people call, and Thou
  Their supplication spurn?
And shall our souls refuse Thee now,
  Their utmost in return?

Though Thou art high, and we are low,
  We are Thy daily care.
Thy hand restrains our fiercest foe,
  And heals our worst despair.

Lord, finish what Thou hast begun,
  In love and grace Divine;
Thy perfect will in us be done,
  And all the praise be Thine.

PSALM 138 (Second Version)

Lord, I adore Thee; all my heart
  To Thee in praises forth shall flow;
The heavens shall hear how good Thou art,
  And all the earth Thy greatness know.

I'll bow me in the sacred place,
  Where prayer and praise are duly heard:
Here magnify Thy truth and grace,
  Here feed on Thine unfailing Word.

341

Whene'er I seek Thy heavenly throne,
   Strength to my soul flows promptly down.
Ye kings of earth, your Monarch own,
   And at His feet lay every crown.

Though God is high, and we are low,
   He still is near His saints to bless;
He shields our souls from every foe;
   He cheers us in our worst distress.

Lord, lead us onward to Thy feet;
   Thy perfect will in us be done.
And in our hearts let grace complete,
   The work that grace has there begun.

PSALM 139 (First Version)

Omniscient God, Thine eye Divine,
   My inmost soul can see;
And every thought and act of mine,
   Is open. Lord, to Thee.

When up I rise, when down I lie,
   Still Thou art at my side.
Where shall I shun Thine awful eye,
   Or from Thy Spirit hide?

If up to heaven my flight I take,
   I meet Thee face to face;
If down to hell, Thy terrors make
   The darkness of the place.

I plunge into the shades of night,
   But Thou art there with me;
And darkness kindles into light
   Before one glance from Thee.

PSALM 139 (Second Version)

From Thee, O Lord, I came at first,
   The creature of Thy hand;
Thy providence my life has nursed,
   And by Thy grace I stand.

Each member of my wondrous frame,
   Displays Thy skill and power;
And countless benefits proclaim,
   Thy love from hour to hour.

Down in Thine arms at night I lie;
   Thou watchest while I sleep.
I wake at morn; Thou still art nigh,
   My soul to tend and keep.

Search me, O Lord; my spirit prove;
   From sin O set me free:
And make my heart return the love,
   It daily shares from Thee.

PSALM 139 (Third Version)

Thou knowst me, Lord. 'Tis Thine to view,
Whatever I am, whate'er I do.
When up I rise, when down I lie,
I still am in Thine awful eye.

My inmost thought, my lightest word,
By Thee is seen, by Thee is heard.
Thy wonder-working hand I find,
Around, before me, and behind.

Where from Thy presence could I flee?
Where find a refuge. Lord, from Thee?
From heaven Thou shinn'st in glory down,
And hell is darkened by Thy frown.

On morning's wings beyond the sea,
I fly, but cannot fly from Thee.
I plunge me in the depths of night;
One look from Thee makes darkness light.

Father of mercy, God of grace,
I cannot, would not, shun Thy face.
No, be it rather mine to prove,
An omnipresent God of love.

PSALM 139 (Fourth Version)

All-seeing God, to Thee is known.
My rising up and lying down;
Thine eye my bed and path surveys,
My public haunts, and private ways.

My secret thoughts are known to Thee,
Yea, known ere well conceived by me.
Thou judgest what my lips would vent,
My yet unuttered heart's intent.

Surrounded by Thy power I stand,
On every side I find Thy hand;
And every member of my frame,
Bespeaks the Source from whence it came.

Let me acknowledge, too, O God,
That since this maze of life I trod,
Thine acts of grace to me surmount
The power of numbers to recount.

Search, try, O Thou that'knowst my heart,
What ill there lurks in every part;
Correct me when I go astray,
And guide me in Thy better way.

PSALM 139 (Fifth Version)

Could I, O Lord, so faithless be,
To think of once deserting Thee,
Where, where could I Thy influence shun,
O whither from Thy presence run?

If up to heaven I took my flight,
Thou dwellest there enthroned in light:
Or dived to hell's unhallowed plains,
There Thine almighty vengeance reigns.

345

If I the morning's wings could gain,
And fly beyond the western main,
Thy swifter hand would first arrive,
And there arrest Thy fugitive.

Or should I try to shun Thy sight.
Beneath the sable wings of night;
One glance from Thee, one piercing ray,
Would kindle darkness into day.

O let me rather seek to fly,
The guilt that makes me dread Thine eye;
Then day and night, at home, abroad,
'Tis joy to feel a present God.

PSALM 140

Preserve me. Lord, from those
  Who meditate my fall,
False flattering friends, and threatening foes,
  Preserve me. Lord, from all.

The tempter's hate or guile,
  The feeblest soul may brave,
The lion's rage, or serpent's wile,
  With Thee at hand to save.

Ere now, in hours of dread,
  I found in Thee a friend;
Thou coveredst my defenceless head;
  And Thou wilt still defend.

Strength of the poor and weak,
   Still faithful, good, and true;
Put down the proud, uphold the meek,
   And bear Thy people through!

PSALM 141

Lord, my spirit flies to Thee,
Haste, O haste, to succour me;
Let my prayer accepted rise,
Like a holy sacrifice.

Guard my lips; let no offence,
Smite Thy hallowed ear from thence;
And, to keep my hands from sin,
Purify my heart within.

Let the righteous kindly chide,
"When they see me step aside;
And while they my faults condemn,
Make me love and pray for them.

Many are my snares and foes;
Vain my efforts to oppose;
Lord, mine eyes are unto Thee;
Haste, O haste, to succour me.

PSALM 142

To Thee, O Lord, in deep distress,
To Thee my suppliant soul would press.
Ill can my burdened spirit plead,
But Thou its untold wish canst read.

I walk 'mid snares on every side,
No voice to cheer, no hand to guide:
A lonely, dark, and rugged road,
But not unknown to Thee, my God.

"When earthly helpers fail or flee,
How sweet to turn, O Lord, to Thee!
And find in Thy exhaustless love,
My rest below, my hope above.

O hear, and set my spirit free,
From foes and chains too strong for me!
My drooping hopes refresh and raise,
And fill my heart with thankful praise.

PSALM 143 (First Version)

O hear my supplication, Lord!
O hear and succour me!
Thy finished work. Thy plighted word,
This, this is all my plea.

With judgment's stem unbending eye,
Let not my works be scanned;
For who could bear that scrutiny?
O who that trial stand?

Thy mercy, Lord, large, changeless, tried,
   On this alone I call:
My sins are great, and hell is wide;
   Redeem me, Lord, from all!

O let the brightness of Thy face,
   Dispel this night of mine!
I seek Thy help, I trust Thy grace:
   Arise, O Lord, and shine!

O keep me when my footsteps swerve!
   Incline me to Thy will!
Lord, whose I am, and whom I serve,
   Bless, guide, defend me still!

PSALM 143 (Second Version)

Lord, hear my prayer, in mercy hear,
   That mercy is my trust.
Who at Thy bar could dare appear,
   If Thou wert sternly just?

But Christ has borne His people's sin,
   And won them from the grave;
And from all foes around, within,
   I fly to Him to save.

My sinking soul revives to trace,
   Thy love in other days;
I fall before Thy throne of grace,
   And prayer turns there to praise.

349

O let that love still round me shine!
 Recall me when I roam!
Strike down my enemies and Thine,
 And lead me safely home.

PSALM 144

Blessed be the mighty Lord!
 Well He arms us for the fight.
With Him for our Shield and Sword,
 Soon we put our foes to flight.
Nature's powers may faint or fail;
God is strong, if they are frail.

Bow the heavens. Almighty God!
 Touch the mountains, they shall smoke!
Launch Thy lightning shafts abroad!
 Break the proud oppressor's yoke!
Dark the flood around us rolls;
Save, O save our sinking souls!

God is gracious; God is strong,
 He has helped His trembling dust.
Be His grace our daily song;
 Be His strength our daily trust.
Hell may rise with all its powers;
We are safe while God is ours.

We are safe; yea, every good
   Man can wish, or heaven can lend,
Light and comfort, health and food,
   All are ours with God our Friend.
Happy who His mercies share!
Happy in a Saviour's care!

PSALM 145 (First Version)

Thee will I praise, my God, my King,
  To Thee my dally homage bring.
Begin it now, and bid it prove,
As endless as eternal love.

Great is the Lord; His praise be great:
Let age to age His works repeat;
Let clime to clime His glories show:
Nor half repay the debt they owe.

O full of goodness, full of grace!
O Father of our fallen race!
Thy meanest works Thy praise proclaim.
Shall not we love and praise the same?

Yes: let my powers, however weak,
Of Thee, of Thee delight to speak:
Till all around Thy mercies see,
And sing and share them. Lord, with me!

Thy hand our daily wants supplies;
Thine ear attends to all our cries:
Thy grace our sinking souls upstays —
O shall our lips neglect Thy praise?

PSALM 145 (Second Version)

The Lord is great; and greatly ought
    His name to be adored;
He rises high o'er mortal thought,
    The dread, eternal Lord.

The Lord is good; His acts of grace,
    Beyond our wishes rise;
His anger moves with slowest pace,
    His willing mercy flies.

How holy is the Lord, how just!
    How righteous all His ways!
How nigh to him whose humble trust.
    For heavenly succour prays!

His steadfast throne, from changes free,
    Shall stand for ever fast;
And they that serve Him here shall see,
    His glorious face at last.

PSALM 146

Praise the Lord; my soul shall praise Him,
    While I life and being own.
Praise the Lord; I hope to raise Him,
    Better anthems round His throne.

Who would haughty flesh confide in,
    Soon returning dust to dust?
Happy who their God abide in,
    Happy who in Jesus trust.

Great His might. His mercy greater;
    All in heaven, and earth, and air.
Own Him for their high Creator,
    Wait upon His daily care.

Thou who suffering souls relieves,
    Thou who sett'st the captive free,
Wants suppliest, guilt reprievest,
    Reign for ever, Lord, in me!

PSALM 147

O praise the Lord, 'tis sweet to raise,
The grateful heart to God in praise;
When fallen raised, when lost restored,
O it is sweet to praise the Lord!

Great is His power. Divine His skill,
His love Diviner, greater still;
The sinner's Friend, the mourner's Stay,
He sends no suppliant sad away.

The lions roar to Him for bread,
The ravens by His hand are fed;
And shall His chosen flock despair:
Shall they mistrust their Shepherd's care?

His Church is precious in His sight;
He makes her glory His delight.
His treasures on her head are poured;
O Zion's children, praise the Lord!

PSALM 148 (First Version)

Praise the Lord, ye hosts on high:
Praise Him, angels through the sky.
Sun and moon, and stars of light,
Praise your Maker day and night.

He commanded, and you all,
Rose obedient to His call;
He commandeth, and you still,
Move submissive to His will.

Praise the Lord, thou earth below;
Praise Him, lightnings, hail and snow,
Ocean, wide His glory roll;
Waft it, winds, from pole to pole.

Seasons, tell it as ye fly,
Forests deep, and mountains high!
Birds and creatures, great and small,
Praise the Lord, the Lord of all!

Let mankind their tributes bring;
Monarchs, own a higher King.
Young and old, His mercies tell;
Men and maids, the chorus swell.

Praise Him, saints, above the rest;
Praise Him, for ye know Him best.
All His love and grace record;
Praise our Saviour, praise the Lord.

PSALM 148 (Second Version)

Ye realms of light and love.
   Exalt your Maker's name;
Ye hosts that round Him move,
   His power and skill proclaim.
      Your voices raise.
       Ye cherubim.
       And seraphim,
      To sing His praise.

Thou moon, that rul'st the night,
   Thou sun, that guid'st the day,
Ye countless orbs of light,
   To Him your homage pay.
      His praise declare.
       Ye worlds above.
       And clouds that move.
      In liquid air.

Let all adore the Lord,
   And praise His holy name,
At whose almighty word,
   They all from nothing came;
      And all shall last,
       From changes free,
       His strong decree,
      Stands ever fast.

Let earth her tribute pay;
   Sing, creatures great and small,
In air and land and sea,
   And man above them all.
      From every shore.
       Let old and young,

With heart and tongue.
Their God adore.

And ye. His chosen race,
Ye more than all beside,
Who know and share His grace,
O spread it far and wide.
His love proclaim,
Till all around.
Shall catch the sound.
And seek the same.

PSALM 149

O praise ye the Lord,
With heart and with voice;
His mercies record,
And round Him rejoice.
Ye children of Zion,
Your Saviour adore!
And learn to rely on,
His grace evermore.

Repose on His arm,
Ye sheep of His fold.
What terror can harm,
With Him to uphold?
His saints are His treasure;
Their peace will He seek;
And pour without measure,
His gifts on the meek.

Go on in His might,
　　Ye men of the Lord:
His Word be your light,
　　His promise your sword.
The King of Salvation
　　Your foes will subdue;
And their degradation,
　　Bring glory to you.

PSALM 150 (First Version)

Praise the Lord, His glories show.
Saints within His courts below,
Angels around His throne above;
Praise Him, all that share His love.
Earth, to heaven exalt the strain,
Send it, heaven, to earth again;
Age to age, and shore to shore,
Praise Him, praise Him, evermore!

Praise the Lord; His goodness trace!
All the wonders of His grace;
All that He hath borne and done,
All He sends us through His Son.
Strings and voices, hands and hearts,
In the concert bear your parts.
All that breathe, your Lord adore,
Praise Him, praise Him, evermore!

PSALM 150 (Second Version)

O praise the Lord in that blest place,
From whence His goodness largely flows;
Praise Him in heaven, where He His face,
Unveiled in perfect glory shows.

Praise Him for all the mighty acts,
Which He in our behalf hath done.
His kindness this return exacts,
With which our praise should equal run.

Let all that vital breath enjoy,
The breath He doth to them afford;
In just returns of praise employ;
Let every creature praise the Lord.

Praise God from whom all blessings flow;
Praise Him, all creatures here below;
Praise Him above, ye heavenly host;
Praise Father, Son, and Holy Ghost!

TALES IN VERSE
ON
THE LORD'S PRAYER

TALE FIRST

'Our Father, which art in Heaven, hallowed be Thy Name.'

HARFORD

'Twas Sabbath morning; and the pleasant sun
From a blue sky looked smiling out upon
The day of God, — inviting man to come
And walk the fields and muse, where even the dumb
Were eloquent in praise, and dewy eyes
Looked up their beauteous worship to the skies
From every bank and hedgerow, and the trees
Gave song or incense to each passing breeze
To waft on to high heaven; for buxom June
Now pranked the fields, and set the woods in tune;
And Nature, priestess-like, in full attire
Stood forth, and called on man to lead her choir.

I envy not his feelings who is dead
To such an invitation; who can tread
With unimpassioned step, at such an hour,
On such a day, the dewy herb and flower
All redolent of God — can look on earth
Young, green, and smiling as it came at birth
Fresh from His hand, nor feel as then was felt,
When every eye and tongue and spirit dwelt
On Him, when morning stars sang joy and love,
And all the sons of God shouted above
A new-born world, where the Creator viewed
His six days' works, and lo they all were good!
I envy not the man who thus can share
Mom's pleasant sun, wild music, and free air,

361

Nor note the present Deity, who stands
There in His temple not built up with hands,
Whose footprints and whose handlings may be traced
On every side now fresh and uneffaced,
And who from all around receives the praise,
Which man, most favoured, most neglects to raise.

'Twas Sabbath morning; but not thus the sun
Reached amidst London's vapours dense and dun[6]
The hero of my tale, and struggling through
The garret's skylight pane of yellow hue,
Shot on his bed a slanting sickly ray,
That just gave notice of returning day,
And roused him up, and called him forth to pass
That morn with Nature on the open grass.
I will not say indeed the Sabbath brought
To him these high emotions; that he thought
Of mingling offerings now with bird or flower;
That on such day, at such unwonted hour
He left his comfortable couch, and strode
So resolute along the City Road,
And sought escape from pavements, rails and bricks,
Before Bow bells rang out the hour of six.

He passed each nuisance of town's Sabbath morn:
The coach's rattling wheel and stunning horn;
The loitering groups collecting in the street,
With oath and jeer that blessed day to greet;
The drunkard reeling from the licensed sink,
Where his week's hire is spent in one night's drink;
The tawdry harlot shrinking from the light;
And other prowlers of the lawless night,
Still found where man his Maker would dethrone,

---

[6] One who persistently demands payment of a debt

And shut out God's creation with his own.
Disgusting all: and yet he passed them by
With small offence to either ear or eye;
For daily use had dulled the finer sense,
That gives such sights and sounds due influence.
Sam Harford had behind a counter lived
For thirty years; was wealthy, fat, and wived.
Early and late still constant at his stand
With ready smile and bow, and yard in hand,
A magic wand, whose touch had influence
To turn whole bales to shillings, pounds, and pence.
None more adroit to wield the shears or quill,
To measure, pack, or item up a bill,
Or deal neat phrases to each customer —
As, 'Pray sit down, ma'am,' 'Pleasant morning, sir.'
His travel through the day was seldom more
Than now and then from counter to the door,
To just look out, and rub his hands, and then
Back like a pendulum to his place again.

Sam Harford's thoughts were like his steps — they moved
One plain small circle, whence they rarely roved.
The world and the world's business occupied
His mind, and left small space for aught beside.
He knew he had a soul, but why or how
Had never brought one wrinkle o'er his brow;
He thought there was a God, and had heard tell
Of Christ, and future being. Heaven and Hell;
But these were matters distant all and dim;
He was, and that was quite enough for him.
He deemed the Bible a good book, and those
That had the time might read it if they chose;
Sunday was useful too, to check and state
The week's accounts, and keep his ledger straight.

363

But as for church, prayers, sermons, and the rest,
He thought the parson managed such things best;
He therefore left them wholly to his care,
And paid his tithes, and kept all matters square.

Still Harford's mind showed one redeeming trait—
This man of tills and ledgers, strange to say,
Loved Nature, loved the earth and skies. A ride
On Sunday coach, a row up with the tide
On the broad Thames were life to him. Each void
Of business was in one small spot employed,
Where a few smoke-dried flowers with sickly smile,
And doubtful fragrance overpaid his toil;
And on his busiest hours of care and din
Would rural hopes and visions oft break in.
And he would pause and think how sweet it were
To change the dingy town for the fine air
And green fields of the country, and retire
lo his own villa a substantial squire.
Perhaps in every human bosom lurks
A yearning toward Nature and her works,
Which neither cooping, smoking, use, or art,
Can stifle quite, or banish from the heart.
This leads the pale mechanic forth to pass
His listless Sabbath stretched along the grass;
This throngs the parks, and fills the one-horse chair,
That wheels the cit [7] through summer dust and glare
His sweltering Sunday ride; and this could lure
Even Harford forth upon this morning's tour,
To roam at will for one whole day, and share
His fill of rural musing and fresh air.

---

[7] City Dweller

Now pavements, footways, walls, and lamps are
passed,
And on the open turf he stands at last,
And breathes and gazes. 'Tis a lovely scene,
So fresh, so bright, so fragrant and so green!
The sun up in the sky; the crops all growing;
The cattle browsing round; the hawthorns blowing;
The meads in flower; the large leaves on the trees;
The bees all out and busy; and the breeze
Just stealing from the bean-field, where he lies
Bathing his wings in balm; the butterflies
Hovering about like winged flowers; the swallow
Skimming the lake that in the grassy hollow
Trembles in cowering loveliness. — The whole
Reached even Harford's unpoetic soul;
He thought it vastly pleasant, and again
Would fetch a Sunday ramble now and then.

But time went on: and even scenes like these,
When limbs are weary lose their power to please.
Harford, I've said, was fat; had trudged some miles;
And climbed o'er sundry hills and gates and stiles;
And now uprose before him steep and high,
Another hill his nerves and breath to try.
He sat down, wiped his brow, and called to mind
The desk and day-book he had left behind:
'The scene indeed was pretty, and all that,
But not to spend a day in looking at.'
And what had next occurred I cannot tell,
Had not the chiming of a distant bell
Broke on his servile musings apropos, [8]
And roused him up to cross the rise, and know
What was it and from whence. It was the sound

---

[8] Timely; At a good time

Which calls to Sunday prayers the parish round;
And as he climbed the hill, more clear and clear
The joyous music rose upon his ear,
Till in a group of elms below was spied
A tall white spire, and there from every side,
Up to the house of God, a chequered train,
They gathered in by every path and lane:
Young lads, and knots of talking girls, and pairs
Of decent parents with their little heirs
Scampering before to pull the kingcups; one,
The youngest, chubbiest, riding blithe upon
The father's arm. The labouring man bedight
In plain smock-frock of more than usual white,
Heaving along each slow and ponderous limb.
As if he carried them, and not they him.
Old goody here in silken cloak of black;
There farmer with his dame on Dobbin's back;
And then their maid, who runs, and rights the while
Her ribboned head, in haste to reach the aisle
Ere prayer begins. And, noted o'er the rest,
With book in hand, white tippet, and brown vest,
The little damsels of the Sunday-school,
Pacing in marshalled file beneath the rule
Of staid instructress. — On they swarm, and all
Enter the porch before him, great and small.
The bell is ceased; the busy crowd is gone;
And Harford stands reflective and alone.

The sun now lorded it aloft in heaven,
And from before his burning face had driven
The bird and brute, who slunk into the glade,
And, meek and silent, through the leafy shade
Eyed the strong monarch. Not a living sound
Or object crossed the solitude around;
Save when by chance a bee that way came humming,

Or the dry grasshopper at hand was strumming
His monotone; or from the house of prayer
The voice of worship floated up the air
Dim, but most sweet, like the faint memory
Of some fair vision. — Harford felt as he
Were a strange outcast there; for once he felt
A wish to bend the knee where others knelt,
And lift his voice with theirs. He onward prest
To enter in and worship with the rest;
And reached the porch just as the psalm was done,
And prayer alternate was again begun.

It might do good to any heart to share
The simple, solemn scene that met him there,
So peaceful, so devotional; where eye,
And lip, and heart, seemed all in harmony,
All turned to one high object — to their God;
As if they felt Him present, and were awed,
Yet not overwhelmed. Humility was there
To check bold zeal, and love to temper fear,
And all appeared in singleness of heart,
To come as to a Father, to impart
Their wants and woes, to tell Him all their cares,
Place in His hands themselves and their affairs,
Pour their thanksgivings forth for mercies past,
And humbly beg His blessing to the last.
It was a goodly presence; and the blood
Thrilled in the veins of Harford as he viewed
Their patriarchal worship. 'Sure,' he thought,
'God is in this place, and I knew it not!'
How suitable the forms of prayer and praise,
In all their antique simpleness of phrase,
For heart? indeed in tune! And how much more
They spoke than when he heard them jabbered o'er
'Mid whisper, cough, and yawn, and rustling gown,

367

And all the nuisances of church in town.
Religion here appeared in truth to be,
A spirit-soothing, sweet reality:
And as he gazed and listened, o'er his soul
Unwonted thoughts and feelings 'gan to roll;
And wants and wishes never felt till now
Yearned at his heart, and bathed his anxious brow.

But still went on the service. Prayers were ended;
And to the pulpit from the desk ascended
The man of God, the delegate of Heaven,
The shepherd of the fold, to whom was given
To break for them the bread of life, to guide
The wandering, soothe the wounded, wake and chide
The slothful and the wayward. On his tongue,
As if athirst to hear, the audience hung;
Till from his lips the text appropriate came —
'Our Heavenly Father, hallowed be Thy Name.'

His air was gravity with mildness blended,
His language strong, yet simple, and descended
As soft at first as snow upon the stream.
But as he followed up his lofty theme,
He kindled like a torch as he went on;
His manner grew more earnest; and his tone
And features seemed new meaning to acquire,
Till living thoughts leaped forth in words of fire;
And round him shone a glory and a grace,
Like that which Israel's prophet on his face,
Awful and bright, from Sinai once did bring,
And told with whom he had been communing.

He showed how God was Father of all men;
First by mere virtue of creation; then
By force of benefits transcended far

Beyond what any earthly parents are.
He showed with what solicitude and care
He watched and kept us, sinners as we were;
Bade earth give up her increase to our hand,
And seasons come and go at our demand;
Bade light and gladness round our senses play,
And health and plenty spring up in our way.
And then His pardoning, long-enduring love,
His angels sent to tend us from above,
His Jesus dying on the cross for sin,
His Heaven wide opened to receive us in;
As if the Father's bliss was incomplete,
Unless the child might have a part in it.
He turned him next to ask how much was owed,
From children such as we to such a God.
Should we not love Him, cherish Him, who thus
So loved, so cherished, pitied, pardoned us?
Was His the Spirit we should lightly grieve?
Was His the service we should loathe and leave?
Or should not rather all within us bum
To do some little, make some poor return,
For so much done? Ah! should not all our aim
Be still to hallow and exalt His Name?

'But set aside the claims of gratitude,
The gift of life, and every living good,
The love of self were plea enough to draw
And bind our hearts to Him and to His law.
His glory and our interests are tied
And linked in bonds which nothing can divide;
And on what head may blessedness descend,
If not on his who calls the Almighty friend?
His yoke indeed is easy, and more light
Than on the bird the wing that speeds his flight,
Bearing its bearer; and His laws are those

Which Wisdom of her own accord had chose
For her own good, and these His love employs
To speed and fit us for eternal joys,
Making a duty of our interest;
Leading us thus through blessings to be blest,
And then in sorrow, sickness, pain, and strife,
And all the chances of heartbreaking life,
How sweet it is to peacefully look up,
And know a Father fills the bitter cup!
To feel 'tis mercy lifts the chastening rod,
To drive us from all other rest — to God!

'When fortune frowns, friends fail, and hopes are
riven,
Where should he fly who knows not Him nor
Heaven?
Where should he turn when earth grows dark around,
To whom all other is forbidden ground?
Where should he turn? From God he cannot turn.
Fly from His smile, we meet Him dark and stern,
Refuse Him for a Father, He will come
A King, a Judge, to strike the apostate dumb.
Seek we the screen of night? Those thousand eyes
Are His that watch us from the silent skies.
Plunge in the grave? The grave must open her womb,
And judgment follow, and eternal doom.
Where then to fly? There is no refuge where
The godless may betake him but despair!
Ah, rather seek Him, seek Him! He is good,
Apt to forgive, and willing to be sued;
More mild, more merciful, more wise and great,
Than heart can wish, or fancy can create:
He gave His Son to wash our guilt away;
And loves to pardon more than we to pray;
The future He can mend, the past atone;

Believe, repent, reform, and be His own.

'If any here has yet to lift his eye,
And feel he hath a Father in the sky,
Has trodden still that dark and downward way
Whose course is madness, and whose end dismay,
Here let him pause. The God whom he has. held
So long in lightness will not be repelled;
He will not give him up: He will not lose
His child. His creature; but even now pursues
His wanderings, haply to perdition's brink.
And calls him while he may to stop and think;
To fly to Him from that devouring gulf,
Who loves him better than he loves himself;
Turn from despair to His protecting breast,
Hallow Him, serve Him, bless Him, and be blest.

'And should some yearning spirit here exclaim,
How should I hallow as I ought His Name? —
Are there not laws of His to keep and do?
Rise not His temples in our land to woo
Our footsteps in? Can nothing for His sake
Be found to yield, resist, or undertake?
Loves He not prayer? Delights He not in praise?
Commands He not to train up in His ways
The infant mind? And do not thousands groan,
Children of His, and brothers of our own,
Whom we may aid? Or if our lot denies
Of outward goods a worthy sacrifice,
We all have hearts to proffer — give Him them: —
The simple offering He will not contemn.'

'Tis done. The blessing given, the service closed;
The rustics to their homes in peace disposed;
And Harford to the city moves again,

371

A wiser and a better man than when
He walked that way at morn. His full heart swelled
Within him now; and from its fountain welled
The unwonted tear: and though words came not,
these
Breathed purer eloquence to Him who sees
The spirit's fine vibrations. He discerned
Melting contrition there, and shame that spumed
Its own misdoings; awe and humble love
That longed, yet feared, to lift an eye above,
And say, 'My Father!' — God beheld the whole,
And sent His Spirit to assure his soul; —
Then praise burst forth, and struggling tears found
vent
And hi heart burned within him as he went.

Duly is Harford now each Sabbath day,
With wife and children, seen in neat array
Amidst his neighbours at the house of prayer,
And none more fervent or attentive there.
From worldly interests his eye is turned,
To those by Wisdom prized, by faith discerned;
He feels that wealth is best employed when spent
In His high service who the boon hath lent:
And if his earthly gains are 'minished.
He has a heavenly treasure in their stead;
And lives to bless the day when forth he trod,
To ramble in the fields, — and met with God.

TALE SECOND

'Thy kingdom come.'

THE MISSIONARY

Rise, King of Glory, rise, resume Thy throne,
And make the empires of the earth Thy own:
Awake, appear, to strike the scoffer dumb,
Assert Thy sway and bid Thy kingdom come.
How far shall guilt and violence advance?
How long deface Thy fair inheritance?
How long shall man Thy dignities invade,
And push Thee from the world which Thou hast
made?
O glorify Thyself! Our toils are vain,
And only mock the cause they would sustain.
But let that voice which through primeval night,
Said from on high, 'Be light' and there was light,
Let that almighty voice again be heard,
To call the nations to their rightful Lord,
And prayer and praise on every wind shall rise,
And Thou be served on earth as in the skies!'

Such were the vows that on the lonely side
Of Mississippi rose at eventide,
And mingled with the jackal's plaintive whine
And with the plash of rushing crocodile,
With the flamingo's scream, and with the breeze
Whose wild wing strayed thro' the magnolia-trees,
And with the river walking on his way

373

Through nations. There before a hut of clay
Knelt an old man, and lifted up his prayer
To the Great Spirit, in whose service there
He long had laboured, zealous to proclaim
To Indian wastes his Master's saving name,
Assert the honours of the dread 'I am,'
And meeken down the wolf into the lamb.

Nor were his toils in vain. Behold yon green
Savannah, reaching down the woods between
To the broad flood, and 'mid the wilderness,
Smiling as sweet as Hope amid distress.
There neat enclosures rise, and cattle graze,
And vineyards bloom, and spots of rice and maize
Dapple the slope, and from a hundred huts
The smoke in wreathy column upward juts;
And where the buskined hunter roved erewhile
Now harvests wave, and hanging gardens smile;
And where the wolf was howling in his den
Ascends the social hum of busy men,
And Christian worship swells to God around,
In language newly hallowed with the sound.

O'er that old man were forty summers flown,
Since from far lands to this wild spot alone
He came, and built his hut, and lodged his store
Among the prowlers of this lonely shore.
Those white locks then were jet, and that meek eye,
Which twinkles yet with immortality,
Looked living fire; and round his form and face
Glowed high romance, and dignity, and grace.

No common man, and with no common aim,
To his bold task the missionary came:
And left whatever else was bright or dear,
To walk with God, and spread His Gospel here.
And lurked there no regret in that bright eye?
Stole from his bosom no half-stifled sigh?
So young, so warm, so feeling as he was,
Thus quitting all, and taking up his cross,
'Mid savage lands and men to live and die,
No friend but God, no home but in the sky?
No! He had known the world, had proved the worth
Of all that wears the stamp and hue of earth;
Had played deep with Experience, and had quaffed
From her stern cup a large and bitter draught:
And finding all was frail and false around,
He turned betimes to build on stabler ground:
Steered his poor skiff from life's tempestuous sea,
And sought a haven in Eternity.

In sooth he ill was fitted for the strife,
The storms, the buffetings, the stabs of life,
His ardent spirit was not formed to bear;
And his had been a stepson's portion there.
In early youth of both his parents reft,
To all the snares of rank and affluence left,
The boy grew up into a world of sin,
With scarce a friend to guide his way therein.
His glowing mind to wild luxuriance ran;
His years passed on without an aim or plan:
Till into life he stepped at last, as wild,
As simple, and confiding as a child.

Yet deem him not, untutored as he was,
A thing of sense, a lump of clay and dross.
His heart was warm and open as the spring,
A rich-toned lyre that thrilled through every string,
Alive to bliss, and prone to melt and move,
At each appeal of friendship and of love.
He banqueted on music; and his taste
Was quick to all of beautiful and chaste.
He looked on Nature with a painter's eye,
And caught the soul of speaking poesy.
And though possessed of no outstanding trait
Which burthened memory cannot put away,
No character energic, bold, defined,
That haunts, and fills, and triumphs o'er the mind;
Yet see him, hear him, and anon there stole
A spell around that riveted the soul;
And a mysterious interest gradual grew,
Till all about him strange observance drew,
And round his influence breathed, and spread a tone
O'er other minds congenial with his own.

Such, and so circumstanced, it was his lot
To dwell with those who knew and prized him not.
His sphere was narrow. Fate had set him down
On the dull confines of a country town,
Where he was made the idol and the dupe
Of creatures to whose arts he scorned to stoop.
Thence friends thronged round him, and professions
loud,
And greeting smiles attended him. The cloud

Fled from all brows before him; and he moved
In every circle courted and beloved.
The ladies thought him sweetly sentimental:
Their mothers canvassed o'er his handsome rental.
And though all thought him odd — nay, some said
mad —
None could esteem his face or person bad,
And then how fine a property he had!
Sure a good spouse and jointure must await
The maid that might secure her such a mate.

Thus many a sigh was breathed, and not in vain.
There was one blue-eyed girl among the train,
Retiring, gentle, graceful, fair and tall,
Who bore the prize away from midst them all.
Little she said; but, oh, that eye! — that eye! —
What did it not in its blue archery?
He shrunk before it; — yet returned to ask
Permission in its milder light to bask;
Was heard, — received, — and nothing now there
needs
But fix the day, and draw the marriage deeds.

I say not how the hours from hence were spent;
I pass each sigh, and look, and blandishment,
The air-built castle, the sequestered walk,
With trembling arm-in-arm, and all the talk
'Bout poetry, and trees, and flowers, and skies,
And young Love's thousand hopes and phantasies; —
Nor can I tell how they had matched for life,
What husband he had made, and she what wife:

For when all else was settled, and there now
Remained but just the priest, and ring, and vow
News came, that one, on whom, as on his soul,
He rested, and resigned to him the whole
Of his affairs, was fled, and with him bore
The bulk of all his patron owned before.

Pursuit was made, — in vain, — and clear away
The perjured villain carried off his prey;
And home his dupe returned, less keenly feeling
His loss of substance than the traitorous dealing
Of one so loved. He felt that he had leant
Upon a faithless reed, that broke, and went
Into his heart. A sweet dream was dispelled;
A thousand beauteous fancies all were quelled:
The world lost half her lustre; her fair dress
Was rent, and through appeared her nakedness.
The tendrils of his heart, that wont to stretch
And twine round every object they could catch,
Were nipped, his sympathies were chilled, and fled
The curdling life-blood to its fountain-head.

But there was more to suffer. Ah! the crew
Were mean and base with whom he had to do!
Much had been proffered, and it was not much
To look for some concern, some kindly touch
Of sympathy to mitigate his shock:
But all fell off, like waves from round a rock.
They that were yesterday all cringe and bow
Stared in his face or swaggered past him now.
At once their smiles and welcomes and respect

Grew cold civility, or proud neglect.
He seemed a dead weight on their hands: his pelf [9]
Was gone, and he a cipher in himself.
But there was yet one breast where he might hide
His outcast head, though all were false beside;
One faithful friend, one gentle comforter,
That would not shrink from him; and O, it were
An Eden still to gather up the wrecks
Of his past wealth, and fly from all the checks
And wrongs of a bad world, and be with her
Beyond the reach of knave or flatterer,
Nestling in some sweet cottage far removed
From man's intrusion, loving and beloved!
On with such thoughts his pathway he pursued
Up to the well-known door, his darker mood
Clearing and brightening as he went. At last
He reached the threshold, and would thence have
passed
On to her presence as he wont; but there
A servant stops him ere he mounts the stair,
And begs, with many a scrape and bow, to say,
That his young mistress can't be seen to-day.

A letter followed cold and brief, expressing
Her thanks for past attentions, and professing
A high esteem; but she regretted much
That circumstances were no longer such
As would admit their union; and in fine,
She begged all future visits to decline.

---

[9] Wealth or riches, especially when dishonestly acquired.

It was enough. He now had known the worst:
He wept not though his heart was nigh to burst:
He raved not, cursed not, though to both inclined;
But calmly turned his back upon mankind.
He made the woods his mate, and to the breeze
Poured out his spirit's baleful reveries.
He walked the mountain-tops; and loved to lie
And follow the light clouds along the sky,
And shape and name them in his moods: he pried
Into the cups of flowers; and o'er the side
Of streams would lean and watch the fish at play:
Or at the close of evening roam away
Among the dews, and linger till the sky
Grew beautiful with stars, and sounds from high
Came to him through the stillness of the night,
And his soul mingled with the Infinite,
And rose from earth; and here it was that first
Upon his intellectual darkness burst
The majesty of God: amid the woods,
The solemn rocks, blue skies, and sounding floods
He grew familiar with Him, learnt to trace
His power. His love. His wisdom, and His grace,
From suns and planets down to the poor blade
That trembled at his foot. His spirit made
A friend of God; and with the flowers and birds,
Breathed up a worship which no earthly words
Could adequately utter; till with Him
Conversing, this poor earth grew dark and dim;
And the large spirit bursting every bond,
Rose on immortal wing and soared beyond

The bounds of time and space, and joyed to roam.
And drink the glories of its native home;
And heavenly longings swelled within his breast.
And his heart thirsted for eternal rest.

'A few more suns and moons,' he thought, 'and then
A long farewell to earth and earthly men;
A full release from guilt, and guile, and woe,
And all the spirit weeps or fears below.
O, it is joy to think the day shall be
When all chains will drop off, and we be free;
When every cloud shall pass from off our sky,
And every tear be wiped from every eye!
Roll on, ye seasons, bring that blessed time
Unstained with grief, unspotted with a crime!
O, wheel this ruin of a world away,
And usher in that long bright Sabbath-day!'

There are fond hearts that cannot do without
Some object upon which they may pour out
Their overflowing love, and his was one;
And now that earthly objects all were gone,
He turned for such to Heaven; and there he gazed
Till every feeling was refined and raised
From earth, and he appeared to stand the last
Lone being of some generation past,
Longing and reaching to a better place,
With little wish to linger on his race;
For he had other aims and views than they
Through whose strange land his transient journey lay.
His eye was fixed on God; and there had dwelt

So long and earnestly, he almost felt
Identified with Him. God was his bliss;
God's glory was his glory; God's cause his;
He had no being but in God; no rest
Nor happiness apart from Him. He blest
The very flower that breathed its balm on high,
And would not trample on it. In his eye
The poorest leaf grew precious, for it bore
The impress of Almighty Hands: nay, more,
The very scorn and hatred he had felt
To faithless men before began to melt

Down into love and pity; for they were
Children of God's and objects of His care,
Although they knew Him not, they loved Him not -
There was a desolation in that thought —
He could not brook to think there should be one
Who knew not Him his soul so hung upon:
And when he turned his eyes the world around,
And thought how many were to whom the sound
Of their Creator's name was all unknown,
His heart bled in him, and he longed to own
An angel's voice. He saw from every shore
Ten thousand hands outstretching to implore
His guidance, pleading for the sacred bread
On which his own more favoured spirit fed;
And God's sweet promise fired him, 'blessed they
Who feed My sheep, and gather those that stray.'

Then came the voice of prophecy, and told
Of whiter days, when all should be one fold,

Under one Shepherd; when the brows that bled
Beneath the plaited thorns should wear instead
The crown of glory, and descend to reign
O'er earth subjected to her God again.
Then Eden's hours once more on golden wing
Should visit man, creation laugh and sing,
The billows clap their hands, and to the skies
On every wind glad hallelujahs rise,
Sorrow and sin, and violence, and fraud
Disperse before one kindling look from God,
And the redeemed around their Saviour prove
On earth a foretaste of the joys above.

Musing on themes like these, his soul took fire,
And sprung up in him an intense desire
To bear the Cross to foreign lands, and dare
A missionary's toils and dangers there.
A momentary pause, a passing swell
Of heart; a line to her he loved so well:
Then rose his sail before the vagrant wind,
And calm he left his native land behind.

'Beloved and lovely' (thus his letter ran),
'Hear the last words of a devoted man.
I write not to implore, reproach, or grieve:
I simply send to say that I forgive:
Blest if that word from any pang may free
A heart I would not have distressed through me,
A heart round which I wish more joys to twine
Than thy repulse once seemed to snatch from mine.
But this is over now. My soul, though late,

Has found a nobler aim, a higher mate;
God is the object of my love; and I
Go forth to distant lands to lift on high
His glorious ensign. We no more shall meet,
Till thou shalt see me to their Judge's feet
Leading my little flock. O may this be
A joyful meeting to both thee and me!
May we be joined in better bonds than e'er
Our fondest thoughts anticipated here!
Farewell! my prayer shall rise when far away
For thy dear sake to Him I there obey;
And, ah! do thou at times a thought bestow
On him who scarce knows how to let thee go,
So loved, so lost; — I feel I must not dwell
On themes like these; once more farewell, farewell!'

The bounding deep is passed, and lo, he stands
A stranger now on transatlantic lands,
'Mid giant lakes, and streams, and woods, and plains,
Where Nature in eternal grandeur reigns;
And as he passes through them to his charge,
He feels his spirit mount, his thoughts enlarge;
And 'here indeed,' he cries, ' are works of Thine
Worthy Thyself, my God! These depths of pine
Are pathless but to Thee; to Thee these floods
Lift up their voices. In their various moods
Of terrible or tranquil they portray
Thy image, show Thy majesty, and say,
'Behold Omnipotence! And thou, bright eye
Of heaven, thou sun, that walkest there on high
A king indeed, methinks one look at thee

Were all enough to set the spirit free.
And chase the mists of error, and declare
The God whose minister thou standest there!'

So spake fond Hope, so thought romantic youth,
But sage Experience told a sterner truth;
And many a toilsome day and sleepless night
Checked his enthusiast zeal, and set it right.
He learnt a simpler, soberer way to try,
And point by plainer precepts to the sky.
He settled 'mid a fierce uncultured train,
Wild as the wind and lawless as the main;
And sought in vain for many a darkling year,
To charm the deaf dull adder in their ear:
To raise to human what before was brute,
And lead the wanderers to their Saviour's foot.
He found them dark, the slaves of sin and sense,
Preoccupied with thoughts and aims intense,
Snatching from danger's lap their daily bread,
And hourly shaking hands with pain and dread,
Strong in delusion, proud, self-satisfied,
Married to earth, and spurning all beside.
Yet patience, perseverance, faith and prayer,
Found in the end their promised blessing there;
And precept upon precept, line on line,
Awoke at length a sense of things Divine:
Gave conscience a new sanction, and o'erawed
The rising passions with a present God.
Upon the night of many a heathen mind,
The Sun of Righteousness arose and shined,

And ushered in that morn serene and bright,
Whose noon goes on into eternal light.
Rapine and force their wonted seats forsook,
The spear was changed into the pruning-hook,
The heart of stone grew flesh, and 'mid the wild
The arts and charities sprung up and smiled.
Old Mississippi saw with proud surprise,
The cot and vineyard on his side arise:
And smoothed his wave, and lingered in his race,
Young Culture's footsteps on his banks to trace,
To kiss the all unwonted flowers, and hear
The voice of Christian worship swelling near;
Then sullen flung him onward to the main,
To meet no more such sights and sounds again.

And, ah! what felt our missionary there?
How looked he on the children of his care?
With what sensations did he watch and trace
The gradual progress of reclaiming grace?
And see the savage scene beneath his eye
Rise into life and form, and harmony?
'Twas bliss, but not for human tongue to show;
'Twas pride akin to that which angels know
Tending their charge to Heaven, all unallied
To earth, and shaming every joy beside.
Here in an Eden of his own he moved,
And led the worship of the God he loved;
Brought the blind sight, and language to the dumb,
And saw the kingdom of his Father come.
Here undisturbed he mused on things above,
And praised amid His works the God of love;

To Him his voice arose with morning's light,
And when above his lonely hut at night
The wind made solemn music in the trees,
God came down to him walking on the breeze,
And brought him awful joy. And thus afar
From earthly heed or hindrance, care or jar,
His life ran smoothly onward. God from high
Looked on his labours with approving eye,
The Spirit loved within his breast to dwell,
And angels often whispered 'All is well.'
With late and gentle call he was removed
Hence to the home he sought, the God he loved.
He closed his eyes to rest one happy night,

To open them wondering in eternal light.
Still may be seen on Mississippi's side
The little hut the good man occupied;
The old oak spreading o'er the grassy mound,
From which he taught his people standing round.
And still the pious traveller loves to stay,
And kneel down by his lowly grave to pray,
And hear his converts tell with honest pride
How holily he lived, how calmly died.

TALE THIRD

'Thy will be done.'

THE WIDOW

'Here, peep in through the window. I will pull
This knot of woodbine back that hangs too full
Across the leaded lattice. Do not fear,
Our presence will not interrupt her here.
She cannot note us: to her aged sight
Nature is blankness now, and day is night;
And all her thoughts are occupied. See, where
She kneels in yonder nook in quiet prayer.
And mark that lifted face, which beams as bright
As if an angel, hovering near, shook light
Down from his wings upon it. Looks it not
Most beautifully tranquil? Then her cot,
You note how orderly and neat 'tis kept,
The tiled floor crisp with sand, the hearth clean
swept.
The dresser with its well- washed range of delf, [10]
Her five good volumes set out on their shelf,
And then the four old chairs with backs so tall,
And all the Bible prints around the wall —
It is a pretty picture. Take one gaze;
Then turn we hence a moment while she prays;
And as we go and come, receive from me
The old blind widow's simple history!'

We crossed the little court, and entered in
Through a latched wicket in a privet screen,

---

[10] a contraction for Delft 'ware a kind of earthenware
originally made in Delft Holland.

388

The fence of a small garden, where there grew
Sweet marjoram, and thyme, and mint, and rue,
And star-eyed marigolds; and in one spot,
Of bashful flowers a solitary knot.
Here the black currants good for colds appear,
And there a few old plums and apples rear
Their mossy trunks. The rest is planted thick
With cabbage and potato, bean and leak,
In useful alternation. At the end
Where yonder group of long lithe osiers bend,
Out wells a little spring, and onward passes
Hiding itself among the flags and grasses,
From whence with playful foot it leaps anon,
And o'er the neighbouring fields runs laughing in the
sun.'
Hard by the well a little arbour stood,
Here we sat down, and thus my friend pursued.
'That poor old widowed thing we just have seen,
Of all the country-side was once the queen;
With temper, form, and manners that could move
Each maid to envy, and each youth to love.
Her father, a substantial churl, had piled
A goodly portion for his only child;
And 'twas his fondest wish on earth to see
His darling Jessy married suitably.

'Young Richard Gray was handsome, frank, and boon,
Pleasant as Nature in her own sweet June;
In all the neighbouring hamlets none could tell
A blither tale, or dance, or sing as well.
Happy the maid who might on holiday,
Walk on the green and chat with Richard Gray;
And merry 'twas in alehouse or in fair,
When rattling Richard laughed and revelled there.
Dressed out on Sunday in his best attire,

He looked and moved as brave as any squire.'

'So thought poor Jessy, in whose simple ear,
Richard had breathed what she had blushed to hear;
He met her oft in lane and field and grove,
And whispered there the music of his love.
Her sire indeed the growing friendship saw,
And sternly tried to check it and o'erawe.
"Marry a clown? my child? who might aspire
To win and wear a captain or a squire? —
Look on an idle, dangling, thriftless sot?
Break with him, girl, this moment; or if not
Take your own course! ay, do! and starve and rot."

'But there were words which soon sent these aside.
"Come, lovely Jessy, come and be my bride!
My little cot stands white upon the hill,
The roses clamber round its porch at will;
Before, my garden and its blossomed trees
All bright with flowers and musical with bees;
Behind, my little farm and sheep and kine; [11]
Come, lovely Jessy, come, they all are thine!
Fly from a frowning father, and with me,
Come live and love, secure and fond and free."

'She went, — they wedded, — and all things awhile,
Save an offended father, seemed to smile. —
Richard was kind, and for his Jessy's sake,
Gave up his jollities at fair and wake;
He laboured hard all day, and home at night
Returned to lay before her with delight
His earnings, and sit down in peace to share
The frugal meal prepared by Jessy's care.

---

[11] Archaic term for cows

And then in chatting, working, reading, fled
The evening swiftly till the hour of bed;
When down in peaceful sleep betimes they lay,
To wake up to their wonted toils with day.

'Thus all went well, and Jessy shortly came
To add a mother's to a spouse's name.
And a fair boy, bounding with health and grace,
Looked up his father in her happy face.
The crops were good, the cattle thrived, the rent
Was paid, and all was comfort and content. —

'Why must I paint this picture's dark reverse;
Why show how canker-like a father's curse
Clung to them? First a rainy season came,
And lodged their corn; and then their horse fell lame;
Their best cow died in calf, provisions too
Grew scarce and dear; and there was nought to do. —
And as his substance 'minished, with it fled
Poor Richard's ease; and gloom and care instead
Grew on him, soured his temper, checked his tongue,
And o'er his brow a cloudy blackness hung.
His house grew cheerless to him, and his farm
Presented nought but ruin and alarm;
While idleness, the sufferer's restless curse,
Hung on him too, and made all crosses worse:
Moody and dark he sauntered from his home,
In fretful discontent to sigh and roam.
His former haunts and habits by degrees
Won on him, promising a transient ease;
Till in the alehouse soon he daily sought
A desperate refuge from himself and thought!

'Jessy with dread beheld the change, and tried
By every art to charm this mood aside;

Made light of every ill, plied all her wiles,
Locked up her cares, and tasked her face to smiles.
She placed her little babe upon his knees,
Hung on his neck, looked up, and sought to seize
His wandering vacant eye — in vain, in vain; —
Instead of answering tenderness again,
Disgust in harsh impatience ill concealed,
Repulsed her efforts and her spirit chilled;
And forth anon she saw him blindly go,
To seek his cups and leave her to her woe.
Still she forbore, nor by one look expressed
The storm of feelings working in her breast
She spoke not, chided not; but conscious shame
Read in her kindest acts reproach and blame;
And brutal violence, the more inflamed
By sense by wrongs inflicted and unblamed,
Burst out on her in language loud and high —
Which, save in quiet tears, found no reply!

'Month after month rolled on, and brought no change,
Till neighbours shunned them, and old friends grew
strange;
Her father in his anger sternly smiled,
On the just meed [12] of a rebellious child,
And he, who should have been her stay, her friend,
Looked but to frown, or spoke to reprehend.
Where could she turn for comfort? Ah, it came
But cold and cheerless through a husband's blame;
And less she deemed it to abide the press
Of boding thoughts, and wrongs, and loneliness
Than words that wounded him. She therefore kept
Her feelings down, and plied her hands, and wept.

---

[12] A fitting reward

'One night her husband o'er his cups delayed,
And she, as oft accustomed now, afraid
And anxious for his safety, took the road,
To find and lead him to his lone abode.
She dared not seek the alehouse, and support
Its drunken inmates' coarse and ribald sport;
But still he must not walk alone where lay
The long canal beside his reeling way.
And here, her little Richard in her hand,
Beneath the silent moon she took her stand
Most desolate, and heard at times from far
Their loud wild laughter, and their brutal jar.
She looked upon her infant, and the whole
Of her lone state came rushing on her soul.
She thought of father, husband, wrong, and crime,
Herself, her helpless offspring, and the time
When she for common food might hear him cry,
Nor have wherewith to soothe his agony.
She saw the waters sleeping 'neath her there,
Breathing, and bright; the frenzy of despair
Came o'er her; here was shelter, here was rest
For her and hers; there now remained no breast
To feel her loss, nor would her baby stay,
Like the young bloom that opens on the spray
In March, ere yet a leaf is on the trees,
To screen the trembler from the bitter breeze.
Strong was the conflict of that trying hour,
And hard she struggled with the tempter's power;
But God at length controlled the desperate strife
And led her back again to peace and life.
Even as in frantic agony she stood,
Strange contrast, o'er that still and placid flood,
And strained her wondering infant to her breast,
And on his lips her last wild kiss impressed,
A light broke in on her, a sudden ray

393

Of hope and comfort (how she scarce could say),
That showed at once her madness and her sin,
And calmed and settled all the storm within.
She deemed herself it was the child she held
Who named the name of God, and with it quelled
Her agonies; who with a random word,
Remembered from the task he daily heard
From her own lips, his erring mother taught,
And bade her turn for comfort where she ought,
Sending her dark and wandering thoughts away
To Him, the widow's friend and orphan's stay.
She paused, she trembled, on her teacher looked
With awe and shame, owned God and stood rebuked
Saw the full, horror of her guilty aim,
And home returning in an altered frame,
In penitence and prayer a course began,
Which on to lasting peace and full submission ran.

'Within her home now Jessy sits no more
In lonely desolation as before.
A Friend is hers who leaves not nor forsakes,
A peace the friendless world nor gives nor takes;
God has looked in upon her mental night,
The clouds are passed away, and all is light.
She sees a plan unveiled to earthly eyes,
Finds all her ills but blessings in disguise,
Learns on her God to rest with faith and prayer,
And trust her cause to His paternal care;
Content in His appointed path to run,
And meekly say, "My Father's will be done."

'But sickness seized at length the man of drink,
And nailed him to his bed, and forced him think.
The long delusion from his spirit passed,
And his true state rushed full on him at last.

Robbed of excuse, and stripped of all disguise,
His guilty self rose up before his eyes;
And crimes and wrongs in fast succession came,
And fanned his inward fever into flame,
He spurned all solace, and refused all aid,
And night and day against himself inveighed:
He called upon his injured wife and child,
And bade them curse him, till his brain ran wild.
They brought him medicines, but he took them not;
The body's pangs were in the mind's forgot;
And every soothing word and act from them
Seemed but anew his baseness to condemn.

'In vain his faithful partner o'er him hung,
Love in her looks, and comfort on her tongue;
In vain his infant round him smiled and played,
His angry conscience would not be allayed;
"Curse me," he cried; "the worst that ye can do,
Is all too little for my wrongs on you." —
A friend of mine beheld him ere he died;
His consort's words and prayers had then supplied
A ray of peace, and taught the poor distrest
To seek his refuge in a Saviour's breast.
There never died a deeper penitent;
And charity may hope the prayers he sent
For mercy to his God were heard in Heaven:
But by himself he never was forgiven;
And his last bitter words and tears in life,
Deplored his conduct to his generous wife.
But it is time we seek her cot again,
And learn from her own lips what may remain.'

We rose, and to the cottage bent our way,
And found her there in the same neat array,
Seated and knitting in a window, where

395

The sun looked warmly on her, and the air
Flung in at times a perfume as it flew.
She heard the sound of our approach, and knew
The steps were friendly, and with pleasant smile
Rose to receive and greet us; in awhile
We freely talked together, and my friend
Induced her thus her simple tale to end.

'It was,' she said, 'a heavy thing to lose
A friend so dear, so needful, when his views
Were now corrected, and his heart reclaimed,
And his new efforts might have still redeemed
Our sinking cause from ruin. But 'twas not
For me to strive, where God had dealt the lot.
They seized our little stock for debt, and sent
A writ to drive us from our tenement;
And sad and helpless as I was (for then
The time was near when I must feel again
A mother's pangs and fears) I took the road,
And left with aching heart my loved abode;
And to the parish workhouse turned to share,
Their coarse hard lodging and unwilling fare,
And take the common pittance of the place,
Without one soothing word or friendly face,
And here 'mid want and sorrow, noise and strife,
My second infant struggled into life;
And a wild fever followed close, and cast
A shroud round thought and feeling; present, past,
And future, all were dark for many a day;
And when the strange delusion passed away,
Ah me! I heard my babe for nurture cry,
And found my withered breast could none supply.
It was a trying season, and my cup
Required but one drop more to fill it up;
And this too came: my angry father came

To curse me at my hour of grief and shame;
Yes, sir, my father came to curse me here; —
But ah! he could not do it. God was near
To check and change his purpose; and one look
At me and my affliction staggered, shook,
Subdued him; tears burst forth without control,
And all the father rushed into his soul.
He fell upon my neck, and sobbed "My child";
And my poor heart within me leaped and smiled.

'Thus in my anguish God forsook me not,
But in His own good time assistance brought.
My father took me to his home once more,
And life flowed swift and smoothly as of yore,
A quiet bypath of my own I trod,
And read my Bible and conversed with God:
And taught my little ones, and saw them rise
Two pleasant plants beneath my widowed eyes.
Peace crowned my nights, and pleasure winged my
days,
And half my prayers were gladdened into praise.

'But bliss like this is not for earthly breast;
And God was kinder than to let me rest,
In any object short of Him and Heaven;
And when at length a darker lot was given,
Though flesh and blood recoiled, the spirit stood
Strong in her sense that He was wise and good.
I knew myself an heir of sin and pride,
And felt it useful for me to be tried;
What He ordained 'twas not for me to shun,
Nor say my will, and not my God's, be done.
My father now was dead, and all he had
Devolved on us; and soon my elder lad,
Bright as the morn and active as the wind,

Took charge of all his grandsire left behind;
Worked, marketed, farmed, bargained, sold, and
bought,
And joy and increase to our dwelling brought.
'Twas balm indeed to a fond mother's heart,
To see her child so nobly play his part;
And blind with joy, and drunk with empty pride,
I saw no foes nor dangers at his side;
I feared no snares to one so young as he,
Even in such dealings, scenes, and company.
My frank, my generous, my manly son!
Why should I tell you how he was undone?
Why call the steps by which he fell to view,
And bid each wound within me bleed anew?
I saw my error, and his change too late,
But had no power to save him from his fate:
He rushed on blindly in his father's way,
And prayers and efforts were in vain to stay. —
The soldiers of a passing regiment
At last seduced him, and before he went
He came to ask my blessing. — Here I took
My last embrace, my last foreboding look
Of my poor boy; and gave with many a prayer
A little favourite Bible to his care,
And bade him keep and read it for my sake,
The last best gift a mother's love could make. —
Then, sir, I gave him up to God; and forth
He went, to bless my eyes no more on earth.

'Excuse these tears; they give my heart relief;
And God forbids not unrepining grief.
The very Saviour wept when He was here;
And nature claims the comfort of a tear.
I would not strive against my Father's will,
Nor reckon aught that comes from Him an ill;

But ah! I felt, I feel the chastening rod!
And it smote hard though in the hand of God.
Five years went by, nor heard I of his fate. —
At last, one night, a man came to my gate,
A war-worn veteran, but of aspect mild,
Who brought, he told me, tidings of my child.

'Sir, I must weep, my feelings must have vent. —
This man had marched, had slept in the same tent,
With my boy Richard. He had been his friend,
And shared his toils and dangers to the end.
He was a Christian and a man of prayer,
Who loved his God, and served Him everywhere.
My wanderer's follies he had seen with pain,
And warned him from them kindly, but in vain;
Yet joined he not the common laugh and jeer,
Nor mocked the precepts he refused to hear.
Thus things continued, till the corps were sent
On foreign service on the Continent;
And there 'mid exile, danger and distress,
A graver mood on Richard 'gan to press;
His eyes were opened to the path he trod,
And his heart yearned to find a friend in God.
He sought his pious comrade's company,
And read his Bible much, and spoke of me;
O sir! that Bible my own hands had given,
And sure my prayers brought down that grace from Heaven.
At length in deadly strife they met their foes,
And my poor boy was missing at the close;
And when they found him he was cold and dead,
And by his side his little Bible spread. —
The old man kept and brought the book to me,
And, O, my soul within me thrilled to see
My child's own life-blood still the pages stain,

A mournful pledge that we should meet again.

'Well, sir, I wept; but they were blessed drops,
And bright with high remembrances and hopes:
I looked too on the youth that still was left,
And felt with him I was not quite bereft.
For he was mild and docile, kind and good,
The light and comfort of my solitude.
He loved his home, and o'er a favourite book,
Would spend whole evenings in our chimney nook.
Our little garden 'neath his culture throve,
And the moss-rose and woodbine learned to rove
Upon our cottage wall; my joys and fears,
My prayers, my occupations, smiles and tears,
He shared with daily love, and sense beyond his
years.
But now it pleased my God again to lay
His hand on me, and take my sight away;
And anxious for the welfare of my son,
Whom my fond eyes no more could look upon,
I forced my heart to give him up, and bade
A kind relation teach my boy his trade.
He wept to leave me; but I hid my pain,
And talked of joy when we should meet again. —
And we did meet, — but not with joy; — a year
Was scarce elapsed ere tidings smote my ear
That George was sick, and that his native air
Was recommended for him. To my care
They sent him. O sir, what I felt to trace
His hollow voice, his wasted form and face!
How have I sat beside his bed, and stayed
His burning brow, and watched, and wept, and
prayed,
And talked of hope, when there was hope no more;
And whispered comfort, while my heart ran o'er

With desolation. But his spirit rose
Above this little world of crimes and woes,
And asked no earthly comfort. Many days
Before he died he dwelt within the rays
Of Heaven; he saw his Saviour face to face,
And stood with angels at the throne of grace;
And spoke such blessed words to all around,
Grief stood rebuked, and love in awe was drowned.
Bright as the closing of a summer's day,
Soft as a Sabbath hymn he passed away.
The soul, they said, departing to its place,
Left a still marble smile upon his face,
A sweet assurance of the bliss he gained,
A pledge of peace to those that yet remained.

'Here, sir, my story closes. I was left
A poor lone thing, of all, save God, bereft.
I now had nought to do but weep and pray,
And kiss the hand that gave and took away.
I know Him good and wise, and scarce would dare
To wish that things were other than they are.
All that I loved are gathered safe above,
Better and happier far than earthly love,
However warm, could wish them. There they live
In all the bliss the Father's self can give,
Or the Redeemer earn; and I shall there
Meet them again, bright, blooming as they were,
To praise the God we served together here,
And dry in glory's rays each earthly tear.
My eyes behold no more this world of sin,
But brighter worlds light up my eyes within.
And here in my lone cot I sit, and try
My soul to keep, my God to glorify,
Take what He gives with thankfulness of heart,
And feel His mercies more than my desert,

And calmly wait His own good time, to say,
"Come to thy rest, poor pilgrim, come away." '

⚘ ⚘ ⚘

TALE FOURTH

'Give us this day our daily bread.'

EDWARD FIELD

Upon a rise near Sydney Grange is seen
A small neat house with lawn of velvet green;
A shrubbery skirts and screens it from the wind,
And a snug garden woos the sun behind.
Here with his wife and rosy children twain,
A man and maid, and chattels few and plain,
Some years ago from distant town or shire,
Came Mister Field, or Edward Field, Esquire,
The neighbouring village gossips o'er their tea
Have not yet settled his precise degree.
Farmer he was not; stock nor land he kept,
A few small fields around his house except;
Nor yet like neighbouring squires he entertained,
Nor drank, nor swore, nor dogs nor hunters trained,
But still he was the parson's friend and guest,
And all the poor around his bounty could attest.

Well, Squire or Mister Field (just call him which
You please) inhabited this quiet niche;
Milked his three cows, and made his bread and beer,
On just four hundred annual pounds in clear.
Sleek were his kine. His yard was peopled thick

402

With turkey, guinea-fowl, and hen and chick,
All of choice kinds; and o'er his lawn there went
Six sheep, kept less for use than ornament.
O'er a neat paddock gate all free and tame,
Neighed his one horse in answer to his name.
I pass swine, ducks, and things of like degree,
He kept them out of sight, and so shall we.

His wife, good Mrs. Field, Heaven bless her face!
Was one might well adorn a higher place;
Accomplished, mannered, lady-like and fair.
Though not quite all that some fine ladies are.
She read few novels, seldom screamed or fainted,
Dangled no reticule, was flounced nor painted;
And thought her hands were made for something
more
Than nursing up in kid, or running o'er
Piano keys. She could both mend and make.
Wash and get up small linen, boil and bake;
And her made wines, her puddings, and preserves, —
What tongue can speak of them as each deserves?

Her dress was simple; but you might suppose
The Graces helped her to put on her clothes.
Her house, too, perfect neatness; yet not such
As makes one half afraid to step or touch;
And all things there appeared to go or stand,
Rather by secret clockwork than command;
Then in the healing art how vast her skill!
How deep her lore in herb and salve and pill!
Buchan and Reece right well she understood.
And even in Thomas dipped, and Underwood.
The ailing poor for miles around confessed
The sovereign virtues of her medicine chest;
And lean the village doctor grew, and bare,

Since Mrs. Field began to practice there.

Her husband had his avocations too:
He kept, I've said, a garden, where he grew
The earliest peas in all the country round,
And fruit for size and flavour far renowned.
Here were his bees in hives of curious form,
And there his green-house, to keep off the storm
From favourite flowers of every scent and hue,
Tended by him, and ranged in order due.
To bud and graft he was supremely skilled,
And aye a pruning-knife his pocket filled.

His other tasks were various. On his land
He commonly employed a labouring hand.
His poultry likewise 'twas his due delight
Himself to serve with barley morn and night.
He taught his boy and girl; and taught them so
That will and duty hand in hand might go.
For he had still for them a smile in store,
A playful word, or tale of pleasing lore:
A happy knack, that tired not while it taught,
And rarely failed to gain the end he sought.
A school then in the village he maintained,
Where boys to write, and girls to sew were trained;
And where on Sunday all the neighbouring young,
Hymns, catechisms, and collects said or sung.
The poor there claimed his frequent inquest too,
For truest suffering oft is least in view;
And not content to notice and redress,
The loud, bold plaint of petulant distress,
He loved affliction to its home to trace,
And by inspection learn its real case;
See who might dress or baby-clothes require,
Or Madame's Thursday soup, or wine, or fire.

He was not one whose charity found vent,
In very fine but empty sentiment;
None of the simpering, soft, poetic crew,
Who talk, and feel, and weep, but never do.
Where'er were wants to succour, woes to share,
There was his haunt, though none might see him
there.
He loved to seat him in the poor man's cot,
And hear the annals of his humble lot,
Joy round the widow's lonely heart to shed,
And weep and pray beside the sick straw bed.
And ' what sweet tears they were, pure, bright, as
flow
From angel's eyes o'er earthly sin and woe!'
'What luxury of sorrow ' (he would say),
'And how unskilled in true enjoyment they
Who ne'er the full uplifted eyes have viewed,
Nor drank the wild warm voice of gratitude;
Seen the poor children's smile their steps attend,
And the dog bark not at his master's friend,
And all the simple joys that God hath given,
To light the steps of charity to Heaven!'
Then, there were other lighter rambles, when
He and his boy went up the neighbouring glen,
Old Walton for their guide, and from the brook
Wiled the lithe trout, but not with baited hook.
Or all together in a one-horse chair,
They went at times to breathe the fresh sea air.
In summer, picking shells along the sand,
Or watching while the ocean o'er the strand
His lordly crest smoothed down, his thunders mute
Crept like a tame thing up to lick their foot.
Or when at eve along the fields they strayed,
Just when the cattle ventured from the shade;
When the tall grove upon the neighbouring rise,

Stood in relief before the western skies;
And pleasant murmurs on the ear would come,
Of lowing kine, and rooks returning home;
And every breeze brought in some varied sweet;
And grass more soft than sleep wooed on their feet:
Till dancing insects humming round their way,
And the wild thrush's lessening roundelay,
And stars faint twinkling through the twilight blue,
Warned them in home from darkness and the dew.

On other evenings, when rough weather brings
Us friends with fires, rugs, shutters, and such things;
And when the Vicar, or some neighbour friend
Dropped not in on them to take tea, and spend
An hour in chat; nor when the county news
Came once a week, nor monthly the reviews: —
The children then would either draw or write,
Or cut out forms in paper blue and white,
Or sing together at their mother's side;
Or while the female part their needles plied,
The others read aloud; perchance with Cook,
From isle to isle their way through ocean took;
Or else with Bruce or Park the desert thrid, [13]
Or learned what other ages felt and did:
And traced the lore of England, Greece, and Rome,
With safer guides than Gibbon or than Hume.
Thus bedtime stole upon them unawares;
And the night closed, as morning ope'd, with prayers.

Such was the dwelling, such the simple life
Of Edward Field, his children, and his wife.
Here from the world, its toils, and snares, he fled

---

[13] To pass through in the manner of a thread or a needle; to
make or find a course through; to thread

To serve his God, and eat his daily bread.
Retired, but active; useful, though forgot;
The world owed much to him that owned him not.
His aim was not men's notice, but their good,
To have his actions felt, enjoyed, not viewed.
And like the tree that bows its head the lower
The heavier it is hung with fruitful store,
He lived humility; — unlike to those
Who wear it in their manners, looks, and clothes,
Who tell their frailties, spread their sins abroad
To man who disbelieves them, not to God:
Then triumph in their hypocritic sham, —
'How humble must the world suppose I am!'
His heart was humble, for he knew its state:
He had no claims to guard and vindicate;
Made no pretensions, took offence at none,
And notice oft but for endurance won;
As in the grass the wild thyme we discover,
Smelling most fragrant when most trampled over.
The judgment of the vulgar, small, or great,
In praise or blame with him had little weight
He chose his path in life, and walked right on,
And yet, if possible, offended none.
Ambitious of no martyr's lot and name
From gibbets, racks, and fires of worldly fame:
Nor swift to take the lists, and hew and hack
In controversial parry and attack,
Where seldom aught is gained, though much is spent
Of temper, time, and breath, and argument.
His object Heaven, and God his Judge alone,
Busy, yet quiet, moved the Christian on.
Like home-bound vessel through life's voyage hied,
Leaving no track along the closing tide:
Took what of joy he might with safety there,
And for his perfect bliss looked on elsewhere.

Who now would think this simple plain good man
Had once been joined to fashion's lightest clan?
Had chased ambition's wildest meteor down.
And shared the idlest follies of the town?
Yet such had Edward Field. The earliest air
He breathed was in a smoky London square;
Where, in a dingy brick and mortar pile,
His high-born parents lived in handsome style,
Kept their state coach, with many a liveried knave,
And large sad parties once a fortnight gave;
Using a world of pother and address,
To make themselves and others comfortless.

To Eton, thence to Oxford, was he whirled,
To make acquaintance there, and see the world.
And then pro forma to the Continent
The graduate dunce was with his tutor sent,
To just learn how to dress, and cook, and stare,
And say of places, 'O yes! I've been there!'
Thence must he pass through fashion's usual paces,
Learn the right manners, jargon, and grimaces,
Acquire the one sublime indifference
To all that smacks of feeling, thought, or sense.
In friendless intimacy day by day,
With grinning things must languish life away:
Must go to bed at four and rise at two,
Then ride out in the Park as others do;
Or lounge at five in Bond Street, with a score
Of just such stiff, starched, stayed poor creatures
more.
To dinner then at eight, and thence away,
To formal route, the club-house, or the play,
For which till the fifth act he never starts,
And talks aloud through all the finest parts.

From thence in time his genius onward passed,
And left this wooden life behind at last.
But who, all inexpert, may think to trace
Each new gradation of his hopeless race?
Now in his tandem, now in ring or pit,
A gudgeon here, and there a blood and wit,
He did in fact what others like him do,
And found in all as much enjoyment too.
Meanwhile his parents their own path pursued,
And with complacency his progress viewed;
Saw their three hundred friends each fortnight still,
And took their share of scandal and quadrille;
Still smiled and simpered with the same dull set,
Kept up appearances, and ran in debt.
Yet while so smooth and fair in public eyes,
They doffed at home the cumbersome disguise;
And fretful words were heard, and frowns were seen,
And angry squabbles with short truce between.
At last one night at cards Miss Farley said
'You've heard the news, that Mrs. Field is dead.'
'Good Heavens! poor Mrs. Field!' another cried.
'Diamonds are trumps, — do tell us how she died.'

The hatchment now was hung up o'er the door,
The family their decent mourning wore;
The spouse went through the usual routine,
And for due time in public was not seen:
And to speak truth, in spite of every cross,
And every pet and humour, felt his loss.
He had no longer one to scold and flout,
To order dinner, and to nurse his gout.
The servants too had all things their own way,
And bills besieged him which he could not pay.
Beset with all these complicated ills,

409

Vexation, ennui [14], pilferers, duns, and bills,
He saw no better speedier antidote,
And so one morning coolly cut his throat.
His property was so secured, no dun
Could claim, he knew, a farthing from his son;
And on his table this advice was found,
'Pay them, my boy, a penny in the pound.'

Edward was shocked, astonished; and decreed
To make no profit of this fearful deed.
A generous spirit that too long had slept
Awoke within him, scorning to accept
At the red purchase of a parent's blood,
And tradesmen's ruin, such ill-gotten good,
And with a nobleness foreseen by few
He sold up all, and gave to each his due.
A monied man of fashion now no more,
A different path must Edward Field explore;
And though it was at first some pain to meet
His old friends tittering by him in the street'
And though his pride some passing shocks received,
His mind upon the whole felt lightened and relieved.
He took to letters, and began to mix
With graver men, and talk of politics,
With authors and new books became acquainted,
And Mister Murray's drawing-room frequented;
Wrote articles for magazine reviews,
And was in high request among the blues;
Kept common-place book, talked in learned strain.
And praised his rivals to be praised again.
Fired with his progress he new courage took,
And sat him down at last to write a book;
A pamphlet by Ignotus. O what paper,

---

[14] Boredom

What pens and ink were spent upon the labour!
What brows were knitted, and what nails were bitten,
Before this mighty work was planned and written!
And lo! in cover blue it now appears,
To set the wondering public by the ears,
To fill the world with envy and delight,
And make the critics bark that cannot bite.
What questions will be asked! what tart replies,
And brisk rejoinders from all sides will rise!
But weeks, now fortnights, now whole months go by,
And no critique, rejoinder, or reply;
The world alas! jogs on the very same,
And neither readers buy nor rivals blame!
At last a friend in some obscure review
Gave it a fillip; but it would not do.
Puffs and advertisements in vain are penned
Copies in vain sent round to foe and friend;
And the whole matter ere six months were shotten [15]
Was born, and dead, and buried, and forgotten.

So much for authorship. His next design
For wealth and fame was in another line.
Lord Littleworth, Prime Minister of State,
Had been his father's friend and intimate;
And many handsome offers once had made
If he would bring his son up to the trade.
He met poor Edward's application now
With many a flattering smile and courtly bow,
And bade him dance attendance with a bevy
Of would-be placemen at his Lordship's levee.
Long were to tell his harassments and trials,
Mid marble looks, smooth lies, and kind denials.
Long were to tell his various dirty jobs

---

[15] worthless or undesirable

In public and in private; and the throbs
Of wounded honour rankling in his breast,
And scorn and wrath that dared not be expressed,
And hopes and fears so tempered as to keep
The heart half drowned, half floating in the deep.
Suffice to say a year or two went by,
And still promotion failed, and still was nigh:
When an event occurred to calm his fever,
And burst his bonds, and set him free for ever.

It chanced that Edward, when at Oxford, had
Among his college friends a lively lad,
Who afterwards assumed the sacred gown,
And held a living threescore miles from town;
And when his friend he happened there to meet
He often asked him down to his retreat;
And Edward now was in a mood and station,
To take advantage of the invitation.
He found the Rector living on the skirt
Of a neat village, safe from noise and dirt,
With sister, wife, and rosy children seven,
Enjoying earth, and looking on to Heaven;
In a fair house with pleasant glebe embraced,
Where grace and comfort well were matched by taste.
There Duty walked; there decent Order dwelt:
There Quiet nestled, and Religion knelt.
There might the needy for assistance turn,
And there the erring ever look and learn.
Amid his books, his children, and the poor.
Loving and loved, the good man dwelt secure;
A sun within his little system shone,
Still bright, and brightening all he looked upon.
Mild on his face good nature seemed to sleep,
Forth at each caU in smiles to wake and leap:
And kindness, cheerfulness, and strong good sense

To higher graces added influence.

With him now Edward sat, and chatted o'er
Their various boyish feats and whims of yore;
Talked of the scenes and facts of other years,
And what was come of these and those compeers.
With him around the village Edward strolled
To see and minister to sick and old,
And learn their simple histories, and gain
Truths that are rarely heard in prouder fane.
Oft with the ladies too abroad he walked
Along the pleasant fields, and sweetly talked
Unheeding, till the evening round them fell,
And roosting blackbirds twitted through the dell:
Or else with music or with books at home
Taught bedtime all unconsciously to come.
And then the little farm and garden too
Were rife with occupation sweet as new;
The children also twined them round his heart,
As in their play and tasks he bore a part;
Nay, even the very family devotions,
So ill according with his former notions.
Grew grateful in the end; and when he knelt
On Sabbath in the decent church, he felt
An awe and interest all unknown before,
A new reality religion wore;
And as the man of God its truths proclaimed,
Rebuked, alarmed, exhorted, urged, and shamed.
His altering mood bore witness to the word,
And listening conscience echoed all she heard.

This simple, useful, unambitious life,
Unwarped by passion, undisturbed by strife,
To Edward's fluttering heart was new and strange;
Yet sense approved, and taste enjoyed, the change.

Weeks rolled away, and still the Rector pressed,
And Edward still remained his willing guest;
And as the time of parting nearer drew,
The more his heart revolted to renew
His former wretched course, and bid his friends
adieu.
'Here man,' he thought, 'his destiny fulfils,
And finds the goods of life with half its ills.
Here mind and heart have both their ample play
And chance grows stable 'neath religion's sway.
Ah, happy life! where simple joys abide,
And calm content makes up for all beside!
Where man exalted, hallowed, and refined.
Lives for his God, himself, and humankind!
How shall I leave thee? how return to trace
My former round of folly and disgrace,
And stand again a blot on fair creation's face?'
And then a conscious shame upon him grew
And his heart sickened at the bleak review,
And awful thoughts arose of God offended,
With strong compunctions and forebodings blended.
A sense of wasted years for ever flown,
And deeds of shame no more to be undone,
And all the fearful images that press
On the lone hours of trembling consciousness.
It was a time of trial, harsh, but good;
His heart was 'neath it humbled and subdued.
Remorse became repentance; and despair
Changed her dark groan at last for faith and prayer:
A sweet assurance o'er his spirit crept.
And at his Saviour's feet he wept, — he wept.
Each day confirmed the temper; and he passed
From strength to strength, till all was Heaven's at last.
His former views and sentiments were gone
And every past ambition lost in one,

And that unearthly; for beneath the sky
He now found little to detain his eye.
Life seemed a passage to a place of rest;
A road the lightest-laden travelled best.
He had no wish to fix his dwelling there,
Or take too largely of its cumbering care;
As much of earthly goods he still possessed
As nature craved, or wisdom would request.
Enough had to a faithless world been given;
It now was time to live for self and Heaven.

His friends with joy beheld the change; and none
Beheld it with more interest than one,
Of whom, though tempted much, I've little sung,
The Rector's gentle sister, fair and young,
Bright and unearthly as a star of light,
Pure! — But I check my fancy in her flight.
I've said before that she could mend and make,
Wash and get up small linen, boil and bake,
Could keep the heart, and keep the house beside,
And elegant with useful well divide.
Their dwelling, mode of life, and all the rest,
My rhyme already hath at large expressed.

TALE FIFTH

'Forgive us our trespasses as we forgive them
that trespass against us.'

THE BROTHERS

Some years ago, remote in Erin's isle,
There dwelt in good old hospitable style,
In huge stone house and large enclosed demesne,
Shane, master, squire, nay prince of Castleshane,
O'er miles of naked, ill-farmed acres round
His woods and walls in lonely grandeur frowned;
And hundreds there of ragged, trembling knaves
Lived on his looks, and joyed to be his slaves.
His cellars with the best of wines o'erflowed,
And groaned his table 'neath its smoldng load;
And poor relations round it day by day
Ate, joked, and sang, and swore their hours away.
The priest and parson met in friendship there;
And all were welcome, so they drank their share.

Shane was a county magistrate; but took
His law from his own brain, and not from book.
And when a puzzling case came up, his worship
Settled the matter by a general horsewhip.
To Dublin every year in state he went
To attend the Castle and the Parliament,
And learn improvements in the useful arts,
And bring down Scottish stewards, ploughs, and carts.
Each guest that came must see and praise in full
His drilled potatoes and Merino wool,
And all his undertakings and expenses,
In breeds, plantations, crops, and drains, and fences.

But these, and much else of his state and glory,
I now must pass and hasten to my story.

Shane (for he scorned all adjunct to a name
Which straight from Erin's ancient monarchs came)
Was married twice, and had from either spouse
A young supporter of his regal house.
An heir indeed had been for years delayed,
While daughter after daughter came instead;
And when at length his prayer was heard, his wife
Paid for the infant blessing with her life.
The widower's vacant eye was after caught
By the fair English governess, who taught
His elder girls, and tempted, yet denied
His suit so well, she was at length his bride;
And ere twelve months had o'er their union sped,
The wife had born a son, the sire was dead.
The land was on the elder youth entailed,
But the young widow on her spouse prevailed
To leave by will both property and heir
To his dear wife's sole management and care.

Strange changes now were seen at Castleshane;
Gone were the dinners, claret and champagne.
No errant friends or poor relations there
Put up their steeds, and took their welcome fare.
The old domestics all were turned away,
The tenants' rents demanded to a day.

Sold were the ploughs, the cattle, horse and hound,
The whole demesne let out to farmers round,
The ancient timber felled, and broken up the ground;
And to complete the wreck, when all beside
Was gone, the lady too to England hied;
And a stem agent to the castle sent

To screw the tenants, and transmit the rent.
The boys were put to school, to college then,
And grew apace, and ripened into men:
But as their minds unfolded day by day,
The more diverse they showed in every trait.
Edmund the elder from his earliest youth
Was free and fearless, full of warmth and truth,
Frank, unsuspicious, sensitive, and kind,
And graced alike in person and in mind.
His brother James was secret, smooth, and sly;
He spoke nor acted but with reasons why:
He weighed each look and word with nicest skill,
And checked and feigned all passions at his will.
He early learned his interests, and the art
To wind him round his brother's honest heart;
And watched his moods and motions, and indulged
In hopes and views that might not be divulged.
While Edmund lives, he best can help his ends;
But Edmund dead, and all to James descends.

On thoughts like these he brooded, till they grew
A part of his existence; gave a hue
And turn to all within him; sent their root
Deep in his soul, and upward bore their fruit;
Grew with his growth, and strengthened with his
strength.
Till in one foul ambition all at length
Was lost; one viper passion filled his breast,
And, like the prophet's rod, devoured the rest.
No pains were spared, no practice was untried.
No tempting lure unsought and unapplied;
And his fell spirit, like a stream up pent,
But gained new strength with each impediment.
Yet on through baffled project, plot, and snare,
Young Edmund walked secure, though unaware:

Till came at last the proud eventful age,
That burst the tedious bonds of pupilage.

Time passed, and still o'er Edmund's easy soul
The son and mother held their strong control.
James, now a lawyer, kept his brother's deeds,
Received his rents, and furnished all his needs:
While the base mother fed his appetites,
And kept him quiet, while they filched his rights.
This was, however, a precarious game,
And soon might end, perhaps, in loss and shame;
But could poor Edmund once aside be thrown,
Then all for ever were by law their own.
At length the troublous year of ninety-eight
Arrived; and on the Castleshane estate,
Oppressed, deserted, as the tenants were,
They blindly rushed into rebellious snare;
Held nightly meetings, laws and arms defied,
And rents and taxes to a man denied.
The case was urgent, and confirmed a vow
Which Edmund long had formed, but which till now
Had always met some hindrance, to go o'er
Their real state in person to explore,
Hear their complaints, their grievances reform,
And quell, if possible, the rising storm;
And 'Come, my friend, my brother, and my guide,
Assist me in the generous task,' he cried.

They went. The kingdom wheresoever they came
Boiled like a crater, ere it bursts in flame;
Rolled like the ocean when a storm is near;
And haste, and trouble, and suspense, and fear
Sat in all faces. Fierce debate was heard;
And fiercer thoughts indulged, that breathed no word,
But kept their angry energy to aid

The avenging arm, the liberating blade.
Edmund, although in England nursed and trained,
Still for his native land a love retained;
And oft had stood the champion of her wrongs
From foreign prejudice, and sneering tongues;
And argument and declamation here
Found quick reception in his partial ear.
His country's claims, and injuries, and woes
Before him through enlarging medium rose;
And Liberty her strong appeal addressed
To a misjudging, though a generous, breast.

Now was the time for James. With villain eye
He watched his brother's moods, nor failed, to ply
His spirit with incentives, and to wind
The chains of error fast around his mind.
From step to step he led his victim on,
Till fear and moderation both were gone;
And forth he stood in Freedom's fancied cause,
An open rebel to his King and laws.
Meanwhile, intelligence was duly sent
Of each proceeding to the Government,
And means soon used their projects to avert,
And bring the leaders up to their desert.
Edmund with sudden consternation learned
All his fond aims detected and o'erturned.
He saw the danger rushing on his head,
One desperate effort at resistance made,
Failed; out escaped pursuit by James's timely aid.
Think not the wolf had now begun to feel;
Think not that any generous appeal
Had reached the heart of James. He only thought
Of what might best advance his fiendish plot.
If Edmund had to open war proceeded,
There was a chance his cause might have succeeded;

If made a prisoner, as matters were,
The law had power, and there were pleas, to spare;
And on himself the office and the stain
Of traitor and accuser must remain.
Besides, he saw another readier way
To gain his objects. In a secret bay
Near Castleshane a lawless privateer,
With his connivance, anchored twice a year.
Thither 'twas easy Edmund to ensnare,
And quietly dispose of him when there,
He knew the crew were fit for any deed.
At least, when (as they should be) duly feed.

The pirates put to sea, their grand concern
Their sanguinary recompense to earn.
But as they came to put their plans in force,
Among thorn rose strange scruples and remorse.
A something in their victim's case and air
Won on their hearts, aU ruffian as they were;
And when the bloody deed was to be done,
They slunk back from the office one by one.
At last three fellows, bolder than the rest,
Took it upon them. Edmund now had guessed,
From certain looks and whisperings, that some plot
Was hatching, though he scarce conjectured what.
But when the villains to the cabin came,
Stealthy and armed, at once he saw their aim,
And rose, and rushed upon them for his life.
The foremost was struck down; another's knife
Just grazed him as upon the deck he sprung,
And snatching up a random weapon, flung
Back on his hot pursuers, and engaged
Hand to hand boldly with them. Fiercely raged
The unequal conflict; back retired the crew,
And stood aloof the deadly sport to view.

Edmund, meanwhile, fought backward o'er the deck.
Till at the poop he held all three at check;
And dealt his blows so ably round him there,
He soon brought one to ground. The other pair
Pressed the more hard on him, all efforts plied,
And wounds were shared and dealt on either side;
But a good cause gave weight to Edmund's blade
And soon another at his feet was laid.
The last assassin fled: and from the rest
A general shout his gallantry confessed.
The captain then stepped forth, disclosed the whole,
Doubt and amaze bewildering Edmund's soul;
Till, all made clear, the feelings struggling there
Passed on through wrath and scorn to blank despair.
He bared his breast. 'Come on, come on,' he cried;
'Here in my heart your murderous weapons hide:
Obey the traitor: let him have his will.'
'Nay, cheer up,' cried the captain; 'take not ill
Our usage: 'twas a job we never loved,
Though bribes like his might better men have moved.
But it shall ne'er be said. that one of us
Killed any man for hire in cold blood thus.
Cast in your lot with us, my lad, and dare
A bold sea-pirate's joys and gains to share.
Thou lovest freedom. We are of the free,
The untamed rovers of the rolling sea.
Quit the false land, its traitors, and its slaves,
And take with us the fortune of the waves.'
Alas, he had no choice; for death was now
On shore, life and the deep before his prow.
He cursed the treacherous caitiff, joined their cheer,
And roamed the world a reckless buccaneer.

No more was heard of him. The contest closed,
And Ireland was to sullen peace composed;

And James, as heir at law, the objects gained
At which he had so long and basely strained.
But rumours somehow rose, that all had not
Been managed well and fairly as it ought.
The neighbouring gentlemen were cool and shy,
And shunned him, though they gave no reason why.
A closer scrutiny he feared to face,
So wisely let the lands, and left the place.

He left the place, but could not leave behind
The heavy burthen of a rankling mind.
Fly whom he might, himself he could not fly;
His worst accuser, conscience, still was nigh;
Made all his riches poor, his splendour dim,
And flattery but a tuneless taunt to him.
From place to place, from scene to scene he pressed,
And found in restless change his only rest;
No friend nor home in the wide world enjoyed,
And all beyond was madness or a void.

Thus matters stood with each. Time travelled on.
At last, when many, years were passed and gone,
To a small parish down in Devon came
A reverend priest of meek and holy frame.
He lived retired, and a strange mystery hung
Around him. Who he was, and whence he sprung
None knew; or how, or where his youth was spent.
Yet there was somewhat in each lineament
That caught the notice he desired to shun,
And told discernment he had seen and done
More than he chose to mention. On his face
Toil more than time had left its harrowing trace:
The hue of other climes was there displayed;
And words at times dropped from him, that betrayed

A knowledge from strange scenes and manners
brought,
And ill consorting with his present lot.

Yet be he who he might, each sterner trait
Religion's influence much had smoothed away.
A moonlight stillness in his looks was seen,
And all has air was thoughtful and serene.
A trace of melancholy thrid the whole,
Entendering [16], chilling not, where'er it stole.
Perhaps dark recollections o'er him came,
Constraining self what God forgave to blame;
Perhaps he long had erred from him, and now
Resolved his penitent for aye to bow;
Retaining still a deep and humbling sense
Of what he had been, and should feel from thence.
Howbeit among his little flock he moved,
Active, though sad, though distant, yet beloved;
Straight by the line of even duty steered,
And fearing God, no other object feared.

This man was injured Edmund. Here he came
Altered in views, in features, lot, and name;
Came to repay by such a life as this
A morn of trouble with a noon of peace.
The long-lost wanderer by his God was found;
The broken spirit by its Saviour bound.
Heaven had recalled him from his fierce career
Of lawless daring, and had sent him here
To give to God the remnant of his days,
And lead in others to his hallowed ways.

The little town where Edmund thus abode

---

[16] to make tender; weaken

Lay, as it happened, on the public road
To a large watering-place upon the coast,
Where Fashion yearly sent her restless host.
One day a carriage, journeying thither, met
Close to the town a frightful overset.
A well-dressed man who sat alone within
Was wounded much, and to the village inn
Was brought, and there in great distress and pain
Now lay, and all assistance seemed in vain.
The faculty at last gave up the case,
And now the priest was summoned in their place.

Edmund approached, upon the stranger looked, —
It was his brother James. — But he rebuked
His strong emotions, and his face withdrew.
'Leave,' said the man, 'the chamber to us two.'
They went. 'Sir,' he continued, 'I have learned
Much of thy worth and goodness, and have yearned
To lay my case before thee, and receive
What comfort thou a dying man canst give.
I feel it is no season to dissemble,
When in a few hours longer I must tremble
At God's dread bar, and all the truth display
In the broad light of everlasting day.
These, sir, are things I've tried to disbelieve,
But am constrained to shudder and receive:
The frail supports such reasonings can supply
May serve whereon to live, but not to die.
I want, I feel it, now a surer stay;
And haply, sir, thy long experience may
Suggest such comfort; only with me deal
In candour, nor compose where thou shouldst heal.
Thou seest a wretch before thee who has erred
Deeply and grossly: if thou hast a word
Of peace for such, say on; I need not add

425

How sounds like these a dying ear will glad.'

Edmund a moment paused. His soul was moved
Within him; but the mood he soon reproved,
And calm replied, ''Tis well to know our guilt:
A sickness to be healed must first be felt.
None are exempt from sin; but grace is sent
To all that look to Jesus and repent.'

'But mine, sir — mine is a peculiar case,
Beyond the reach of ordinary grace.
No venial errors, common to mankind,
Have stained my life, and now oppress my mind.
But guilt so black, that tears of blood might fail
To rase it. Memory sickens, Hope turns pale
To look at it. And here upon the verge
Of that dark ocean, whose next rising surge
May sweep me in, I tremble now, nor find
Whereon to rest before me or behind.
If, then, thou ownest aught of stronger power
To comfort such a wretch, at such an hour,
O speak it!'

'Sir, this language makes me bold,'
Said Edmund, 'and were all more plainly told,
Some mitigating feature might arrest
Another's eye; the case itself suggest
Its own peculiar comfort: but be sure,
Whate'er thy guilt, it is not past a cure.
The Saviour died that none might feel despair
 Who turn to Him with penitence and prayer.'

'Suppose, then, sir, the blackest and the worst
Of all that's mean, base, devilish, and accurst.
Suppose the use of every trick and art

That mars and desecrates the human heart;
A show of candour o'er a knot of wiles,
A soul of hell beneath a face of smiles,
Worth undermined, and confidence betrayed,
And love and truth with wrong and hate repaid.
Suppose one mammon project long pursued,
And sealed at last with perfidy and blood —
Suppose the victim of all this to be
A brother. — O! the kindest! best! — and he
Duped, beggared, outlawed, murdered — all by me! —
Is there still hope?'

                  'Thy guilt indeed is great;
But God forbids me to set bounds or date
To His redeeming mercy. So the thief
Who on the cross found pardon and relief!
To the same Saviour be thy prayer up sent,
For sure thy language says thou dost relent.'
'Relent! O yes! If days and nights of tears;
If sorrow eating on my joyless years;
If this false head, all prematurely grey;
If pangs that cannot rest, and dare not pray;
If Heaven grown black above, and earth beneath
Become one gloomy vault, one waste of death;
If taunt and scorn descried in every face,
And hunting me forlorn from place to place;
If to seem less among my fellow-men
Than the poor scribble of some idle pen;
If envy of the meanest thing that crawls,
The idiot's leer, the maniac's chains and walls;
If death desired, yet dreaded —— '

               'Hold, O, hold!
Enough, enough to mortal ear is told.
Turn to thy God. With Him for mercy plead:

All is not lost while He can hear and heed.
My heart bleeds for thee. Lift with me thy prayer.
Why shouldst thou yield to Satan and despair?'

'I cannot pray. I dare not look on high.
My brother's form is there to meet my eye.
His voice is there my conscious plea to drown.
Yes! his least glance will hurl me headlong down
From Heaven, will be enough my soul to scare
Down to its place of judgment and despair.
See where he stands! my murdered brother! See,
He turns his still reproachful eyes on me!'

'O! calm this mood! thy wandering thoughts recall!
Thy brother? O! he pities, pardons all!
Has he not sins himself to be forgiven?
How could he look up to his God in Heaven,
And ask the mercy which himself denied?
Has he not seen thee? has he not descried
Thy deep remorse, thy bitterness of soul?
He has, he has. He knows, forgives the whole.
He was not wont to own a mood like this:
And anger cannot dwell where Jesus is.'

'Ah, could I think it so!'
                              'Then look on me.
This face is not so changed but thou mayst see
A brother's likeness in it. — Yes, I live! —
Live to console, to cherish, to forgive!'

There have been looks of power; and souls have
shook
And shrunk and quailed before one awful look.
The eye of Marius struck the slave to stone,
Who came to slay him fettered and alone.

A look from Christ pierced Peter like a sword
In Pilate's hall, when he denied his Lord.
The hosts of Pharaoh in the deep were awed
And checked, and scattered by one look from God.
As strong, as thrilling, though with love they gushed,
The looks of Edmund on his brother rushed.
He started up as lightly from the bed
As if his pain and weakness all were fled;
Held back and glared awhile in Edmund's face,
Then dropped exhausted in his spread embrace.
'He lives! thank God! thank God!' he faintly cried,
Then back upon the pillow sank, and died.

❧❧❧